What type of lifestyle is yours?

Are you among the *need-driven*?

> Are you a *survivor*—earning only $5,000 a year and past the age of ambition and achievement?

> Or are you a *sustainer*—rebellious, anxious with the feeling of being left out, yet not ready to give up hope?

Do you fit instead among the *outer-directed*?

> A *belonger*—middle-class, traditional, conservative, and family-oriented, eager to know rules and follow them?

> An *emulator*—seeking to stand out and be like those you consider successful?

> An *achiever*—one of the builders of "the system," hardworking, self-reliant?

Or do you consider yourself *inner-directed*?

> An *I-Am-Me*—a student, perhaps, running the gamut from narcissistic to self-effacing?

> An *experiential*—looking for vital, direct experience from life, either in involvement with ideas and issues or in the search for joy?

> Or are you *societally conscious*—successful, influential, involved in single-issue politics, seeking simplicity in your life?

Or have you reached the level of the *integrated*?

> Have you found the balance, calm, and purpose that enable you to realize the fullness of life?

Chances are your lifestyle is a combination of these nine, but identifying yourself—finding out where you fit—can help you focus your personal and business life and make the most of your American opportunity.

> "Mitchell's surveys…have set the stage for a whole new way of looking at marketing products and services….the inner-directed marketplace is a reality right now. It has literally spilled over to touch all aspects of our lives."
>
> —*Daily Journal of Commerce,*
> Portland, Oregon

THE
NINE
AMERICAN
LIFESTYLES

WHO WE ARE
AND WHERE WE'RE GOING

Arnold Mitchell

WARNER BOOKS

A Warner Communications Company

Warner Books Edition

Copyright © 1983 by Arnold Mitchell

This Warner Books edition is published by arrangement with Macmillan Publishing Company, Inc., 866 Third Avenue, New York, New York 10022.

Warner Books, Inc., 666 Fifth Avenue, New York, NY 10103

A Warner Communications Company

Printed in the United States of America

First Warner Books Printing: May 1984

10   9   8   7   6   5   4   3   2

HM
73
M567
1984

Library of Congress Cataloging in Publication Data

Mitchell, Arnold.
    The nine American lifestyles.

    Includes bibliographical references and index.
    1. Life style.   2. Social values.   3. Social change.
4.   United States—Social conditions.   I. Title.
HM73.M567   1984   303.3'72   83-21873
ISBN 0-446-38067-9 (pbk.) (U.S.A.)
        0-446-38068-7 (Canada)

Contents

PART III
USING THE TYPOLOGY
151

PART IV
SOCIETAL PATTERNS AND THE FUTURE
197

APPENDIX
235

NOTES AND INDEX
289

Preface

WHY THIS BOOK

Why should you or I or anyone want to know about the values and lifestyles of Americans? Perhaps the single most compelling reason is that they tell us so much about who we are—as individuals, as citizens, as consumers, and as a nation. But there are other reasons, too. People's values and lifestyles say a good deal about where we are going, and they help explain such practical, diverse questions as: why we support some issues and oppose others; why some people are strong leaders and others weak; why some people are economically brilliant and others gifted artistically—and a few are both; why we trust some people and are suspicious of others; why some products attract us and others don't; why revolutions occur.

By the term "values" we mean the entire constellation of a person's attitudes, beliefs, opinions, hopes, fears, prejudices, needs, desires, and aspirations that, taken together, govern how one behaves. One's interior set of values—numerous, complex, overlapping, and contradictory though they are—finds holistic expression in a lifestyle. This book analyzes and systematizes the values and lives of Americans today in such a way as to yield insights into why people believe and act as they do. It attempts to provide a fresh way of looking at the dynamics of individual and societal action. The system is foremost a conceptual scheme based on the findings of developmental psychology, but, as established in field research, the approach reflects the real world. In our research we have looked at well over 800 facets of people and find that different lifestyle groups have unique patterns in almost every area. We now have powerful evidence that the classification of an individual on the basis of a few dozen attitudes and demographics tells us a good deal about what to expect of that person in hundreds of other domains. Further, the approach often enables us to identify the decisive quality-of-life factor or factors in a person's life. For example, the lives of people in our "Need-Driven" categories are characterized by extreme poverty. Yet great numbers of people who are equally poor nonetheless are not need-driven in a psychological sense; for them how they feel—their values and attitudes—overcomes the external reality of poverty.

Our findings, of course, are statistical, meaning that the correlations are tendencies, some strong and others weak, and are by no means inviolate.

The perspective this book presents is intended to help us gain insight not only into ourselves and others as individuals, but into the dynamics of societal change and the phenomena of everyday living. People's values have increasingly become crucial determinants of the course of events, although, of course, they are not the only determinants: natural events such as storms or earthquakes, for example, fall beyond the realm of values. So do the advances of science and technology, to an extent, but the "technological imperative" nowadays is often tempered or even reversed by human choice—witness debates concerning genetic engineering, use of many drugs, or nuclear power. It appears that more and more people are driven by an inner vision of what they think should—and hopefully can—be, and less and less by acceptance of what is. In short, choice based on value is coming to dominate over mere capability. The time seems at last to be arriving when many people are able to employ the full range of their powers to choose what kind of lives they truly want to lead.

RESEARCH BACKGROUND

Some readers of this book may wish to know something of its history. From the professional standpoint the origin of this book came in 1960, when the author teamed up with an anthropologist, Kenneth J. Cooper, and an economist, Hawkins Stern, to write a report called *Consumer Values and Demands*.[1]* In that first groping effort we tried to suggest that a neglected area of market research lay in how people's values influence their spending patterns. The report, written for a business audience, hazarded some guesses as to the direction of influence of selected values on a dozen spending categories and explored the consequences of the hypothesized trends. The paper had no discernible influence on its readers, perhaps because it was ahead of its time but more likely because the arguments were ingenious rather than demonstrable.

A series of further reports followed over the next seventeen years.[2] All were published on a proprietary basis for clients of SRI International (then Stanford Research Institute) and hence have received only restricted distribution. Each was a substantial research effort and reflected considerable literature. Three of these studies were of particular importance to the development of the approach described in this book.

*References are listed at the end of the book.

The first was *American Values*,[3] coauthored with Mary Baird and published in 1969. In this study we adopted Abraham H. Maslow's celebrated "needs hierarchy"[4] of human motivations as the framework for characterizing the values of Americans. Maslow suggested that growth toward full psychological maturity can be defined in terms of five sequential stages which he called Survival, Security, Belonging, Esteem, and Self-Actualization. In our report, a variety of values associated with each needs level was hypothesized and described in considerable detail. We next postulated a numerical profile of adult Americans for 1965 in terms of Maslow's needs levels and then described how that profile might change by 1990. A considerable portion of the report consisted of an analysis of the business and social consequences of this postulated shift in the numbers of people at each needs level. The study received an enthusiastic reception as a pioneering effort—a happy happening that no doubt had much to do with our continuing pursuit of this line of research and our borrowing of many of Maslow's terms and concepts in developing our own system of lifestyles.

The second study important to this book was *Life Ways and Lifestyles*,[5] published in 1973. A potent reason for writing that report was our discomfiture with hierarchical schemes like Maslow's: If I am at level 3 and you are at level 4 (and I know it), it's hard for me not to despise you because of your superiority. And you, of course, have a marvelous put-down weapon at your disposal! To avoid this dismal prospect we devised a system of "ways of life" based on distance from the cultural mainstream. On one side of the cultural center were groups we dubbed Preservers, Takers, and Escapers. On the other side were groups called Makers, Changers, and Seekers. In some sense the groups could be depicted as a ring, with Seekers and Escapers not far removed at the bottom and Preservers and Makers side by side at the top. Each of these six types was described in psychological terms. The paper went on to suggest that conflict between Preservers and Makers would eventually require the emergence of still another way of life, called Movers. The Movers, it was postulated, would be able to meld the best from all the groups into a higher-order solution and thus resolve their differences. Although the terminology is different, the concept of a Mover will be recognized as similar to the lifestyle we now describe as Integrated.

A final earlier report significant to the evolution of the present volume was a slim paper by Duane Elgin and me, published in 1976 under the title of *Voluntary Simplicity*.[6] (Duane Elgin has since published a book of the same title.[7]) In this paper we described what we perceived as an emerging lifestyle, "voluntary simplicity," which we defined as living in a way that is "outwardly simple and inwardly rich." We set forth the principal tenets of this lifestyle (which include frugality, conservation, preference for things natural, and attention to inner growth), speculated about its future evolution, and commented on implications for business and the society should voluntary simplicity develop into a substantial trend. The paper, slight as it was, received considerable attention in business circles and in the press. One result was that SRI International decided to "put the show on the road." Consequently, in 1977, Duane Elgin, Marie Spengler (cofounder and later director of SRI's Values and Lifestyles program), and I presented a series of seminars in cities across the United States on the topic of values and business. Voluntary simplicity was the focus of the seminar, but one segment of the program presented an early version of the values and lifestyles schema that is the subject of this book.

In response to the interest stirred by these values seminars, in late 1977 Marie Spengler and I (Duane Elgin had resigned from SRI to write his book on voluntary simplicity) developed a proposal for a three-year program we called Values and Lifestyles, or VALS for short. SRI International endorsed the proposal, and VALS was launched in May 1978 with thirty-nine corporate sponsors. I served as founding director, with Marie Spengler as associate director. As new sponsors joined the program (reaching seventy-three after three years), we were able to expand our research efforts to a total of about $2 million by the end of the initial three-year period. During this period I wrote or coauthored numerous reports[8] published by the VALS program. The present volume draws heavily on those reports and, in many sections, on selected other publications issued by VALS[9] and other parts of SRI.[10]

So it was that over the years I had become convinced that the roles played by people's values and lifestyles were absolutely central to their personal development, to their actions as citizens, and to their behavior as consumers. I knew this partly from personal experience: Retrospection showed me that every major turning point in my life—and there have been many over the decades—was profoundly associated with a change in self-perception, heralding a new set of priorities. I believed it also as a result of exploring how and why societies change and why people act and consume in such distinctive ways.

Acknowledgments

My first professional acknowledgments are due to SRI International, a leading applied-research organization located in Menlo Park, California. My debt to SRI is at two levels: first for appointing me a 1981 Fellow, thus freeing for me a major block of unimpeded time in which to write much of this book, and second for allowing me to use many of the conceptual and a few of the statistical findings of the initial three years of SRI's Values and Lifestyles (VALS) program. For the most part in this book I have drawn from VALS reports that I wrote; where I have cited other VALS reports, specific credit is given. Much important, innovative, and sophisticated research continues in the VALS program. Without doubt, some of this ongoing work will refine and advance findings reported in this book. That, happily, is the way of progress.

The book owes a general debt to scores of my colleagues at SRI, particularly those with whom I have had the good fortune to collaborate in writing reports and papers. I should like specifically to acknowledge the contributions of Mary K. Baird, Duane Elgin, William S. Royce, and Peter Schwartz.

Because the VALS research program has been very much a joint undertaking, essentially all members of the core staff, and those working with us, have contributed in substantial ways to our collective wisdom. It is therefore a pleasure to thank the following: James Barrell, Richard Carlson, Barbara Casey, Catherine Chavez, Stephen Crocker, Gloria Esdale, Richard Ferguson, Bill Huckabee, Robert Kimball, Paul Kohlenberg, Klaus Krause, Dustin Macgregor, Christine MacNulty, Thomas Mandel, Betsy McConnell, Donald Michael, Bonnie Miller, David C. Miller, Jane O'Connor, James Ogilvy, Meimei Pan, Louis Perica, Lynn Rosener, William Royce, Susan Russell, Daniel Schneberk, Peter Schwartz, Marie Spengler, Peter Teige, T. C. Thomas, Joop de Vries, J. W. Waters, and Ian Wilson. My particular gratitude goes to Marie Spengler, gifted associate director of the VALS program from the start and now its director, and to Tom Thomas, our supporter and administrative chief for the first three years of the program.

In summary, this book has developed over several decades with input from many colleagues and insights drawn from hundreds of scholars in many fields. Many have been explicitly acknowledged in the text, but undoubtedly many have been inadvertently overlooked or forgotten.

I have saved the most important for the last. She is my wife, Connie. Without her the book might not have gotten written and, certainly, the writing of it would have been far less rewarding and fun.

PART

I

LIFESTYLES AS A SYSTEM

1

The VALS Typology

More than anything else, we are what we believe, what we dream, what we value. For the most part we try to mold our lives to make our beliefs and dreams come true. And in our attempts to reach our goals, we test ourselves again and again in diverse ways, and in doing so we grow. With this growth comes change, so that new goals emerge, and in support of these new goals come new beliefs, new dreams, and new constellations of values. Some unusual people grow and change many times throughout their lives. Others change hardly at all with the decades. Most experience one or two periods when what is most important, most compelling, most beautiful shifts from one comprehensive pattern to another. These are the times when a person's values change—and lifestyles are transformed.

Further, studies made by developmental psychologists indicate that change is not random; it progresses step by step from relatively simple, immature states toward more complex, wider-ranging, more balanced states. Human growth can be thought of as an ordered sequence—a hierarchy—advancing in response to changing drives from the undeveloped toward the developed.

The values and lifestyle (VALS) typology that is the subject of this book incorporates the above concepts. In addition it rests upon data obtained in a major mail survey conducted by VALS in 1980. The Appendix describes this survey in detail and gives selected demographic, attitudinal, and financial data drawn from it. The survey asked over 800 specific questions on a great range of topics. Sample size exceeded 1,600. Respondents constituted a national probability sample of Americans aged eighteen or over living in the forty-eight contiguous states. Statistical analysis of survey results quantified and enriched the basic concepts of the VALS typology and enabled us to provide detailed

3

quantitative and human portraits of the VALS types, together with their activities and consumption patterns. Essentially all of the specific data presented in this book are derived from this survey, although we have space to touch only on highlights.

The VALS typology comprises four comprehensive groups that are subdivided into nine lifestyles, each intended to describe a unique way of life defined by its distinctive array of values, drives, beliefs, needs, dreams, and special points of view:

Need-Driven Groups
    Survivor lifestyle
    Sustainer lifestyle
Outer-Directed Groups
    Belonger lifestyle
    Emulator lifestyle
    Achiever lifestyle
Inner-Directed Groups
    I-Am-Me lifestyle
    Experiential lifestyle
    Societally Conscious lifestyle
Combined Outer- and Inner-Directed Group
    Integrated lifestyle

Each of these groups is characterized in the pages that follow.

NEED-DRIVEN GROUPS

At the lowest levels of the lifestyles typology come the the Need-Driven groups, called Survivors and Sustainers. The two groups are very different, but they share the burden of being poverty-stricken, so that their lives are driven by need. The luxury of choice in many economic matters is a relative rarity. This means, in effect, that they are less able to express their values in everyday living in the contemporary American society than are more affluent people. This overwhelming fact shows up dramatically in the activity and consumption patterns of the Need-Drivens: Their poverty forces them into patterns that deviate greatly from national averages, and the greater the poverty, the larger the deviations. One might say, then, that the Need-Drivens are, from an economic perspective, a values-based group more in the sense of denial of values than of expression of them. But happily there are many exceptions. Thus, many Need-Drivens occasionally splurge—accounting, for example, for many color TVs and splendid automobiles in "poor" neighborhoods. More significantly, many activities—such as gardening or baking—and virtually all the emotional and spiritual aspects of life do not involve appreciable income, and in these the Need-Drivens are as able as others to find rewards and self-expression.

Much evidence shows that the Need-Drivens are the farthest removed from the cultural mainstream of any of the VALS groups. They are the least flexible psychologically and least aware of the events of our times. They tend to be distrustful, rebellious, left out, and to think things are changing too fast. Hopelessness causes many to lead shrunken lives with little sensitivity to the wants of others and little vision of what can be.

Survivors

Located at the foot of the lifestyles typology, the nation's 6 million Survivors are the least favored segment of the population. Terrible poverty marks them. Only 22 percent of Survivor households made over $5,000 per year in 1979, and none made over $7,500. And the direction is down. Very few Survivors experienced improved finances in the 1977–1980 period, and only about 12 percent expected to be able to keep up with inflation in the years ahead. Many are old—the median age is sixty-six. Many are ill, without the energy to fend for themselves. Most are poorly educated—over a third haven't gone beyond eighth grade, and half have not graduated from high school—and hence find it difficult to take advantage of whatever opportunities come their way to better their positions. Not surprisingly, Survivors tend to be despairing, depressed, withdrawn, mistrustful, rebellious about their situation, lacking in self-confidence, and finding little satisfaction in any aspect of their lives. Their focus is on the elemental needs of survival and security; the aim is less to get ahead than not to slip backward. For many, existence has shriveled to the bleak reality of the moment and the fantasy world of television. As a group, Survivors are traditional, conservative, conventional. Of all the segments of the U.S. population, they are the most likely to think things are changing too fast.

There appear to be at least two rather distinct classes of Survivors. One consists largely of those ensnared in the culture of poverty. Generation after generation are born, live, and die in unchanging, paralyzing poverty. Few expect to escape, and even fewer do, for the experience of these people shows there is little reason to put out the enormous mental and social effort of trying to move upward through classic means— education, work, leadership. Those who do achieve financial success usually chose other channels, such as athletics, or drugs, or various rackets that can pay off hugely. The proportion of minorities in this class of Survivors is very high. Most live in urban ghettoes and some in rural backwaters of the South. In general, minority group Survivors are younger than other Survivors, probably less well educated, and certainly farthest (but not wholly) removed from the trends and ideas that power the society. Our portrait of Mrs. Washington and her son Peter (see Part II) attempts to capture this aspect of the Survivor lifestyle.

The other class of Survivor is less likely to have been born into the predicament; rather, through bad luck, lack of enterprise, or the onslaughts of old age, they have slipped back into the Survivor lifestyle, after following most of a lifetime spent as a Sustainer or Belonger. This, the largest group of Survivors, tends to be older than the other and is more likely to be white, to be in better touch with the events of the world, and to have larger resources, especially a home. Some live in city slums and ghettoes, but many inhabit the aging frame houses of small towns or the porches and shuttered rooms of old folks' homes.

For most of these people, the years of ambition and achievement have passed. Life has become a waiting game. Television is their main entertainment. Their homes are filled with mementoes of the past. Most are retired, and at least 80 percent are widows. They lead lives full of echoes, for most of their friends are dead or have moved to places unknown. Our sketch of Paddy reflects this kind of Survivor.

Sustainers

Sustainers are angry, distrustful, rebellious, anxious, combative people who often feel left out of things—but, unlike Survivors, they have not given up hope. Their life problem is less merely to survive than to secure and sustain hard-earned gains and, if possible, to move ahead to a better life. They live at the edge of poverty, probably with erratic incomes, for over a fourth are looking for work or work only part-time. Average income of Sustainers in 1979 was about $11,000, with only 22 percent exceeding $15,000. Few get much satisfaction from their jobs, which are heavily skewed to machine, manual, and service occupations. It is not surprising to find that Sustainers are the least satisfied of any lifestyle group with their financial status and the most anxious to get ahead economically.

Sustainers have the largest families despite the fact that over 25 percent are divorced, separated, or living together unmarried. They contain the highest fraction of minorities—13 percent are of Hispanic origin and 21 percent are black. More than any other group Sustainers see themselves as having low social status. Only a relative handful have gone beyond high school. They rank second lowest of the lifestyle segments in self-evaluation of overall happiness.

Mistrust of the system goes deep. Sustainers have less confidence in elected officials and corporate leaders than any other group. They are least likely to think products are getting better or safer or that labeling is improving. More than any other group they think the energy crisis is imaginary. They also rank high in thinking things are changing too fast.

Despite all this, Sustainers see themselves as financially expert— probably a reflection of their adroitness in stretching a dollar and, perhaps, their ability to operate in the so-called underground economy. Over 80 percent look forward to better things. And many support some contemporary social trends—for example, unmarried sex and legalization of marijuana. At the same time, deep insecurities seem evident in the high need Sustainers express to have social status and to feel part of a group.

There appear to be several distinct types of Sustainers. First is the street-smart operator of urban slums and ghettoes, where much organized and disorganized crime originates. Sometimes of minority descent, these Sustainers know the ropes of the illicit economy—dope, liquor, gambling, prostitution, and the like. Extreme violence, threats, payoffs, and gang agreements are common. Business is done in cash; the spoken word is the only record. Life is dangerous and uncertain but often spectacularly rewarding.

Far more common and less dramatic is the crafty Sustainer, who makes ends meet through barter, side jobs done for cash, and, sometimes, adroit manipulation of the welfare system. This variety of Sustainer is likely to be other than the hard-crime type, less systematic, less urbanized, less exclusively male. They may think of themselves as taking advantage of a system that asks for it, but they do not see themselves as criminals. The Flame—one of our portraits of the Sustainer lifestyle—deals chiefly with this kind of situation.

A very different kind of Sustainer is found in the impoverished family struggling to keep going on minimal wages supplemented sometimes by food stamps, sometimes welfare. The lone mother, divorced or separated, with several children—like Lucia in our sketch—is frequently a Sustainer. So, too, are members of the family whose wage earners are frequently unemployed or whose income is minimal. Because they are subject to intense ups and downs financially, these people often consider that they're in the grip of temporary hard times, and they promise themselves the revved-up muscle car and the new TV as soon as the corner has been turned.

A final type of Sustainer, less common today than early in the century, is the recent immigrant trying to make a go of it in a new world. Without much English, without appropriate skills, without sophistication, sometimes without real friends or family, this individual finds that only substandard jobs are available. But these are enterprising, hardworking, ambitious people with faith in the system and drive sufficient to keep striving. Many of them will not escape from the Sustainer pattern, but their children may do so, driven by the conviction that here indeed is the land of opportunity.

Psychologically, Sustainers are more advanced than Survivors in that they ask much more of their world. They do more planning, are more self-confident, and expect more of the future than Survivors. At the same time, like Survivors, they are not trusting of people, they are unhappy, and in particular they often feel left out. Although many are unemployed, it is clear that they seek work and place enormous importance on financial security. Many Sustainers will move up to Belonger or, more likely, Emulator levels in the years ahead. These are people learning the ways of outer-directed America; indeed, many would qualify as outer-directed except that their resources remain so restricted as to force them into need-driven living patterns.

OUTER-DIRECTED GROUPS

The Outer-Directeds make up middle America. It is a huge category, including about two-thirds of the adult population, or well over 100 million people. It is also highly diverse, consisting of three distinct lifestyles we call Belongers, Emulators, and Achievers. Belongers, at about 57 million adults, are the largest group in the typology. They are followed in size by Achievers at about 35 million, and about 16 million Emulators.

The common denominator of these three groups is what we call Outer-Direction. Outer-directed people respond intensely to signals, real or fancied, from others. They conduct themselves in accord with what they think others will think. Since "out there" is paramount, this tends to create ways of life geared to the visible, tangible, and materialistic.

Attributes shared (especially by Belongers and Achievers) include a sense that most people are honest, a lack of rebelliousness, a sense of being "with it," conventional behavior, and insistence that the family is the most important thing in their lives.

Outer-Directedness is a major step forward psychologically from the need-driven state in that the perspective on life has broadened enormously to include real concern for other people, affiliation with a host of institutions, a developed sense of the nation, and an array of personal values and options far more diverse and complex than those available to the Need-Drivens. Because they dominate the economy, the Outer-Directeds have much greater control over the events of their lives than do the Need-Drivens, and hence they are far less despairing, less suspicious, and less fearful. In general, the Outer-Directeds seem to be the happiest of Americans, being well attuned to the cultural mainstream—a fact that does not surprise because, in truth, they are the mainstream.

Belongers

Belongers typify what is generally regarded as middle-class America. Traditional, conforming, conservative, "moral," nonexperimental, family-oriented, Belongers are a mighty force for stability in a world of tumbling change. As a group, Belongers prefer the status quo if not the ways of yesteryear. Old-fashioned values still shine bright: patriotism, home and family, sentimentality. These are people who above all cherish shared institutions such as the family, church, and loyalty to nation, job, and old associations.

The key drive of Belongers is to fit in, not to stand out. Their world is well posted, and they follow the rules. About 95 percent are white. Most are middle-aged or older and have middle incomes and middle levels of education. Women, largely housewives, predominate; in fact, 30 percent are housewives, the highest fraction of any values group. Belongers tend to live in small towns or the open country and to shun big cities. They are not much interested in sophistication or intellectual affairs. All the evidence suggests that Belongers lead contented, happy lives relatively little vexed by the stresses and mercurial events that swirl around them.

Belonging as a lifestlye in the United States is almost always associated with the "middle middle" class. Belongers are the people for whom soap operas and romance magazines are created to fill their emotional needs. The needs of Belongers reflect the fact that many were exposed to much rejection or ridicule in their formative years, resulting in an excessive need for acceptance. Family mores were usually conventional; as children Belongers often were criticized for unusual ideas or punished for experimental actions (which often were called "bad" or, worse, "deviant"). Dependency and conformity were cultivated in family life through reward and punishment. The usual message was that the parents (or the church) knew what was right.

People brought up this way tend to be puritanical, conventional, dependent, sentimental, nostalgic, mass-oriented, outer-directed, xenophobic. Most Belongers have exceptionally strong matriarchal feelings because the first belonging relationship for most people is with their mothers, and mothers provide the classic image of the most unselfish, forgiving, nurturing, belonging symbol.

Belongers see safety in numbers; they think it is important to be an insider; alikeness, togetherness, and agreement are important measures. But closeness with others tends to be quite formalized; open emotionalism and sensuality are embarrassing. Tolerance for ambiguity is low. They feel the system should reward "virtue." They prefer to follow rather than to lead; to avoid hostility they will accept the lowest common denominator. They are threatened by the aberrant. Adherence to tradition and the status quo is essential. "Should" and "ought" are dominant words.

Belonging of this sort has the strength and virtue of providing a reference point, a sense of stability and often tradition, a set of agreed-upon rules, a charted road, a nest. At the same time, unalloyed belonging tends to exclude unaccustomed ways and in that sense is prejudiced, authoritarian, and closed. The Belonger thus tends to be accepting and following within the group and rejecting of anything outside it. Group interests and concerns come first; the individual tends to be suppressed. The world the Belonger feels most comfortable in is a well-posted, well-lighted place whose outer limits are in view at all times.

Belongers are easily the most old-fashioned and traditional of the VALS groups. This stance is taken against a background of much happiness and intermediate levels of satisfaction and trust in people. Although they are not particularly affluent and their financial progress is not above average, Belongers are satisfied with their situation. Generally they seem a contented, unambitious group. Traditional values emerge clearly in their opposition to "women's liberation," moral and sexual freedom, and rights for blacks. Belongers feel strongly that obedience is a prime virtue in children and that the military deserves much confidence. They tend, relatively, to abstain from alcohol; they are heavy TV watchers. This description is to a degree overdrawn, yet it captures the sense of the Belonger seeking security through avoidance of surprise, comfort through being surrounded by the familiar, and happiness through acceptance by the group.

In terms of psychological maturity Belongers are ahead of the Need-Drivens in many ways: Their concerns extend to a wider range of institutions and people; they plan for the years ahead; they match their consumption to their means; they are much more trusting of people and less rebellious. They feel better attuned to events around them and find more satisfaction in job, hobbies, and friends; and they are markedly more supportive of military leaders, elected officials, and corporate leaders.

For our sketches we have selected Belongers of two distinct types: Spunk Clarenden has lived a busy, useful life as a telephone lineman in Maine. He enjoyed life as he led it, and in retirement he enjoys recalling it. Myra and her husband live on the outskirts of a small Southern town. Their lives are well regulated, and the rules are clear. They expect their children to adhere to the same rules that have served them so well.

Emulators

The outer-directed world of the Emulator is totally different from that of Belongers. Emulators are intensely striving people, seeking to be like those they consider richer and more successful than they are—that is, Achievers. They are more influenced by the values of others than any other lifestyle group. Whether man or woman, they tend to be ambitious, competitive, ostentatious, unsubtle, "macho." They are also hard-working, supportive of contemporary social trends, and fairly successful. Despite a relatively young median age of twenty-seven, Emulator households in 1979 had an average income of over $18,000. But they are spenders and tend to be in debt. The problem for Emulators is that they do not really understand the values and lifestyle of those they emulate. Nor are their life patterns very similar. The important area of occupation illustrates the mismatch: 29 percent of Achievers hold professional or technical jobs, but only 9 percent of Emulators do; 17 percent of Achievers are managers or administrators vs. 6 percent of Emulators.

Emulators are more likely than any other group to have attended technical school. Unusually large numbers have one or two years of college but have not graduated. Self-assessed social class is strongly skewed to the low side, although the Sustainer pattern is more extreme. On the other hand, educational patterns of the fathers of Emulators are surprisingly high—higher, in fact, than those of Survivors, Sustainers, or Belongers, even when age differences are taken into account. Our data provide some support for the hypothesis that the Emulator stage is a key resting place for many upwardly mobile members of minority groups. Blacks and Hispanics both are materially overrepresented in the group, but not as much as they are among Sustainers. Despite this, Emulators appear to include many raised in favored circumstances but who, for one reason or another, have conjured up ambitions inappropriate for their achievements and perhaps for their abilities. Although many surely sense this—witness their anger at and mistrust of "the Establishment"—they seem unable, or unwilling, to realign their goals.

The information that Emulators have about Achievers tends to be secondhand—from movies, romanticized magazines, gossip columns. The result, naturally, is that they experience much rejection, inevitably generating a pervasive sense of anger, mistrust of individuals, and little faith that "the system" will give them a break. Emulators wind up with a poor self-image: for example, only 5 percent (vs. 41 percent for Achievers) regard themselves as upper-class; many often feel left out of things; they are below average in considering the inner self more important than fame or power; they rank next to lowest (after Survivors) in their self-confidence; they are unable to get much satisfaction from job or friends; their levels of confidence in institutional leaders are low, and they distrust information coming from institutional sources. It comes as no surprise to find that Emulators rank near the bottom of the lifestyle groups in overall self-ratings of happiness.

Although Emulators are probably the most upwardly ambitious of the lifestyle groups, it appears likely that most of them will not make it to Achiever status. One reason is that their blind upward striving seems to force many into leading lives of deception—lives filled with acts calculated to mislead others. Hence Emulators tend to be "operators" and to embrace conspicuous consumption, follow the voguish fashion, and spend only where it shows. This profoundly secondhand or imitative lifestyle accounts for the extraordinary lack of differentiation of Emulator activity and consumption patterns from those of other lifestyles. Thus Emulators seem in some sense to lead hollow lives—solid in appearance on the outside, empty inside. This characteristic is central, in different ways, to both of our sketches of Emulators. In Roger it is blatant and crippling; he is one who will not make the transition to the

Achiever level. For Sheila the inner neglect is more silent, more subtle. Our sketch concerns itself with the unexpected inner leap that frees her to grow.

Psychologically, Emulators represent a turbulent transition stage between the established, solid, self-confident, well-adjusted lifestyles of Belongers and Achievers. Scornful of the first, Emulators have not yet attained the second emotionally, intellectually, economically, or socially. Emulators, nonetheless, are psychologically a step ahead of Belongers in the sense that they ask more of themselves and the system and have taken on greater responsibility for getting ahead, instead of drifting with events in the style of many Belongers.

Achievers

Achievers are at the top—at the pinnacle of Outer-Direction. They are the driving and driven people who have built "the system" and are now at the helm. Including almost one-fourth of the adult population, they are a diverse, gifted, hard-working, self-reliant, successful, and happy group.

Achievers come in many shapes and forms. The ambitious, competitive, effective corporate executive is one familiar type. But there is also the skilled professional—lawyer, doctor, scientist—the adroit politician, the money-oriented athlete or entertainer, and the artist whose goal is fame and "the big life." Then there is the vicarious Achiever— the individual who expresses his or her achievement needs through others as much as through personal attainment. Our vignette of "D.J." represents the executive kind of Achiever. Our portrait of Elizabeth comes closer to the vicarious kind.

To some, Achievers typify the stereotype of the wealthy, successful American. To social critics, Achievers represent the Establishment. But more than anything else Achievers have learned to live the comfortable, affluent, affable, outer-directed life, and in so doing they have set the standard for much of the nation.

In things material Achievers are far in the vanguard among the lifestyle groups. Average household income in 1979 exceeded $31,000; over 20 percent were self-employed, and two and one-half times as many Achievers as any other VALS group held managerial or administrative jobs. Almost half had total household assets of over $100,000 in 1979, compared with 31 percent for the next highest lifestyle group. Life appears to be comfortable: almost half of Achievers live in the suburbs, 87 percent own their own homes, and they top the lifestyle groups in recent financial improvement.

Importantly, this success enables Achievers to feel good about themselves: 94 percent rate themselves as "very happy." They lead all groups in trusting people, in considering themselves upper-class, in having self-confidence, in not feeling rebellious or left out of things, and in supporting many national issues, such as encouraging industry growth, spending on the military, and supporting U.S. involvement in world affairs. They are more satisfied with their financial situation than any other group. They feel that products are getting better and safer. They support technology and go for the "new and improved" product. Achievers are staunchly Republican and conservative. Politically they do not want radical change. After all, much of the culture is of their making; they are on top, and radical change might shake them off.

The demographics of Achievers show them to have a mean age in the early forties, but with a wide spread. Over 95 percent are Caucasian and only 2 percent black. A third are college graduates, and many went on to attend graduate school. Contrary to popular impression, the evidence is that they are more happily married (that is, with fewer broken marriages) than any group other than Belongers. It is clear from data on their fathers' educational attainment that Achievers tend to be self-made people. Regionally they are a bit underrepresented in the South and overrepresented in the West.

No doubt because they are leaders, Achievers tend to be conservative, not only politically, but socially as well. Only Belongers rate themselves as more conservative in their general behavior. Specifically, they are far down the list in support of such issues as sex between unmarried people, working women also being good mothers, legalization of marijuana, or air pollution as a world danger. But they are not full of resentments. Indeed, Achievers show their psychological maturity by their success in bringing their ambitions into good alignment with reality.

But Achievers have contributed to the development of American values in a fashion they did not anticipate. By building an economic system of unprecedented affluence in the years following World War II, they made possible the emergence of postmaterial values. Further, it was largely the children of Achievers who spearheaded this change toward valuing the nonmaterial in the 1960s and 1970s. We are referring, of course, to the advent of inner-directed values, especially as expressed by members of what we have called the I-Am-Me lifestyle.

INNER-DIRECTED GROUPS

The Inner-Directeds are so named because the principal driving forces of their lives are internal, not external. That is, what is most important is what is "in here," not what is "out there." This extends to attitudes toward job, personal relationships, spiritual matters, and the satisfactions to be derived from everyday pursuits. Inner growth—sometimes sought through the great Western religions or analytic techniques, but often through transcendental meditation, yoga, Zen, or other Eastern spiritual practice—is central to many of the Inner-Directeds. Most seek intense involvement in whatever they are doing; the secondhand and vicarious are anathema. Their sensitivity to their own feelings enables them to be sensitive to others and to events around them. Many are active in social movements such as consumerism, conservation, or environmentalism, while others express their concerns more privately in artistic pursuits. As a group the Inner-Directeds are highly self-reliant and notably indifferent to social status. Money is of relatively little concern to them. They are powerfully supportive of such modern trends as women working, sex between unmarried people, or legalization of marijuana. They tend to be self-expressive, individualistic, concerned with people, impassioned, diverse, complex. (It should be noted that the term "inner-directed" was made famous by Riesman, Glazer, and Denney in *The Lonely Crowd*[1] some thirty years ago. Although we have borrowed the expression, our use of the phrase is quite different from Riesman's; he used it to mean selfish rather than self-aware. Employed that way, the term applies better to Survivors and Sustainers than to other groups in our typology.)

Most Inner-Directeds are members of the postwar generation. Most have excellent educations and hold good jobs, often of a professional or technical nature. Except for the most youthful among them, incomes average around $25,000 per year. Politically, the Inner-Directeds are heavily independent.

Essentially all Inner-Directeds were raised in the predominantly outer-directed society of the United States—especially in Achiever families. As children and adolescents they learned and internalized outer-directed parental and societal values, but at some point, usually in mid- or late adolescence, Outer-Directedness began to seem less than the way to live a lifetime. Their family affluence was such that money and materialism no longer had to dominate existence as it has for almost everyone else in industrial societies. Relieved of incessant economic pressures, prosperous parents tended to raise their children permissively, perhaps thinking thus to improve upon their own upbringing. A natural effect was to emphasize noneconomic aspects of life, and this aspect became the focus of many of the most socially favored youths of the 1960s and '70s. In dramatic distinction to strictly raised Belonger children, the offspring of most Achiever families were freed (if not invited) to reject the economic values of the society. And so, in a sense as a result of the success of the U.S. economic system, a new class of lifestyles was born—lifestyles focused on the inner world rather than the external world of tangibles. Inner-Direction, of course, has always been part of the American romantic tradition—witness Emerson and Thoreau—but until the past twenty years it has been confined to a relative few. Today it is a mass movement. And it is assuredly one of the most significant sociological phenomena of the post–World War II period, although it is remarkably little noted in these terms.

If the Inner-Directeds tend to be the children of prosperous, outer-directed families, one implication is that inner-directed people tend *not* to come from need-driven or even inner-directed families. The best explanation is that some measure of satiation with the pleasures of external things seems to be required before a person can believe in—or take deep satisfaction from—the less visible, incorporeal pleasures of Inner-Direction. This does not mean that the joys of the outer world disappear (our typology is a nested model), but that inner needs become more imperious than the outer.

We have identified three inner-directed lifestyles, which we call I-Am-Me, Experiential, and Societally Conscious. Emerging as a major trend in the early and mid-1960s (when the first big wave of the postwar generation was reaching age eighteen), Inner-Direction has now reached major proportions. Survey results for 1980 indicate that about 20 percent of American adults are now more Inner-Directed than Outer-Directed or Need-Driven. This amounts to over 30 million individuals, the majority of whom are in their twenties or thirties with their years of greatest influence as citizens, parents, and consumers still ahead of them.

In the American culture Inner-Direction represents a psychological advance over Outer-Direction in that it adds another "layer" of values to the old, offering the individual new options for self-expression, new perspectives to consider, new ways in which to find satisfaction. In inner-directed cultures, such as those of India or old Japan, the psychological advance would clearly be represented by a switch from Inner- to

Outer-Direction, for that would add the missing dimension. Hence it is not possible to say that Inner-Direction is "better" than Outer-Direction, or vice versa, any more than one can say a dog is "better" than a cat or age twenty is "better" than age forty. They are simply different. It may be, however, that one lifestyle is more effective than another for certain purposes, just as a dog is a better guard and a cat a better mouser.

I-Am-Mes*

This is a stage of tumultuous transition from an outer-directed way of life to Inner-Direction. It is usually short-lived—no more than a few years—and marked by spectacular emotional ups and downs and sidewise veerings. It is a stage of much anxiety brought on by fear of losing the old and uncertainty concerning the new. As a frantic result, I-Am-Mes are both contrite and aggressive, demure and exhibitionistic, self-effacing and narcissistic, conforming and wildly innovative. To give the appearance of solidity and direction, they have developed whims of iron.

The immediate shift is usually from the comfortable, established, well-defined, deeply outer-directed lifestyle of Achiever parents to the evanescent, fanciful, mercurial, flighty styles of I-Am-Me peers and contemporaries. The change is powered by both love and hate, admiration and disgust, envy and resentment of outer-directed ways of life. The stage thus is not only I-Am-Me but also I-Am-Not-You. Clearly it is a time full of confusions, contradictions, uncertainties, excesses, and protean changes. But the style also involves genuine inventiveness, for the shift from the outer to the inner dimension often brings with it the discovery of new interests and new interior rewards that redirect life goals. It is this aspect of the I-Am-Me lifestyle that is of central significance, not the accompanying flamboyance expressed through conspicuous dress, spectacular behavior, or the famed insolence of the modern teenager toward parents.

The picture we have, then, is of youths raised in favored circumstances seeking out—often ungraciously and noisily, to be sure—a new way of life for themselves. Average age is about twenty-one, and almost none are over thirty. The majority are students, and only a few have been married. Many still live with their parents and identify strongly

---

* We use the colloquial phrase as more appropriate despite the command of grammar that this be I-Am-I!

with them—a fact that complicates their sense of personal identity. Interestingly, in 1980 only 36 percent of I-Am-Mes were found to be female, in contrast to a majority of women ten or fifteen years earlier. Because the I-Am-Mes learned to understand Outer-Direction as children and adolescents, they can afford to leave it behind as adults. The evidence is that the new way of life, once found, is a permanent change. The I-Am-Mes of ten and more years ago retain the essence of their old values. But the I-Am-Mes of the 1980s appear in many ways to be less extreme than the I-Am-Mes of yesterday.

As a lifestyle, the I-Am-Me mode is expressed more through activities and demographics than through attitudes. Indeed, many I-Am-Mes appear not to have thought in great depth about many societal issues, but they have no problem in being and acting. Their actions mark them as energetic, enthusiastic, daring, and seeking the new. Intellectual and cultural activities attract them as well as social pursuits and physically demanding games. Overall, in fact, I-Am-Mes display the most distinctive activity patterns of any group in the values typology save the Survivors. I-Am-Mes represent the zippy, high-energy, enthusiastic end of the lifestyle spectrum, Survivors the withdrawn, despairing, weary end. In our two portraits of I-Am-Me people, we have tried to capture their combination of rejection and discovery. In "Softy" Stevenson we portray a wildly successful entertainer who is in intense rebellion against his parents. For Sally the struggle has a more dreamlike quality.

Experientials

Next in the typology of American values and lifestyles come the Experientials, the name deriving from the fact that above all these people seek direct, vivid experience. For some what matters most is deep personal involvement in ideas or issues, for others it is intense hedonism; for some it is the challenge and excitement of great physical exertion, like rock climbing; for many the quest of inner exploration is all-important; for a few the core of existence is a lifestyle of voluntary simplicity— what Emerson called "plain living and high thinking." For most of the Experientials life at one moment is a noisy parade and at the next a journey, often touched with the mystic, through the silent inner domains of thought, feeling, and spirit. For them, the secondhand, the inhibited, the unfeeling is not living. Action and interaction with people, events, and ideas—pure and strong—is the essence of life.

Most such people passed a few years earlier through the chaotic, exhibitionistic I-Am-Me stage. A few years hence many will extend their perspectives to the society—perhaps even the globe—and become more activist and mission-oriented. But for now it is not things that count, but emotion. The intangible and evanescent is likely to loom larger than the plain and visible. Experientials tend to be artistic people attuned to subtlety and nuance. "Right-brained," they will often follow the dictates of the sudden tear or prickled skin in preference to logic and the reasoned advice of others.

Psychologically, the Experientials have the most inner-directed of the lifestyles. Their independence and self-reliance goes deep, enabling them to try anything once, if only for the experience of it. So this inventive, experimental group is given to the unusual, the one-of-a-kind, the daring, the dramatic, the impulsive, the quaint. Their self-understanding makes the Experientials excellent judges of what is authentic and decisive about rejecting what comes across to them as fraudulent. Energetic, they engage in many social activities ranging from vigorous outdoor sports, to the van life, to wine tasting, to participating in artistic events.

Experientials are youthful—mostly in their late twenties—excellently educated and with incomes averaging between $23,000 and $24,000 annually. Many hold technical and professional jobs. They are happy, self-assured, well-adjusted people with faith in the trustworthiness of others and great assurance that they are on top of things. They tend to be liberal politically and highly supportive of such phenomena as the women's movement, unmarried sex, legalization of marijuana, conservation, consumer movements, and limits to industrial growth. Many are intensely opposed to spending on military armaments (for they are part of the "Vietnam generation") and have little faith in institutional leaders.

Most Experientials have a deep sense of the natural and a belief in the innate rightness of nature. As a result they prefer natural products to the synthetic; almost as much as Belongers, they like to grow their own flowers and vegetables. Many preserve their own food or shop in organic food stores. Many have much faith in holistic medicine. It is they who do most of the rock climbing and backpacking. It is they who love above all to get out away from it all, where the signs of civilization are few.

Finally, one of the powerful forces in the lives of most Experientials is a feel for the mystic. Usually this is not connected with the formal Western religions, but is more likely to reflect personal insight and perhaps the study of Zen, Yoga, and the *Tao Te Ching* or other ancient Eastern works. For some Experientials, marijuana and other drugs play an important role in mystic experience; for others the way lies through transcendental meditation; for still others self-hypnosis or learned deep introspection works best.

The Experientials tend to be happy individuals, not because they don't have their depressions and frustrations, but because they feel they are growing and changing and any day may bring a fresh new insight— a peak experience—to illuminate all that has gone before. In its way, the Experiential phase is an untroubled time, not in the sense of being motionless (it is far from that), but in the sense that most of what happens is considered self-induced and is welcomed as one more step on the very long road of life—a road that many of the Experientials think may, in fact, be eternal.

From the psychological standpoint the Experiential lifestyle is much less self-centered than I-Am-Me, is concerned with a broader range of issues, is more participative, is more self-assured. Experientials are notably self-reliant, whereas I-Am-Mes, being in transition to Inner-Direction, are more dependent on peer support and social status for their self-image. The Experientials appear quite able to risk a wide range of inner-exploration techniques. They have begun to leave their flamboyance and aggressively conspicuous behavior and are moving on to more spiritual, intellectual, and artistic preoccupations. Our sketches of Mary and Michael, in Part II, deal with such transitions.

Societally Conscious

The focus of the inner-directed drives of some 13 million Americans is not rejection of other lifestyles (as in the I-Am-Mes) or intense personal experience (as in the Experientials) but concern with societal issues, trends, and events.

The range of concerns and the styles of dealing with them are great. Consumer issues are foremost for some people, who become leaders or supporters of movements concerned with such issues as pricing, additives, labeling, and advertising. Other individuals concentrate on conservation; their concerns range from national lands to energy, packaging, and a host of practices regarded as wasteful. Other concerns are with issues of product safety, environmental pollution, protection of wildlife. Stylistically the Societally Conscious range from aggressive political antagonism, to the more muted collaborative resistance of networks with a commmon interest, to withdrawal to lives of voluntary simplicity.

As a group the Societally Conscious are successful, influential, mature. They are, in a sense, the inner-directed equivalent of outer-directed Achievers, but they differ attitudinally in fundamental ways. Most Societally Conscious people share some key beliefs: that humanity should live in harmony with nature and not try to dominate it; that nature has its own wisdom; that small is usually beautiful; that this truly is one world; that nonmaterial aspects of life are in some sense "higher" than the material; that each person can, and should, help remedy societal problems; that outer simplicity often goes with inner richness; that simplicity may be the most powerful lifestyle of the future.[2]

Few of the Societally Conscious live fully the life of voluntary simplicity, but all act on at least some aspects of it (although, of course, they are not the only ones who do). Thus, for example, they may ride a bicycle or drive an economy car, insulate their home or install solar heating, eat only foods grown without pesticides or prepared without additives.

As a group the Societally Conscious are a sophisticated and politically effective lot. At an average age of almost forty, they have arrived at positions of influence in their jobs and communities. An extraordinary 39 percent have attended graduate school and, even more extraordinary, 59 percent hold professional or technical jobs. Average income in 1979 exceeded $27,000. These outward trappings of success combine with a consistent attitudinal pattern to create a high degree of political activism. Most try to lead lives that conserve, protect, heal. Their confidence in outer-directed leadership is minimal. They have returned unsatisfactory products or complained to a store more than any other group. They are much worried about air pollution, support more spending to protect the environment, believe industrial growth should be limited, and feel more than most that military spending is too high. Societally conscious people place a high importance on energy conservation in the home—more than any other group they have looked into solar heating—and, again leading the groups, they believe the energy crisis is real.

The fact—and action—of societal awareness is of course the psychological hallmark of this lifestyle. Although numbering only 8 or 9 percent of the adult population (but rapidly expanding), the Societally Conscious have had, and are having, a very substantial political and corporate impact on the country. They more than any other group have used the powerful technique known as "single-issue politics"—a technique that has enabled tiny percentages of the population to block causes supported by far larger numbers. The style of the Societally

Conscious has often been aggressively confrontational, reflecting the assuredness of the group. In corporate areas they have spearheaded consumer issues and have powered attacks on corporate practices ranging from investment policies to product safety to more diverse representation on corporate boards.

The overall picture is of a well-educated, prosperous, politically liberal group driven by social ideals that they take with high seriousness. Our portrait of two sisters sketches a gentle variation of this lifestyle in an urban setting. For Mort, activism has taken a scientific turn.

COMBINED OUTER- AND INNER-DIRECTED GROUP

Integrateds

Maturity, balance, and a sense of what is "fitting" are prime characteristics of the Integrateds. These are people who have put together the decisiveness of Outer-Direction with the penetration of Inner-Direction. To these rare individuals Outer-Direction and Inner-Direction are equally good, powerful, useful, and needed; the two styles are simply different, each appropriate in its own place. Psychologically mature, the Integrateds have an unusual ability to weigh consequences, to consider subtlety along with flamboyance, to see the small within the large and the potential within what has gone wrong.

These qualities of mind and spirit enable Integrateds, we think, often to pluck the best from opposing views and combine them into a solution that subsumes both perspectives. Abraham Lincoln—surely an Integrated human being in his later years—was able to do this in trying to mend the wounds of the Civil War. Such tasks are not easy but the Integrated person is unusual, seeing things from a perspective hidden from all but a few. And so it was that Lincoln (and countless heretics and pioneers over the centuries) was excoriated by many on one side and slain by the other.

Such people elude the common ways, hence are recognized less by exterior measures than are members of the other categories. Most of us know some few people who seem to have a kind of inner completeness, a kind of deep-core certainty, that commands respect, admiration, sometimes awe, and not infrequently love. These are people one truly trusts and seeks to be like. These are people who seem to have more wisdom than the rest of us. Very likely these people are Integrateds.

Because of the elusiveness of the Integrated lifestyle, we have not yet been able to identify Integrateds on the basis of the demographic and attitudinal items we have used to categorize the other eight lifestyle groups. One reason is that there are not many people who have attained a truly integrated outlook on life. Our estimate for the fraction of American adults that qualify is 2 percent. If this is correct, our main survey should have included thirty-three Integrateds—not a large enough number to identify with confidence. A second and more compelling reason is that Integrateds undoubtedly are highly diverse, subtle in their responses, complex in their outlook. The "golden mean" characterizes many of their reactions. These attributes make it exceptionally difficult to capture such people in the agree/disagree terms of our survey. A third and very real problem is that the issues and problems of greatest concern to Integrateds involve subtleties and perspectives (as in the case of Lincoln) that either are not understood at all or are badly misinterpreted by people of other lifestyles. The latter may respond to a questionnaire item in the same fashion as the Integrateds yet mean something wholly different—a fact that the data analyst cannot determine. Work in the Values and Lifestyle program at SRI International is continuing in an effort to find means of defining the Integrateds through the development of more discriminating items, but as of now reliable results are not available.

Our sense is that Integrated people adapt easily to most conventions and mores but are powerfully mission-oriented on matters about which they feel strongly. They are people able to lead when action is required and able to follow when that seems appropriate. They usually possess a deep sense of what is fitting and appropriate. They tend to be open, self-assured, self-expressive, keenly aware of nuance and shadings, and often possessed of a world perspective. Our guess is that they are able to do their best, to be satisfied with the result, and to move on to what is next. We would expect them to be quick with laughter and generous with tears, to have found ways to meld work and play, to combine close relationships with people with the drive to accomplish (rather than visibly achieve). We think they are both makers and movers, observers and creators—people who believe in themselves and in what they are doing.

Our surmise is that Integrated individuals score high both as Achievers and as Societally Conscious types. If this surmise is correct, we can draw some inferences concerning the demographics, attitudes, and financial status of the group.

We would expect most Integrateds to be people of middle or upper middle years, many of whom have lived decades as successful Achievers or Societally Conscious. They find it wise or necessary to move from those ways of life to the integrated pattern usually as a result of changing basic values as to what is important. A smaller but particularly interesting group probably consists of much younger people, in their thirties or even twenties, who have had the good luck, the means, and the gifts to find themselves early in life. Our portrait of the Storall family represents the first path of evolution, and the vignette of Tree Sammath the second.

Reflecting Achievers and the Societally Conscious, we would expect Integrateds to be slightly more male than female, generally married, heavily Caucasian, very well educated, working in well-paying occupations, with average incomes of $30,000 or more. They probably would be less conservative than Achievers and less liberal than the Societally Conscious.

The Integrateds probably would not feel rebellious or express much need for social status—although they would have it. Our sense is that they might remain quite divided on controversial social questions that now distinguish Achievers from the Societally Conscious. These probably would include issues such as legalization of marijuana, industrial growth, military and environmental spending. We would expect them to draw closer together, however, on more personal issues such as women working, unmarried sex, trust in organizational leaders, or most consumer trends.

We also believe the Integrateds play a unique and crucial role in the operation of our society. We shall, however, defer discussion of this role until Part IV.

2

The Double Hierarchy

The array of lifestyles sketched on the previous pages is far from random; rather it is bound together by underlying principles and organized to fill specific needs and to answer explicit questions. The initial problem involved devising a comprehensive conceptual framework of values and lifestyles that would bring the various observations we made over the years together into an integrated whole. Ideally, the framework would be of such a nature that a change in one part would point to compensating changes in other parts.

We started from the premise that an individual's array of inner values would create specific matching patterns of outer behavior—that is, of lifestyles. Neither values nor lifestyles alone, we thought, would be sufficient to provide the framework we were seeking. The idea was that behavior—private, economic, social, or political—is not random but reflects specific sets of inner drives. These drives, of course, may have their origins in external reality, such as poverty. They may also originate in internal reality, such as the dream of being a great athlete. We hoped that a framework linking the outer and the inner might yield the comprehensive system we were looking for.

We knew that, to be useful, the framework would have to be simple enough to understand easily and consist of elements vivid enough to identify with. This meant, among other things, that it could not have more than nine parts—a number selected because the human mind seems unable easily to retain more than this level of complexity. (It would be much easier, if not so useful, to devise a typology of 20 or 50 or 100 segments.) The scheme should be applicable to the large majority of adult Americans and, we hoped, to other Western cultures as well.

One further requirement was evident. If our work was to be of practical usefulness in forecasting societal change, it would be clearly essential that the model provide some means of connecting events with shifts within the framework. What this meant to us was essentially two things: (1) some of the measures relied upon to define the groups within the typology should be highly projectible, such as age, education, and other demographic attributes of people; more significantly, (2) the framework would have to reflect an underlying theory that would tie it together into a coherent whole, so that we could say how a change at point y would be likely to affect conditions at point x and point z. This requirement for a comprehensive concept bonding the typology into a coordinated entity was easily the most difficult criterion we imposed on ourselves. However, it was also the criterion that promised exceptional power to any system that could meet it.

THE LIFESTYLE STAGES

Our work over the past twenty years has exposed us to a great variety of schemes calculated to serve as frameworks for characterizing various attributes and qualities of people. (These schemes are briefly summarized a little later.) What we ultimately came up with after much sieving and screening was a typology—that is, a series of types—running from psychological immaturity at the Survivor level to full psychological maturity at the Integrated level. Being a step-wise progression, the system is of course a hierarchy. Each level is characterized by its unique inward needs and values, which are manifested outwardly through a matching style of life.

The progression defined by the typology consists of distinct and discrete stages, each of which can be thought of as a lifestyle. Stages 1 through 5 are at heart outer-directed and include the need-driven lifestyles. Stages 6 through 8 are at heart inner-directed but take off from outer-directed lifestyles. Stage 9 combines outer- and inner-directed ways of life. Here is the essence of the pattern of growth:

Stage 1. Central concern with survival—just to make it from day to day is enough.

Stage 2. Central concern with sustaining and solidifying gains made from the Survivor stage and, if possible, extending them.

Stage 3. Central concern with belonging, being accepted by others, fitting into a closed, sharply defined, local network.

Stage 4. Central concern with breaking free of the local network to make it as an individual within the major system, emulating leaders of the system.

Stage 5. Central concern with achievement, success, leadership, and power in the major system.

Stage 6. Central concern with breaking free of outer-directed patterns and discovery of the inner self.

Stage 7. Central concern with living intensely, vividly, and experientially, so as to widen and deepen the inner experience.

Stage 8. Central concern with societal issues, especially those affecting the less material qualities of life.

Stage 9. Central concern with melding outer and inner perspectives so as to combine the best of the two into higher-order views.

Change and movement up the typology take place only when life's events satisfy to a considerable degree the special needs, goals, and values of a given stage. When this occurs, the individual is free to "graduate" to the next level. Progress up the typology thus consists of a series of transitions or transformations (sometimes called "passages") from one stage to the next, more complex stage. The drivers of change tend to be different at each stage. By definition, achievement of each new stage brings with it a fresh set of inner values, which find outward expression in a new lifestyle. The total array is thus a nested model, with all preceding steps buried within each existing stage, like the rings of an onion. The significance of this is great. For example, it explains why highly developed people often "see themselves" at various VALS levels at different times—they *are* all of these levels! The nested model further implies that individuals at all levels of development understand their present stages plus all earlier stages but—not having been there—have little comprehension of the value structures, rationales, and inner logics of people at more advanced levels of development. Some far-reaching implications of this phenomenon are examined in Part III.

The values and lifestyles typology explicitly considers psychological maturity. Very generally, psychological maturity is marked by a progression from partial toward full realization of one's emotional, intellectual, and spiritual potentials. It involves a steady widening of perspectives and concerns and a steady deepening of the inner reference points consulted in making important decisions. In general, progression is step by step, with no omissions. There may be exceptions, however; if there are, the personal and social consequences may be severe (as we shall see later). It is also worth noting that people born into favored circumstances often live through early stages, such as the Survivor or Sustainer levels, only vicariously. Such people go through their lives with no deep appreciation of these earlier stages and to that extent are less whole human beings.

It should be recognized from the start that lifestyles are, happily, not fixed and immutable. People change levels as children, as adolescents, and as adults. Many people—possibly most—move one or two levels upward from their "entry point" into our typology at about age eighteen. Some very few may move from the bottom to the top in a lifetime. "Slipping back" is also a common phenomenon, as discussed later. To make the situation even more complex, some people seem to exhibit different lifestyles in various areas of their lives. There are fiercely Achiever corporate executives who are mild Belongers at home and strictly Survivors on the golf course! (Such a person almost surely would test out as an Achiever, since that is the "highest" of the three and the style that calls for the most complex and demanding support system of values. Put another way, the Achiever style is that person's "outermost" layer of values, even though he or she may spend much time operating at less demanding levels.) Despite such complications the concept of lifestyle is a powerful and convenient shorthand way of describing the main thrust of a person's way of life.

The notion of lifestyle may be likened to the bullfighting term *querencia*.* Every bull, it seems, has his favorite spot or turf in the bullring. That is where he feels most comfortable, most in control. When prodded or lured, he may sally forth into other parts of the ring, but soon, in response to his *querencia* (or homing instinct), he will return to the piece of ground where the world seems most familiar. So it is with people. Under stressful conditions an individual may temporarily move up or down or across to another lifestyle pattern, usually in some limited life domain such as work or marriage. Yet, unless the stresses mount and the new lifestyle pattern seems more satisfactory than the old, that person will gravitate back to the place that is best understood and least threatening—the home lifestyle.

---

* We are indebted to Howard Leonard of Young & Rubicam for this felicitous analogy.

The typology we have devised is conceptual in its origin. We identified, named, and characterized the nine lifestyles and their supporting
attributes on the basis of theory—that is, on the basis of our understanding of the way people are. As we shall see shortly, key elements of
the theory were drawn from developmental psychology, but these were
sifted not only through our sense of the values that would be connected
with each developmental stage, but through probable associated activities and consumption habits and an array of allied demographic
features. In the course of our search we looked at and discarded numerous market and social typologies developed by others. These typologies
and the reason for discarding them are cited in the Appendix.

DEVELOPMENTAL PSYCHOLOGY

Many readers will recognize that the values and lifestyles typology is
eclectic; we have plucked ideas and terms from many places. Much its
greatest debt, however, is owed to the works of personality theorists
working in the area of developmental psychology. The needs hierarchy
of Abraham Maslow, which formed the basis of our 1969 report called
American Values,[1] has contributed most notably to the thinking behind
the VALS typology.

Personality theorists have attempted to identify the key steps in the
growth of people from immaturity (at whatever age) to full maturity
(also at whatever age). Most of the developmental typologies are hierarchical in that growth is said to proceed along a specified path, moving
"upward" from one stage to the next. Developmental hierarchies of this
sort have been proposed in explanation of many human characteristics,
such as psychological maturity, motivations, personality, morality, in-
tellect, communications, and so on. These schemes share the notion
that growth can be usefully divided into steps or levels. Some of the
theories identify but three stages, others ten or more. To provide some
sense (but, of course, vastly oversimplified) of key commonalities
among these schemes, we have prepared Table 1, which shows the main
terms used by some leading theorists to identify the stages of growth as
perceived by them. The VALS scheme appears first for comparison.

What is most important about the typologies outlined in the table is
that each, in its own fashion, suggests a pattern of development deemed
to reflect the innermost evolving growth patterns of humans, whether
for the total personality or for some facet of it. Maslow is explicit in

TABLE 1 Selected Typologies of Human Development

SOURCE	IMMATURE			MATURE
VALS	Survivor & Sustainer	Belonger	Emulator, Achiever, I-Am-Me, Experiential, Societally Conscious	Integrated
Maslow[2]	Survival & security	Belonging	Esteem	Self-actualizing
Graves[3]	Aggressive and animistic	Belonging and ordered existence	Materialist	Personalistic and being-motivated
Loevinger[4]	Impulse-ridden	Conformist	Autonomous	Integrated
McClelland[5]	Protection and support	Expressive and regulation of emotion	Master of external world	Self-direction and support
Erikson[6]	Basic trust	Industry	Initiative	Identity
Porter[7]	Security	Social	Esteem and autonomy	Self-actualizing
Fromm[8]	Receptive	Hoarding	Marketing & exploitative	Productive
Harvey[9]	Very concrete (I)	Fairly concrete (II)	Fairly abstract (III)	Highly abstract (IV)
Peck and Havighurst[10]	Amoral & expedient	Conforming	Irrational-conscientious	Rational-altruistic
Kohlberg[11]	Preconventional, stages 1 and 2	Conventional, stages 3 and 4	Postconventional, stage 5	Postconventional, stages 6 and 7
Athos[12]	Knowledge absolute	Knowledge situational	Knowledge relative	Knowledge normative
C. Kluckhohn[13]	Physiological	Social	Individual	
McGregor[14] and Maslow[15]		Theory X	Theory Y	Theory Z
Kantor[16]	Discord	Homeostatic		Unfolding
Shostrom[17]	Immaturity	Adjustment		Self-actualizing
Bruner[18]	Enactive	Iconic		Symbolic
Riesman[19]	Inner-directed	Tradition-directed	Outer-directed	Autonomous
Levinson[20]	Childhood & adolescence	Early adulthood	Middle adulthood	Late adulthood
Bridges[21]	Novice period	Settling down		Forest period

saying that neither intellectual capacity nor educational attainment are substantial considerations in progress up his hierarchy. Indeed, it is a fascinating fact that the concept of self-actualization was developed by one of Maslow's teachers, Kurt Goldstein, when working with brain-damaged children. So it is the concept of sequential stages—the flow—of the maturing individual, whatever his or her predicament, that is the central theme of these diverse schemata. And so it is also in the VALS typology.

THE DOUBLE HIERARCHY

Given the nine lifestyles sketched earlier, the next question is how they fit together into a system. The obvious model is that of the single nested "onion," running from the Need-Drivens through Outer-Directeds and Inner-Directeds to the combined Outer- and Inner-Directed. But this does not work in a practical sense, for the outer-directed styles of Emulator and Achiever seem to overlap the inner-directed styles of I-Am-Me, Experiential, and Societally Conscious in many dimensions of maturity. One may properly argue, as we do, that Inner-Directeds are (in the American culture) in a more complex and diverse psychological stage than Outer-Directeds because almost all American Inner-Directeds learned Outer-Direction as children and adolescents—and Inner-Direction was *their* way of growing. But, despite this, it certainly is not true, for example, that I-Am-Mes are more mature emotionally, or intellectually, or spiritually than, say, Achievers. They are, in fact, markedly less mature in these ways, if only because they are twenty years or so younger and have correspondingly less experience in living. In these dimensions of maturity Emulators seem to correspond most precisely to the I-Am-Mes and Experientials and Achievers to the Societally Conscious. Key demographics such as age and income are roughly aligned in these groupings, and they even share some attitudes, especially those relating to the so-called new values that burst into prominence during the 1960s. These commonalities are substantial enough to suggest that, in a hierarchical array, Emulators should be roughly the equivalent of the I-Am-Me and Experiential inner-directed stages, and Achievers the equivalent of the Societally Conscious.

But how about the relationship of these groups with Belongers? It seems obvious that Emulator and Achiever types and the three inner-directed groups all are post-Belonger and pre-Integrated. The reason they must follow the Belonger stage is that a deep sense of belonging is a prerequisite to coping with the shifts and surges and uncertainties of growing through the upper stages of Outer-Direction and the levels of Inner-Direction. At the Belonging stage the individual acquires the sense of home and solidity and safety so essential to support further growth. Without the personal and cultural roots developed as a Belonger, the individual cannot withstand the buffeting of winds to come. Without a sense of a rock-ribbed homeland to return to—whether family, church, nation, or another—few people dare venture forth on paths that lead into unknown regions.

These lines of reasoning finally led us to the idea that our system of lifestyles is not a single system but a double hierarchy over the zone from Belonging to Integration. If this is the case, the VALS typology can be drawn as shown in Figure 1.

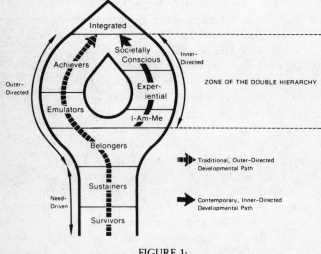

FIGURE 1:
The Lifestyles Double Hierarchy

Since we are suggesting that people can arrive at the Integrated level over the distance of the double zone by either an outer-directed or an inner-directed route, we are also saying that both routes must provide, in their own ways, appropriate satisfactions and insights to cope with the fundamental human needs over that span of development.

The Inner-Directed Way

At the Belonger level the individual is concerned primarily with extending him- or herself beyond the Need-Driven immediacy of self to the family, the church, the organization (often the school), the nation, and a diversity of other groups, cliques, and tribes. This crucial stage of development is an essential predecessor to branching out into an unknown and sometimes hostile world as a person on one's own, which cannot be done successfully unless the individual has a sense that there are safe and friendly domains (i.e., the areas of belonging) to which to retreat if the going gets too rough. And so it is that belonging (but not necessarily belonging as the basic level of functioning) often plays a clear role in Inner-Directedness—for example, in the communal living common among inner-directed adherents to the emergent lifestyle of voluntary simplicity.

Typically, in the postwar United States, the age of branching off into the inner-directed line is young—middle to late teens. The familiar syndrome is what we have described as I-Am-Me. It seems clearly transitional, marked as it is by both highly visible, showoff outer-directed behavior and an often hidden inner seeking for meaning, emotion, and motivation. Rejection of familiar parental patterns is often blatant, giving rise to behaviors, dress, appearances, and attitudes that are studiously designed to be opposite from those of one's roots. A decade or more ago few things could have signaled this transition more clearly than long hair, dropoutism, opposition to Vietnam, hippie dress, experimentation with drugs, strikes on campus, and parading against the establishment. Such actions of course partook both of true developmental behavior and of fad behavior, the latter being more common as the trend widened. Today the signs tend to be less flamboyant but, as we shall see in Part IV, they are nevertheless apparent.

It is clear that most of those taking the "new values" seriously came from prosperous backgrounds. Their family upbringing had satisfied their taste for materialism; their youthful rejection of parental values satisfied their needs for power and recognition: They knew they belonged, and they had no need to emulate. And they were free—few had imperative economic responsibilities. As a result, they did not have to repeat the outer-directed evolution of their parents; they could, and did, move straight from the broad cultural mainstream represented by the Achiever lifestyle into their inner-directed evolution.

Of course, the mere fact of veering away from the familiar in no way means that all the virtues, reasons, limitations, and other aspects of the old pattern are fully understood or appreciated. In other words, I-Am-

Me types may be reacting most explicitly with respect to Achiever values and lifestyles, but that does not imply that they are in any way superior to the Achievers, and certainly not that they are as emotionally or intellectually mature. For this reason it is appropriate to locate the I-Am-Me group opposite the earlier outer-directed style of Emulator and, for the reasons discussed earlier, just above the Belonger level.

We have pointed out that the I-Am-Me stage tends to be short-lived—despite many social incentives to delay maturity. This may be related to the fact that at this stage of development the drive toward something—the allure of what could be and the vision of how things ought to be—as distinct from the drive away, seems rather lacking in most I-Am-Me individuals. Concerns are very close-in, short-range, and shallow in perspective. This overemphasis on rejection perhaps explains why I-Am-Me individuals seem usually to have to work their way back into involvement through an intense, often prolonged, Experiential stage.

The Experiential phase represents a broadening of I-Am-Me perspectives beyond the narrow confines of the individual and his or her small clique. The individual begins to probe more deeply inside and more widely outside. Although often intensely hedonistic, this is a time for developing interest in the arts, in interpersonal relationships, and in political and world affairs. The Experiential is the stage that is the most purely inner-directed in the VALS typology—hence, in the double hierarchy we have drawn it farthest removed from the Outer-Directed line of development.

As the years pass, the hedonism of Experientials tends to yield to the artistic and spiritual drives of Inner-Directedness; intellectual pleasures are on the ascendancy; a sense of responsibility to others looms larger. Spurring this maturation is a general satisfying of many needs through wide-ranging experiences. Further, there usually is a growing realization that intense personal experience alone will not satisfy many basic needs, especially without an improvement in life's general circumstances. And so it is that the Experiential phase gradually transforms for many into the Societally Conscious stage. One might say that from the I-Am-Me stage the individual has passed through a We-Are-Ourselves phase to the comprehensive perspective of We-Are-Together.

As we have said, the Societally Conscious are the inner-directed equivalent of Achievers. Both groups are successful, affluent, self-assured, and in positions of influence. The Societally Conscious, however, tend to be especially concerned with the affairs and workings of the world and at the same time intensely interested in their own inner growth. Many are active in promoting social movements and causes they see as needed to restrain the power of "the system." Some act out their beliefs and hence find themselves in political opposition to Achievers. Others today respond at a more personal level and withdraw from the "big life," preferring lives of voluntary simplicity.

Whether active or passive, the Societally Conscious person's engagement with the Achiever-dominated world affects him or her just as much as he or she affects the Achiever. In the early stages of the inner-directed way there usually is a deep need to be different from the mainstream. If one really hears a different drummer, how can one be like everyone else? As that almost pathological need to be different fades, real inner motives can begin to emerge, and the inability to see anything good in another's viewpoint happily disappears. It is our sense that the "advanced" Societally Conscious and "advanced" Achievers share more views and appreciate what the other believes in. Ambivalence appears common: Both want to do well while doing good (and vice versa). Probably this is one reason why the two groups sometimes find themselves on the same side of issues that earlier seemed wholly divisive. For example, the self-reliance of those living lives of voluntary simplicity dovetails politically with the laissez-faire view of many Achievers; similarly, some inner-directed advocates of minority rights heavily emphasize bootstrapping in the classic tradition, in preference to a philosophy of entitlements and quotas. This coming together of experienced, effective people of wide perspectives, despite some basic differences in personal orientation, explains why we have drawn the lifestyles double hierarchy to suggest a rapprochement at the top of the two stages.

This rapprochement, of course, is prelude to the melding that is the essence of the Integrated level topping the VALS hierarchy. The Integrated individual possesses the psychological maturity to appreciate many sides of an issue, the confidence both to doubt and to believe, and the experience to evaluate the various positions. This is by no means to say that such people are effective leaders; our impression is that many are not. But they do tend to play useful behind-the-scenes roles as balancers, agents of change, and gap spanners.

The Outer-Directed Way

The picture we are painting is of a steadily widening range of concerns and deepening insight into one's self as one moves up the inner-directed way. The development on the outer-directed side parallels this growth.

The rewards there, however, are less likely to be internal and emotional and more likely to be visible, external, material; the vehicles are more likely to be system-oriented (often corporate) and less likely to be personal; the style is more likely to be competitive, market-oriented, and quantitative.

Emulators adopt the traditional outer-directed route to development because, as maturing children and youths, they usually did not experience the pleasures and rewards of materialism, power, recognition, and the big life. Most were brought up in Belonger or Need-Driven families. The Emulator's vision of the Achiever's world may be extreme and unrealistic, but it is above all compelling. Few drives in Western societies are more powerful or universal than that toward overt success, provided one is ready to respond to the drive. Emulators are doubly ready. Not only are they dissatisfied with the have-not Need-Driven phase and with the sedate, conservative Belonger phase, but (unlike the I-Am-Mes) they respond intensely and positively to a culture that provides countless models and images of the rewards of Achiever status. They are motivated by both the fear of not being good enough and the promise of being great.

Emulators in their early stages share the flamboyance and narcissism of the I-Am-Me stage. The sensational $1,000 costume, the flashy car, bombastic oratory, the boastful T-shirt all proclaim the Emulator. This style is so similar to the blatant I-Am-Me style that we have shown a joining of the early Emulator and early I-Am-Me levels in the diagram of our typology. The raucous stage soon passes, often yielding in corporate or bureaucratic ranks to what Michael Maccoby called the Jungle Fighter, whether fox or lion.[22] If Emulators are lucky enough to get exposure to real Achievers, their flamboyance and machinations usually abate. At this stage Emulators adopt a cool, buttoned-down, conspicuously correct style—a style very different from the unclassy, homey pattern of the Belonger. In time, they may become Achievers.

Achievers, as we have said before, include many leaders in business, politics, and the professions. It is they who have built the American system and who represent the Establishment. In general they are able, confident, effective people who have every reason to think their lifestyle is a good one—it has put them on top. It is this very "proof" that makes it so difficult for many Achievers to accept the Inner-Directedness of their I-Am-Me children or the viewpoints of Societally Conscious activists.

But two significant kinds of changes often occur in successful Achievers over the years. Achievers, especially those in corporate life, must cope with the ideas of inner-directed people as expressed in social movements ranging from consumer activism to affirmative-action programs to governmental regulations. It is by no means unusual for their interaction with, say, enlightened Societally Conscious individuals to produce important areas of agreement—or at least of less disagreement. Understanding and appreciation of non-Achiever perspectives is often deep and genuine. It is not uncommon for top business leaders to regard social responsibility as a critical corporate priority and to take actions that win more approval from the Inner-Directeds than from the ranks of Achievers.

The second change has to do with more personal concerns. Achiever values and lifeways sometimes begin to pall, just as some inner-directed types may conclude that, say, country living is not all that gratifying. This sometimes happens, for example, when the successful Achiever has no new fields to conquer; it can also happen more mysteriously in response to some deep shift in private priorities. If Achiever values no longer challenge and inspire and drive, the individual begins a search for motivations and activities with more meaning and more excitement. It is this sort of search that produces the spectacular life changes we sometimes hear about: the eminent businessman who embraces the simple life or the vice president who drops sales management to take up painting. Such changes—which seldom are as sudden as they may appear—could be represented as leaps across the gap in the double hierarchy.

But even if the break is not complete, successful Achievers can, like their inner-directed colleagues, acquire the balance and the maturity that mark the Integrated level. Frequently personal habits change in response to newfound values; seasoned executives may start to take longer vacations, get interested in various "good works," perhaps learn to meditate, develop friendships with people to whom they once were not attracted, drop old hobbies and begin new ones, and so on. (Comparable changes occur among inner-directed leaders who have begun deeply to understand the values of Achievers.) It is our guess that many top executives at this stage remove themselves from day-to-day operating responsibilities and seek a position where, less visibly, they can serve their firm by integrating into its activities the broader and more diverse values they have come to appreciate.

3

Mechanisms of Change

We have thus far sketched nine lifestyles and suggested how they fit together into a coherent system. Implicit in the discussion is the assumption that adults move up, down, or across the double hierarchy. Such change is one of the most fascinating and significant hallmarks of our times. The common statement that the rate of change is accelerating seems really to mean that *we* are changing rapidly as individuals, for our external world is no more changeable than it has been in the past several generations. Indeed, one could argue that more truly massive physical changes in our living environment occurred in the early years of this century than in the post–World War II years. But changes in people's attitudes, expectations, inner needs, and the nature of their dreams have shifted and flowed and transformed with unprecedented rapidity in recent times.

But it is important to understand that not *everything* changes when something—such as a lifestyle—changes. In fact, some argue that the psychological consistency of people over time is more impressive than the degree of change. For example, individual personality traits, such as cheerfulness, seem seldom to change over time. We have no reason to dispute these findings, but we would call attention to two explanatory conditions.

First, some people do not change appreciably in a psychological sense after having reached about age eighteen. We have no reliable numbers on how many do and how many don't. Our sense is that a far smaller fraction of people reaching majority in the pre–World War II period have radically changed their values as adults than is true of those maturing in the 1960s or later. Hence, contrary to common sense, the longer the period over which measurements of the stability of personal values are taken, the less likely they are to reveal changes.

Second, in our model, change is by definition incremental. Each transition to a new lifestyle adds an increment to the old, as specified by the nested nature of our schema. To the individual, who sees him- or herself from the inside, the attainment of a new lifestyle seems a total transformation, for he or she is now aware largely of what is new, the old being of much less interest. But in truth some values and attitudes and most personality traits have not changed. Thus personality inventories are likely to yield a picture that is accurate from one perspective, but not one that the individual would find particularly pertinent, revealing, or even descriptive.

DYNAMICS OF CHANGE

Irrespective of the problems of measuring change, there can be no doubt that personal change and growth are widespread phenomena in all segments of American society. Psychologist William Bridges in his book *Transitions* writes eloquently of times of change.

> Throughout nature, growth involves periodic accelerations and transformations: Things go slowly for a time and nothing seems to change—until suddenly the eggshell cracks, the branch blossoms, the tadpole's tail shrinks away, the leaf falls, the bird molts, the hibernation begins. With us it is the same. Although the signs are less clear than in the world of feather and leaf, the functions of transition times are the same. They are the key times in the natural process of self-renewal.[1]

Bridges writes of the growth process from old to new in terms of three stages: Endings, The Neutral Zone, and Beginnings. Endings are seldom recognized as such by the person undergoing change. The period is marked by such distressing symptoms as disengagement, disidentification, disenchantment, and disorientation. As Robert Frost put it, you must be "lost enough to find yourself."

The Neutral Zone is like a river separating Endings and Beginnings. In crossing the river comes a sense of emptiness, of being neither in the familiar land of yesterday nor the unreached land of tomorrow. The problem at this stage, as stated in the *Tao Te Ching*, is to "savor that without flavor." The individual is struggling to perceive another reality, to let germinate the seed of Ending discontent.

And only when that seed has sprouted does the Beginning begin.

Beginnings start with a hint, an image, a dream, a premonition. An inner realignment takes place, and out of the dissatisfaction of Endings and the emptiness of The Neutral Zone comes the transition to new perspectives and new activities.

To be successful in this most difficult of transitions—psychological growth—requires a special combination of inner and, to a degree, of outer circumstances. These are set forth with splendid simplicity by psychologist Clare Graves.[2]

Graves says that a person must possess three attributes if he or she is to make a substantial psychological step forward:

○ The individual must be deeply dissatisfied. Otherwise why change?

○ The individual must possess much psychological and physical energy. Few things are harder to break than old bonds, old views, old prejudices, old convictions, old loves.

○ The individual must have or acquire the psychological insight to know what will slake the driving dissatisfaction. Without this, the effort to change will be directionless, ceaseless, and pointless.

Only when all three of these factors are present simultaneously will a person have the motivation to change, the drive to act on the motivation, and the perspicacity to know where to go and when he or she has arrived.

The power of Graves's trio is revealed by the radically different results if any of the three conditions are not met:

○ Dissatisfied, with energy but no insight: someone who rides off in all directions at once; full of sound and fury, signifying nothing.

○ Dissatisfied, with insight but no energy: a wailer and complainer; a lazy know-it-all, who gets nothing done.

○ Insightful and full of energy, but not dissatisfied: a leader in his or her chosen field, but not a changer.

Graves's analysis suggests that what happens when people grow is something like this: A person is living a life that seems fairly satisfactory. With the passage of time, however, for one or more of many different reasons a certain sense arises that some old answers, some previous solutions no longer work as well as they used to. The conviction emerges that the explanations heretofore accepted contain unnoticed discrepancies, that some new ideas simply don't fit into the old schema, that once-forbidden feelings unaccountably surface when they seem least appropriate. In brief, the old familiar paradigm of beliefs and thoughts no longer holds the comprehensive explanatory power it once did and no longer covers everything important. One is, so to speak, awakened in the chill night because one's toes are sticking out beyond the blanket.

Naturally this is disquieting, and the individual tends to become distrustful, angry, and confused, simultaneously assertive and uncertain. For a period the doubts may be resolutely rejected and the old beliefs embraced with exaggerated vehemence. But over time, if the individual remains at least partly open to fresh feelings and ideas, the doubts will tend to deepen and to spread until they have penetrated to the realms of innermost values. Almost inevitably the unconscious and conscious minds working together will explore approach after approach, concept after concept, idea after idea in search of resolution. Ultimately, if the person is lucky, persistent, or perhaps skillfully guided, he or she will hit on a new paradigm that explains all the old plus the new "misfits" as well. And this exciting and creative burst of insight opens a new and shining way of looking at things. The emergence of insights (if they come!) may be a "flash of genius," but far more commonly insights come forth haltingly in bits and pieces until, looking backward perhaps years later, it amazingly is revealed that the person has grown, silently and largely unaware, from one stage of human development to another, more complex, more comprehensive, more subtle, more sensitive state of being.

CAUSES OF CHANGE

Given this basic pattern of change, it is appropriate to ask: What powers or blocks such transitions? Certainly there is no simple or single answer. Indeed, the question lies at the heart of an unending sociological argument that is parallel to the age-old nature-vs.-nurture dispute so prominent in discussions of IQ. The question is: Do external forces, internal psychodynamic forces, sociological processes, or other kinds of pressures trigger change in people? Very likely all do at different times for different people and in different circumstances. Below we have tried to summarize the main categories of influence that seem to govern whether people do or do not change as adults.

Events and circumstances.   There is no doubt that events and circumstances both cause and block human growth. Bridges[3] believes that events associated with love and work are the main drivers of change, and he names such items as marriage, divorce, death of a loved one, birth of a first child, job change, being fired, financial reverses. Other kinds of events that might trigger change include serious illness, going to war, discovery of an overwhelming new idea, meeting an unusual person, exposure to another culture or way of life. One's particular life circumstances also have much to do with personal change because they tend to control the nature of subsequent life events. Thus incessant poverty, illiteracy, or even such circumstances as being black in the United States tend to obstruct many channels of growth. People who manage to break loose from these kinds of cultural bonds usually move swiftly up the VALS typology.

Age.   The central thesis of psychiatrist David Levinson in *The Seasons of a Man's Life*[4] is that age per se drives the "macro-structure of the life cycle." The basic notion is that people encounter different problems at different ages, and attempts to cope with these problems induce change. Age-driven change implies advancing maturity rather less than many theories. Levinson correlates certain types of psychological concern, and hence pressures to change, with four somewhat overlapping stages: (1) childhood and adolescence (ages 0–22), (2) early adulthood (ages 17–45), (3) middle adulthood (ages 40–65), and (4) late adulthood (age 60 and up). Gould[5] also emphasizes the age-related nature of many adult crises that lead to change, but, as we discuss below, he sees the main drives as reflecting unresolved childhood issues.

History.   History-as-driver underlies the analytical approach known as cohort or generational analysis. (A "psychological generation" usually extends six or seven years on either side of the individual.) The notion is that people raised in a particular era such as the Great Depression, the World War II period, the halcyon 1950s, the rebellious 1960s, and so forth, forever carry a certain characteristic psychological bent. In this view history is regarded more as a constriction of growth than as a spur. Far more elegantly and profoundly, philosophers like Carl Jung[6] and Joseph Campbell[7] have utilized archetypal images out of history to help explain the drives and growth patterns of people.

Unresolved childhood and other experiences. Freud, of course, first made famous the notion that unresolved experiences dating back into early childhood often lie at the roots of adult problems that trigger the need for psychological change. Many others also have explored this realm. For example, fairly recently Eric Berne[8] and others, in the psychological theory known as Transactional Analysis, have emphasized the role of the "child ego state" in the behavior of people. Even more recently the psychiatrist Roger L. Gould in *Transformations*[9] advances the argument from still another perspective. The thrust of his analysis is that each advance we make as adults is painful because it represents a reluctant leave-taking from the comforting but unrealistic assumptions, rules, and fantasies established in childhood.

Changing paradigms. This view holds that a major driver of change arises from the reshaping of basic beliefs, concepts, ideas, and assumptions that underlie our cultural image of reality. Thus, for example, a couple of centuries ago abandonment of the notion of the divine right of kings wholly transformed the standard political view. Today belief in the reality of parapsychological phenomena or deep acceptance of the principles of voluntary simplicity may change traditional ideas concerning what is possible and what is good. Shifts in paradigms as a societal force have been treated with exceptional insight by futurists such as Peter Schwartz and James Oglivy[10] and Willis Harman.[11]

Natural development. Many developmental psychologists—Abraham Maslow among them—believe that progression toward full maturity is innate and wholly natural and is, in fact, inevitable unless circumstances impede natural development. The concept is that each person has a distinctive natural mode of growing; the problem is to discover that distinctive mode and then concentrate on removing impediments to it. Impediments are enormously diverse and depend almost exclusively on the individual. For some, for example, poverty or social rejection halts growth, but happily many overcome such blockages and move swiftly up our typology.

Evolution. Overlapping with the other factors, the last-mentioned in particular, is the theory that the natural order of things involves the evolution of life in an unknown but nonrandom direction. This is a basic tenet of many ancient religions and a point of view increasingly accepted in contemporary America. Albert Einstein phrased the viewpoint well:

Everyone who is seriously involved in the pursuit of science becomes convinced that a spirit is manifest in the laws of the universe—a spirit vastly superior to that of man, and one in the face of
which we, with our modest powers, must feel humble.

Each of these kinds of explanation of forces spurring or blocking
human growth seems to have validity for some people at some times;
the nature of the drivers of growth shifts not only with the characteristics of the individual but with lifestyles (although Levinson and others
would probably argue that the influence of age is relatively independent
of personality or developmental level). The dynamics of growth at
Need-Driven levels seem especially dominated by "pitchfork" events
and circumstances, especially those relating to financial and social ambitions, since they often propel the individual to seek new channels of
self-expression. At Outer-Directed levels the roles of history and unresolved experiences seem especially prominent—and, of course, "pitchfork" events and circumstances continue to shape the drive to change.
At Inner-Directed levels the more conceptual, intellectual, and spiritual
forces are likely to be critical—those associated with changing paradigms, natural development, and the evolution of life. There is much
less of the pitchfork than at Need-Driven levels and more of the drive
toward what could be.

FLOWS IN THE TYPOLOGY

The Rhythms of Growth

Human growth is cyclic. Both psychologists and classic macrohistorians have observed the rhythms of change in individuals and in
societies, which involve relatively short periods of dissatisfaction, cast-
ing about, confusions, and inner turbulence followed by longer periods
of relative inner quietude and content. According to Roger Gould in
Transformations[12] the transition period for a substantial psychological
change in an individual lasts at least four years but not over six. For
societies, of course, the swiftest of contemporary transitions is likely to
require decades; in the past a major cultural shift often consumed centuries.

The values and lifestyles typology we have been discussing encom-
passes the rhythm of individual growth—inner turbulence followed by
quietude followed by turbulence, and with each lifestyle change a wider

perspective, a more complex set of values, an increasingly elaborate personality structure emerges. Here is the pattern of the VALS staircase:

Survivors—period of quiet, despair, often hopelessness, and sometimes the final wait.

Sustainers—cycle of rage, resentment, distrust, often accompanied by desperation.

Belongers—time of peace, content, security; probably the lifestyle stage where it is most pleasant to linger.

Emulators—return to anger, suspicion, mistrust; sense of not being accepted, of being a misfit.

Achievers—stage of hard and rewarding work, well-defined goals, and usually gathering success; despite high levels of stress, this lifestyle is well attuned to the dominant society and often carries with it a sense of considerable control over key life events.

I-Am-Mes—cycle of independence with a vengeance; this is a chaotic, unsure, volatile interval marked by a change-everything-instantly mentality.

Experientials—a self-absorbed, high-pleasure period that, although vigorous, experimental, and challenge-seeking, is neither rebellious nor resentful; a happy time of "doing my own thing."

Societally Conscious—interval of social activism and attempts to impose personal views on the system; much vehemence, stress, anxiety, aggression.

Integrateds—the ease of balance is here, along with calm that comes from wide experience deeply felt; these are people who swing easily on matters they consider of little consequence, but they are powerfully mission-oriented when the stakes seem important. In brief, they are able to feel both turbulence and quietude and apply each as seems fitting.

The Individual: Upward Flows

Irrespective of the rhythmic nature of human change it is important to examine the main flow lines of the individual in progressing up the lifestyles double hierarchy.

It must be remembered that VALS begins at age eighteen—that is, the flows that concern us relate only to people age eighteen and over. This, of course, does not imply that changes do not take place in earlier years, only that an individual cannot be considered to have developed his or her "own" set of values until around age eighteen. By age eighteen the maturing youth will generally have rather fully internalized the value system of his or her parents and will have accumulated a good deal of insight into the value patterns of relatives, family friends, schoolmates, job associates, and the like. It is well established, however, that a fresh cycle of psychological growth often accompanies departure from home to take a full-time job, attend college, get married, or in some other fashion strike out as an independent person. As we have seen, the popular notion that a person's psychological structure is formed and fixed at eighteen—or any other age—is simply in error. It is one of the glories of human nature that growth can and does occur at any age.

There are, we think, three major paths of flow of maturing individuals moving up the VALS double hierarchy, along with three flows of lesser size but equal interest. These are shown in Figure 2. These flow patterns are strongly suggested by available data but, it should be emphasized, are not yet incontrovertibly established.

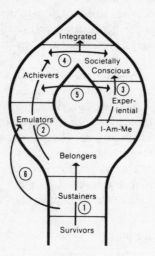

FIGURE 2:
Upward Flows of the Individual

Flow 1:   This is the flow of people from the stultifying depths of overwhelming poverty at the Survivor level, through marginal poverty at the Sustainer level, to the mid-income, satisfying Belonger lifestyle.

This is a natural and healthy progression for people psychologically, economically, and socially; it is also part of the American legend. Simplistically, it represents the profound economic transition from being governed largely by lacks and limitations to the freedom to buy and act as preference dictates.

As we shall see later, by no means all of those at the Survivor level make it upward. This is partly because many Survivors are old and infirm and, in fact, have slipped back into this stage from the higher levels of their younger years. Further, especially in large urban slums, poverty afflicts generation after generation of many families. But those who do escape from the grip of the Survivor pattern often move fast and far. For example, earlier in this century it was not unusual for the children of Need-Driven immigrants from Europe to pass swiftly through Sustainer, Belonger, and Emulator stages to become highly successful Achievers. Although it still occurs, such speedy upward movement from deep poverty is relatively less common today.

We shall treat the special case of some Sustainers unable to penetrate the Belonger level later as flow 6.

Flow 2: The flow from Belonger through to Achiever has traditionally been the most-noted and perhaps the most-trod path in the double hierarchy. This is the highway to success—the lure to countless immigrants and the dream of millions still bound by poverty, ignorance, or cultural prejudice.

Our data indicate that the largest flow is between the Belonger and Achiever lifestyles. Fully half of all Achievers resemble Belongers more than they resemble any other group, suggesting that not too long ago they were Belongers and that identification with their roots remains strong. Further, 48 percent of Belongers are more like Achievers than they are like any other group, suggesting that they are either nearing the time for an upward move or that hard times have forced some Achievers "back" to the Belonger level—a phenomenon we'll discuss later. These close links point to the reality of a powerful if unspoken cultural collaboration between Belongers and Achievers. Together they constituted about 57 percent of the adult population in 1980. The groups share high happiness indices, and their general attunement to the mainstream setting no doubt reflects the fact that the American culture is very largely of their creation. (In Part IV of this book we shall have reason to explore whether this long-standing and productive collaboration is coming to an end.)

The Emulator lifestyle seems an anomaly, lodged as it is between Belongers and Achievers. Our data reveal clearly that Emulators come primarily from the Sustainer and Belonger lifestyles. Well over half are "closest" to one or the other of these styles. The striking thing is that only 11 percent of Emulators are most like Achievers: The inference is clear that Emulators emulate people whom they really do not much resemble. This sad fact helps explain the extraordinarily high anger and mistrust levels of Emulators—a topic to which we shall return in discussing flow 6—and substantiates our sense that many Emulators never make it to the Achiever level, although their children may.

Flow 3:   The inner-directed way discussed earlier is represented by this flow. This growth from the transitional I-Am-Me stage through an Experiential phase to Societal Consciousness did not exist as a substantial trend until the affluence and permissiveness of the 1950s and 1960s opened up the inner way to millions of young people. But today, with over 30 million people holding inner-directed values, the trend is established, basic, permanent, influential, and—it appears—worldwide.

In the United States women were the first to take the inner path in large numbers. In the late 1970s and 1980s, however, more men than women have embraced the early stages of Inner-Direction. This is a fascinating finding we shall examine in detail in another connection.

Inner-Direction remains the favored path for children of prosperous parents; overall about a fourth of those turning eighteen move toward Inner-Direction—the balance prefer an outer-directed lifestyle or are "stuck" at a Need-Driven level. The youthful I-Am-Me stage is essentially generational—that is, I-Am-Mes are typically children of Achievers. The phase is highly transitory, the large majority moving on to the deeper, more satisfying Experiential phase within four or five years. The Experiential lifestyle is more prolonged, averaging well over a decade. At this point in history we have no way of knowing how long the Societally Conscious stage lasts. Median age of the group is thirty-nine. It could be that large numbers will move on to the Integrated stage in the years ahead or that the lifestyle will pall for many, driving them to Achiever patterns or to some new kind of lifestyle.

Flow 4:   This flow is small quantitatively but crucial qualitatively. Something like this happens: Achievers, as they mature, tend to leave behind many of their Belonger traits and adopt more of the values and perspectives of Societally Conscious people. This often comes about through the influence of the Achiever's children and through business and social dealings with successful Societally Conscious people. The "advanced" Achiever comes to accept the validity of many quality-of-life issues and their importance to the building of a humanly responsive society. Similarly, maturing Societally Conscious people begin to perceive the necessity of implementing many Achiever values and techniques if standards of living are to be maintained and many high-technology industries (transportation, communications, agriculture, defense, etc.) kept viable. This reasonable coming together of mature and successful people of differing value sets is prelude to a small number of them moving up into the Integrated zone.

Flow 5: Another interesting pattern is not a flow, but a leap, across the gap separating the outer- and inner-directed sides of the double hierarchy. Although the double arrows of flow in Figure 2 run from Achiever to Experiential, there also are many leaps from Emulators to Experiential, some leaps from Emulators to Societal Consciousness, but (judging from our "proximity" data) almost no leaps to the I-Am-Me style, which, as we have observed, comes about almost exclusively as a result of generational shifts.

During the 1960s and most of the 1970s (but perhaps less so in the 1980s) most of the leaps were from the Outer-Directeds to the Inners. Such leaps make excellent copy, so we probably hear more about them than the numbers justify. The classic case is that of the nineteenth-century French painter, Paul Gauguin: stockbroker one afternoon, artist the next morning. (In actual fact, as is so often the case, Gauguin's transition was far from overnight; he had painstakingly discussed it with friends and family.) But the spectacular contemporary case of Jerry Rubin represents a leap in the other direction: from vehement Yippie a few years back to commodities broker and three-piece-suited entrepreneur today.

Flow 6: One final flow is of particular sociological interest: the upward paths taken by Sustainers in their efforts to improve themselves. It will be remembered that many Sustainers are angry, streetwise people—outside the mainstream, active in the illicit economy, and plagued by incessant financial pressures. Typically, good years are followed by bad. Sustainers find it difficult indeed to get ahead, but they have not ceased their effort.

The usual next psychological step up for Sustainers is to move to the Belonger level, where, in the process of becoming insiders, much of their inner harshness and distrust is eased. In normal circumstances this is exactly what happens: The Sustainer of yesterday becomes an enthusiastic member of a church, company, community, or extended family, and all the associated values of Belonging replace those of the hard Sustainer years. Too often, however, this does not occur. Sustainers feel the doors of the mainstream culture lock them out; acceptance, if given at all, is grudging and partial; they are not welcomed, for they do not belong. Probably a good many Sustainers rejected in this fashion have minority backgrounds. Belongers, it is well established, tend to be uncomfortable with "strangers"—people out of the mainstream. Indeed, it is interesting to note that the groups flanking Belongers have far higher fractions of ethnic minorities: 36 percent for Sustainers, 21 percent for Emulators, but only 5 percent for Belongers.

When normal progression to the Belonger level is blocked, what is a Sustainer likely to do? Some, of course, simply retreat and abandon the attempt to move ahead. But some apparently burrow under the Belonger level, so to speak, and surface again as Emulators. The reality of this phenomenon is shown by data indicating that more Sustainers (38 percent) are like Emulators than like any other group and more Emulators (30 percent) are like Sustainers than any other group. Under conditions of normal progression one would expect both Sustainers and Emulators to be more like Belongers than like each other. Further, Sustainers and Emulators share such attitudes as distrust of people, anger at society, much unhappiness, low levels of satisfaction in their jobs, financial frustration, and many more.

This sad and disturbing situation has several implications. First, it is clear that the anger already present in Sustainers is redoubled if they are denied the Belonger lifestyle and must enter directly into the Emulator level. More profoundly, such people have missed a crucial stage of psychological development—that of acceptance by and acceptance of groups and organizations larger than themselves. They do not learn the sense of obligation and reciprocity so emphasized by Belongers, and they cannot tap the mainstream support system. Lacking the sense of safety and security that belonging gives, the Sustainer-turned-Emulator has an internal psychological gap or hole; his or her personality is likely to be fragile, unstable, defensive, even "paranoid." Conditions are being created for some kind of rebellion, possibly terroristic, at a higher level than the city riots of the 1960s or the union battles of the turn of the century. If systematic terrorism and thievery develops into a major trend—as many think it may—the phenomenon we have just described could be in large part responsible.

The Individual: Blockages to Growth

Not all adults continue to grow, perhaps because of personal insecurities or ineptitudes, but very often because of other kinds of blockages to growth. Some people tend to "get stuck" at some lifestyle levels more than at others: At the Survivor level even the young segment of the population is so overwhelmed by the "culture of poverty" that it is essentially impossible for most youths to break the social suction of the slums. Traditional routes of upward mobility—education, consistent work, helpful connections—usually are either not available or go unrespected by family and peers. In this case the traditional stereotype is true to life in that there are few real-life success models to follow other than the athlete, the pusher, the pimp, or the thief. So personal and societal forces tend to combine to keep many Survivors from rising to higher levels. The evidence shows that, among the minority groups, blacks are hardest hit by these negative influences. Hispanics are far more likely to be Sustainers or Emulators than Survivors. The "other" ethnic category—largely Orientals—is most numerous among the Inner-Directeds.

Sustainers, we believe, are less likely than Survivors to get blocked in their growth. The reasons include their greater awareness of the channels of upward mobility, greater financial resources, much higher expectations of success, greater family and peer support, and probably greater freedom from afflictions such as drug addiction, alcoholism, and disease. Those Sustainers most likely to get stuck seem to be the just-barely-making-it mothers of small children who are either unmarried or without support from a spouse. Streetwise males and, especially, ambitious children of recent immigrants probably have the greatest success in overcoming the Sustainer lifestyle. Many of these people are precisely those the traditional Caucasian Belonger tends to reject, giving rise to the skip-a-level phenomenon described earlier.

It seems likely that many Belongers are born and die wholeheartedly practicing this lifestyle. Those who do so probably live relatively isolated lives in the country or in small towns; events have not propelled them to college or given them much exposure to the siren calls of big-city life. Unsophisticated and untempted, they do not change. It is evident, however, that many other Belongers do change: In youth many move upward to become Achievers or Emulators; in old age some move downward to become Survivors or Sustainers. The age pattern of Belongers demonstrates their upward migration in youth; only 7 percent of them are aged eighteen to twenty-four, compared with our national sample of 15 percent. Less than 9 percent are aged twenty-five to twenty-nine, in contrast to the sample figure of 14 percent. Indeed, underrepresentation by age continues up into the forties. This pattern of upward migration of the younger, more enterprising Belongers—leaving behind the more traditional, more rigid—has implications that we shall explore in Part IV.

Blockage for Emulators is of a very different nature. We have pointed out that Emulators lack a perception of reality: They have naive notions of how Achievers live, what their values are, and what gives them real satisfaction. Few Emulators seem to possess the background, the insight, or the familiarity with Achiever habits to find ready acceptance by members of that lifestyle—although their children probably will. The data on similarities among lifestyles are decisive: only 11 percent of Emulators are most like Achievers, and only 6 percent of Achievers are most like Emulators. Part II of this book documents some of the many dimensions of this discrepancy between Emulator ambition and Achiever reality. The upshot is that it appears to be actually easier for Emulators to move *across* the double hierarchy to the Experiential phase than it is for them to move up to the Achiever level. And even more emphatically, it is easier for them to slip back to Belonger or Sustainer levels. So it may be that the Emulator stage is, psychologically speaking, the high-water mark for many young men and women trying to make it big after having been raised (as they see it) in less than middle-class surroundings: They crest at the Emulator level, and in decades to come they may recede to lower levels. This tidal action would help explain the youthfulness of the group (median age twenty-seven) and its relatively small size (10 percent of the adult population).

Generally speaking Achievers, the Inner-Directeds, and the Integrateds are probably less systematically prone to blockages in psychological growth than others. By this we mean that their blocks tend to be personal or subjective rather than societal or system-induced. These people, have exceptional resources—financial, social, and psychological—and typically have the means and the sophistication to seek out professional counsel when frustration levels get too high. This is not to imply in any way that these people live stress-free or uncomplicated lives—indeed, the reverse is spectacularly the case. But they have options not always open to those with fewer resources. Despite such advantages it seems to be part of the human condition to find psychological growth difficult, painful, and slow. And no doubt this is why there are so few who have attained the encompassing level of maturity we have sought to describe as the Integrated lifestyle.

The Individual: Flows Under Adverse Conditions

The overall progression up the VALS ladder could be reversed under adverse societal conditions such as prolonged hard times, national catastrophes such as defeat in war, drastic declines in international competitive standing, persistent social or economic uncertainty, or any other event that serves to undermine the national image severely and to render people deeply uncertain about their own and the national future. The principal results of these broad situational crises are twofold: (1) a radical increase in the number of Need-Driven people, especially if the crisis is chiefly economic, and (2) sharp reductions in the size of the psychologically fragile transition groups of I-Am-Mes and Emulators. The first would occur as a direct result of widespread unemployment and the inability to sustain former standards of living. The second would occur because, in tough times, voguishness and showy consumption simply would not be acceptable.

Other groups in the typology would be less affected. The solid traditions and fiscal reserves of Achievers and Belongers render them less subject to change under the impact of societal adversity—indeed, their solidity would tend to attract less well-grounded groups, and their numbers might even rise. The Integrateds would be relatively immune to this kind of adversity, and similarly, Societally Conscious people would be relatively unaffected by hard times, partly because they appear to anticipate shortages and constraints more than most and because their lifestyle already honors frugality and a degree of indifference to the trappings of affluence. We would expect that some Experientials would move in the direction of entrepreneurial Achievers and others would gravitate toward Societal Consciousness. A simpler but satisfying lifestyle reflecting many of the tenets of voluntary simplicity would probably emerge, drawing its main strength from the Inner-Directeds and the Integrateds.

Personal circumstances might also influence the progress of individuals up the VALS typology. The impact patterns of these reversals would be very different from those of across-the-board hard times, though. Personal misfortunes affecting lifestyle include severe financial difficulties, death of a spouse, prolonged illness, job problems, accidents, and the encroachments of old age. Reverses from such causes are not, of course, inevitable, nor need they be permanent.

Old age and severe financial problems are probably the most important personal events affecting lifestyle. The data definitely suggest that a fair number of Achievers wind up in their latter years as Belongers; still more evident is the existence of large numbers of former Belongers at the Survivor level. In both cases the prime reason for the downward slip appears to be a combination of lowered incomes accompanying retirement, lowered energy levels, and an increasing loss of contact with events and challenging ideas induced by the frailties of age. Such people tend to be predominantly female (given mortality patterns); a disproportionate number are the less sophisticated members of the former group.

The likelihood that perhaps 10 or 15 percent of Americans "drop" a level or two in the VALS typology raises complex issues concerning the nested nature of the model. The simplicity of the nested model becomes confused when, under adverse conditions, an individual "slips back" to an inner ring. The outer ring(s) wither(s) away, so to speak.

From a values standpoint we could call recidivist Survivors "echo Belongers" and such Belongers "echo Achievers." The term is intended to suggest that memories of the earlier "better days" tend to be attentuated like an echo—still there, but no longer clarion and imperious. As William Bridges puts it in *Transitions:* "We're like the shellfish that often continue to open and close their shells on the tide-schedule of their old home waters, even when they have been transplanted to the laboratory tank or the restaurant kitchen."[13] This phenomenon helps explain why almost half of Belongers are more like Achievers than any other group and especially why 60 percent of Survivors are more like Belongers than any other group. Attitudinally, nostalgia and perhaps a certain bitterness may accompany thoughts of earlier times. But it seems to be common for people to make the emotional best of difficult circumstances. Far from seeing themselves as having abandoned loftier standards, they may instead feel that they have discovered a new, more halcyon outlook less troubled than before by the vexing pressure to keep up with friends, neighbors, and events.

Generational Flows

Another useful way of looking at flows within the values and lifestyles typology is in terms of generational shifts. The question is: Where do the *children* of each lifestyle type tend to migrate as they mature? These flow patterns are interesting for what they tell us about the future shape of society and the marketplace and what they indicate concerning the limits of change over time.

Figure 3 indicates the four sets of flow patterns we consider of greatest importance.

Flow 1: This set of flows indicates that those who shake free of paralyzing poverty often move swiftly up the typology to the Achiever level. We mentioned earlier the able and ambitious children of able and ambitious immigrants as examples of people who make this giant step

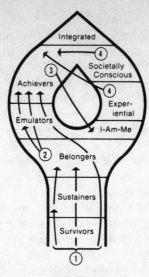

FIGURE 3:
Generational Flows

forward. Far more common is the child raised "on the other side of the tracks" who moves a shorter step forward, from Survivor to Sustainer or Belonger or from Sustainer to Belonger.

Flow 2: This pattern is similar to flow 1. Over half of the children of Belongers leave the homestead between ages eighteen to twenty-four and become Emulators or Achievers. At ages twenty-five to twenty-nine the fraction abandoning the Belonger lifestyle drops to about 35 percent, then continues to decline with the years. The more experienced and better educated Belongers tend to become Achievers and the less favored Belongers tend toward Emulators or remain Belongers. Most Emulator children probably become Achievers, while some remain Emulators or revert to Belonger or (if economically unsuccessful) even to the Sustainer or Survivor levels.

Although the phenomenon is not common today, we think that in the years to come an appreciable number of Belonger youths will adopt the Achiever lifestyle fleetingly, then abandon it for the I-Am-Me or the Experiential styles. Our thinking on this trend is set forth in Part IV.

Flow 3: Earlier we discussed the dramatic separation of I-Am-Mes from the Achiever lifestyle in which most were raised. It is distinctly and almost exclusively a generational event, unlike the situation in any other lifestyle. The embracing of Inner-Direction is in many ways less important at this stage than the snubbing of Outer-Direction. Still, it is less rebelliousness, in the sense of hating or even disrespecting parents, than it is the drive to be free and independent—to be unencumbered. A few I-Am-Mes may come from Belonger, Societally Conscious, or Experiential backgrounds, but almost none, we think, come from Need-Driven families or from the ranks of Emulators.

Flow 4:   By all odds the most interesting and perhaps the most significant of the generational shifts relate to the children of Experiential and Societally Conscious parents. Thoughts here are necessarily speculative because these two VALS types are still so young (median age of Experientials is twenty-seven, of the Societally Conscious is thirty-nine) that we are only beginning to see how their children react on reaching age eighteen.

Our thesis is that the children of the Inner-Directeds will tend to become a new, subtle, and effective kind of Achiever. We foresee developing in the coming decade and beyond a "new convert" Achiever group that will be fleeing the Inner-Direction of their parents just as current I-Am-Mes are abandoning outer-directed family values. The notion is that if you were raised without dolls, you'll collect them as an adult; if you have not visited the pasture on the other side of the road, you must journey there.

There are several reasons why we think this potential addition to the VALS typology could be of crucial importance. First, this new kind of Achiever will, we believe, bring an introspective entrepreneurial spirit to the driving outer-directed segments of society. We expect this to have a profoundly rejuvenating affect on the American system.

Why? Because there is reason to believe that Inner-Direction plus Outer-Direction is more effective in getting things done than either alone. We suggest that this combination is at the root of the remarkable economic success of Japan. Although the American experience surely will not be identical to that of the Japanese—for many reasons of history and culture—it does seem reasonable to anticipate that we, too, will benefit from melding inner- and outer-directed approaches into a single approach in which the division between the means and the end is eliminated. By eliminating this division, the new approach would become more coherent, better coordinated, and more encompassing.

The new class of Achievers will surely be creative and different, just as the I-Am-Mes of the 1960s and 1970s were. They will insist on seeing things and doing things in their own way—and they are not likely to be slavishly imitative of any model. Further, we speculate that they will turn out to be the nation's most important source of leadership by the year 2000, for by then some will have matured into the Integrated stage. These will be people long out of Inner-Direction and recently out of Outer-Direction. This history, we surmise, will equip them to be particularly effective leaders. (We suggest some far-reaching implications of this possibility in Part IV.)

A second significant implication of the generational flow from Inner- to Outer-Direction is simply that a mechanism will emerge to establish a numerical stability between the two groups: very roughly, "leakage" of Achiever children to inner-directed I-Am-Mes will be balanced by "leakage" of the children of Experiential and Societally Conscious people to Outer-Direction. Interestingly, our "renaissance" projections for 1990 (given in Part IV) for the number of Achievers and combined Experientials and Societally Conscious are identical: 36 million each. If these projections turn out to be accurate, the flow patterns suggested above will have substantially evened out the growth rates of the two groups, and a population equilibrium will be in the process of being established.

PART

II

NINE LIFESTYLES: PORTRAITS AND STATISTICS

4

The Nine Lifestyles:
Introduction

This section consists of brief sketches or portraits of typical members of each of the lifestyle types with a detailed statistical analysis of the characteristics of each of the types in five areas: demographics, attitudes, financial status, activities, and consumption patterns. The statistical information comes from a national probability survey of 1,635 individuals, representing the national population distribution, conducted in March and April of 1980. A description of the survey, the methods employed in conducting it, a list of the questions asked, and key quantitative results for each lifestyle group in the areas of demographics, attitudes, and financial status are given in the Appendix.

Respondents to the survey and their spouses or "important others"—a total of 2,713—were grouped into lifestyle types on the basis of their answers to sixty demographic and attitudinal questions. Subsequent to this work we were able to shorten the classification inventory to thirty-two questions without serious loss of discrimination. These thirty-two questions appear in the Appendix under the heading of "The 1980 Algorithm." Work is proceeding both to reduce further the number of items and to identify questions that discriminate among the lifestyle types more sensitively.

To devise the classification system, or algorithm, responses to all questions were judgmentally weighted to reflect the characteristics conceptually associated with each values and lifestyles group. For example, an individual whose inner drives are centrally concerned with conformity, being middle-of-the-road and morally conservative (i.e., a Belonger) would be expected generally to reflect these concerns in his or her attitudes and even in key demographic attributes, such as education, income, politics, occupation, or social class. The example below illustrates the overall procedure. In this case the question related to satisfaction with current finances. The question and weightings in the 1980 VALS algorithm are as follows:

Question: *How satisfied are you with your present financial situation?*

RESPONSE	SURVIVOR	SUSTAINER	BELONGER	EMULATOR	ACHIEVER	I-AM-ME	EXPERIENTIAL	SOCIETALLY CONSCIOUS
Very dis- satisfied	10	10		10				
Mostly dis- satisfied	6	6		6				
Mostly satisfied			10		6	4	5	3
Very satisfied			6		10	3	4	5

To determine what lifestyle type a given respondent is, the scores for his or her responses to all questions in the algorithm are totaled for each VALS type. Each respondent thus gets a score as a Survivor, a Sustainer, a Belonger, an Emulator, an Achiever, an I-Am-Me, an Experiential, and a Societally Conscious person. No score is calculated for Integrateds because we are not yet able to separate this group out from the others in a simple algorithm. Scores for some people vary over a large range—well into the 70s for some lifestyles and 10 or lower for others. Other individuals have a much flatter profile. The former tend to be decisive people, and the latter are more moderate in their opinions. The 1980 classification formula cannot be given here because it is proprietary to SRI International's Values and Lifestyles program.

Based upon the 1980 survey, the following numbers were derived for eight of the lifestyle groups and estimated for the ninth (Integrated), which could not be separated out on the basis of the 1980 classification formula. The data refer to numbers of adults—that is, those eighteen or over. To derive the numbers certain adjustments were made to compensate for known biases in return patterns of lengthy mail questionnaires—notably, that low-income, low-education segments of the population underrespond.

One compelling fact is that two-thirds of the American population is outer-directed. The two classic groups of Belongers and Achievers—the

TABLE 2
Sizes of Lifestyle Groups, 1980

LIFESTYLE	PERCENT OF ADULT POPULATION		MILLIONS OF ADULTS	
Need-Driven	11		17	
Survivors		4		6
Sustainers		7		11
Outer-Directed	67		108	
Belongers		35		57
Emulators		10		16
Achievers		22		35
Inner-Directed	20		32	
I-Am-Me		5		8
Experiential		7		11
Societally Conscious		8		13
Integrated	2		3	
TOTALS		100		160

essence of the American culture for almost all of our history—constitute well over half the total.

The Need-Drivens at 11 percent of the population are a substantial segment, but perhaps smaller in size than most would anticipate. Two factors tend to keep the numbers in this category materially smaller than expected. First, many people with low incomes cannot be classified as Need-Driven because their attitudes identify them as members of another values group. For example, 27 percent of Belonger households (15 million individuals) had annual incomes under $10,000 in 1979, as did over half of I-Am-Mes. Hence we see that there is much more to being psychologically need-driven than mere lack of money. Indeed in some cultures, such as West Germany, the two are scarcely related. The other factor is age. We hear so much about crime and disruption in city slums that many assume that millions are involved. Instead, crime statistics show that a relatively small fraction of the impoverished population is involved, and many of the most active members are unemployed youths less than eighteen years of age—a segment that would not show up in our data.

For many, the most surprising number from the lifestyle survey is the 20 percent, or 32 million individuals, who came out as Inner-Directeds. This is a fifth of the adult population, and a remarkably high number considering that the large majority of Inner-Directeds were members of the post–World War II baby boom and hence could not have reached age eighteen until the mid-1960s. The implication is that the ranks of the Inner-Directeds grew by an average of some 2 million per year between 1965 and 1980, although the growth undoubtedly was not at a constant rate. This astonishing growth, coupled with the fact that many adherents are among the most intellectually, socially, economically, and artistically favored elements of the population, helps explain the extraordinary impact that Inner-Direction has had on the American scene. In Part IV of this book we shall examine future trends in the number of Inner-Directeds.

Our figures for the Integrateds are strictly guesses. We are sure there are not many people today who qualify as Integrateds in terms of our definition. Yet most of us know one or two who seem to us to combine outer and inner perspectives into a whole that somehow subsumes both viewpoints. So we have selected 2 percent of the adult population, or some 3 million men and women.

The 1980 national lifestyle survey probed many, many details in addition to the numbers cited in the lifestyles groups that follow. Indeed, it covered over 800 different subjects ranging from demographics and attitudes to activities and pursuits, consumption patterns, household inventories, and many more. A list of the survey questions appears in the Appendix. Highlights of these findings are presented, lifestyle by lifestyle, in the following pages. It should be emphasized that the full research contains enormously greater detail than is given here.

The vignettes that open each lifestyle section are, with a few exceptions, based on real people. Obviously, names and details have been altered to protect identities.

5

Struggling:
The Need-Driven Groups

SURVIVORS

Portrait: Mrs. Washington's New Home

Mrs. Washington was telling the observer how much better things were here in the Boston black ghetto than in Alabama[1]:

"Well, we does O.K., I guess. Peter here [Peter is her eight-year-old son], he has it better than I did, or his daddy. I can say that. I tell myself that a lot. He can turn on the faucet over there, and a lot of the time, he just gets the water, right away. And when I tell him what it was like for us, to go fetch that water—we'd walk three miles, yes sir, and we'd be lucky it wasn't ten—well, Peter, it doesn't register on him. He thinks I'm trying to fool him, and the more serious I get the more he laughs, so I've stopped.

"Of course, it's not all so good, I have to admit. We're still where we were as far as knowing where the next meal is coming from. When I go to bed at night I tell myself I've done good to stay alive and keep the kids alive, and if they'll just wake up in the morning, and me too, well then, we can worry about that, all the rest, come tomorrow. So there you go. We do our best, and that's all you can do."

Mrs. Washington and her family had moved to Boston a couple of years before, on impulse, when racial tensions in Alabama turned ugly. They did not seek the ghetto—it was simply the only place they could find. She accepts this. She says: "God wants us to have a bad spell here, and so maybe it'll get better the next time—you know in Heaven, and I hope that's where we'll be going."

About a year after the Washingtons arrived in the North Mr. Washington woke up in the middle of the night vomiting blood. He bled and bled and vomited and vomited until he died. That left Mrs. Washington and five children. Peter and his baby brother share a bed in one bedroom. The three girls sleep together in the living room in one big bed. Mrs. Washington sleeps on a couch. There is very little furniture. The kitchen has a table with four chairs, only two of which are sturdy. There is one more chair and a table in the living room. Jesus looks down from the living room wall, and an undertaker's calendar hangs on the kitchen wall. The apartment has no books, no records. There is a TV set in the living room. It is on all day long and through much of the night.

Family health is a big problem for Mrs. Washington. When the children get sick, the welfare worker sends a nurse. The nurse advises dental care, vitamins, and checkups. But when Mrs. Washington took them to the dentist they were supposed to see, he told them to come back in a couple of weeks. Each trip costs Mrs. Washington carfare, and she has to pay a neighbor to look after the children left at home. So Mrs. Washington has given up on taking the nurse's advice. As she puts it, "You can't have everything, that's what I say, and that's what my kids have to know, I guess."

Peter attends school, but he notes, "I wasn't made for that school, and that school wasn't made for me." He knows the streets, the alleys, the rats. He's been bitten more than once and keeps a big stick by his bed to use against them. He wants to be a pilot (sometimes), a policeman (sometimes), a racing-car driver (sometimes), and a baseball player (most of the time). But Peter won't be any of these, for he has a rheumatic heart. At some level he may know this, for he also says, "I don't know what I'll be. Maybe nothing. I see men sitting around, hiding from the welfare lady. They fool her. Maybe I'll fool her, too. I don't know what you can do."

Portrait: Paddy's Last Home

As happened so often these days, Paddy's mind was adrift among the events of the past. Most often he thought of childhood scenes in the old country, on his father's flax farm in County Kerry; the once-a-year trip by wagon to the big town of Limerick, where his father did mysterious business and more than once left him and his older brother to sleep alone in the wagon; the day his mother died screaming and screaming and then sudden silence except for the tiny whimpering of little Molly.

Molly, it turned out, was the smart one of the family. It was she who moved to America and found work as a maid in a splendid New York home. It was she who persuaded Paddy to leave Ireland and join her in New York—and she sent money to back up her persuasions. And when she, like her mother before her, died giving birth, the one solid element in Paddy's life vanished. He held job after job—construction worker, carpenter, farmhand, watchman, truck driver, warehouseman, assembly-line hand, even bouncer in a bar—but never for long because there was always what Molly used to call "the black bottle." After especially bad bouts of drinking Paddy would swear to his priest he would never touch the stuff again.

But there always was an again. And so it was that Paddy, once tall, Irish-handsome, and strong, now sat rocking on the porch of St. Michael's old peoples' home, his face lined, his frame stooped, his eyes rheumy, and his mind wandering endlessly up and down the episodes of his life, seeking to quarry some little pocket of happiness that once was his.

Demographics

Survivors, as shown in Table A-1 in the Appendix, are full of extremes demographically. They are dramatically the poorest of the lifestyle groups: Almost none had household incomes over $7,500 in 1979, and their average income of around $5,000 annually was less than half that of the next poorest group, the Sustainers. They are much the oldest group, on the average some fourteen years older than Belongers, the next-oldest group. Their median age of over sixty-five makes them the most heavily female group (because women outlive men), the group with the largest number of retired people and the smallest number of employed, with the fewest children still living at home, and (except for the very youthful I-Am-Mes) the least likely to be currently married. They are by far the least educated of the lifestyle groups, being six times less likely to have reached ninth grade than the population as a whole. Finally, Survivors contain a larger black segment than any other group. Our data indicate that 26 percent of Survivors are black. This figure is surely on the low side, since only 5 percent of the survey sample is black as opposed to a true national average of about 10 percent of the adult population. (This result is to be expected because blacks and some other minorities are known to underrespond to complicated mail surveys.)

It is interesting that Survivors are the most likely of any group to be Democrats (and strong Democrats, too), yet are second only to Achievers in considering themselves conservative. This, perhaps, is in keeping with their overrepresentation in the South (almost 43 percent) and underrepresentation in the West.

Attitudes

The attitudes of Survivors are generally consistent with their disadvantaged economic and social positions. They are more mistrustful of people than any other group in the typology. They are most likely to see themselves as rebelling against the way things are in general, least likely to feel that achievements lie ahead, most likely to depend on TV for entertainment, most likely to feel little self-confidence, and—to top the list of negatives—least likely to consider themselves very happy. Three-fourths feel it is important to be part of a group; their removal from the mainstream is shown by the startling statistics that 91 percent feel things are changing too fast, 56 percent feel a woman's place is in the home (compared with 26 percent of Achievers and 3 percent of Societally Conscious people), and 57 percent often feel left out of things.

Conservatism is a Survivor trait. This shows up in their opposition to sex between unmarried people, their strong objection to legalization of marijuana, their tendency to be conventional rather than experimental, and their feeling that the nation overspends on protecting the environment. On consumer issues Survivors show up as distrustful. For example, they are less likely than others to feel that products are getting better and safer or that labeling practices are improving. Most are convinced that the consumer movement has increased prices.

In many ways the saddest aspect of Survivor attitudes is the small amount of satisfaction most get from jobs or (more significantly, in view of their work patterns) from nonwork activities. Even in the area of obtaining satisfaction from relationships with friends Survivors are materially lower than the sample average.

Despite being far removed from the societal mainstream, Survivors feel more strongly than most about several issues. For example, they favor limiting of industrial growth more than most; they think too much is spent on military armaments; they tend to agree that the oil crisis is real; and, finally, they are considerably more likely than most to feel the federal government is an accurate source of information on energy.

Financial Status

Although Survivors have much the lowest incomes of any of the lifestyle groups—and things seem to be going swiftly from bad to worse—they are strikingly less dissatisfied financially than Sustainers. Their total resources appear also to be lowest of all the groups, but their debt levels are also minimal, so that they may actually be better off than Sustainers, especially since Sustainers are almost twice as likely as Survivors to be spenders rather than savers. It is clear that Survivors tend to be fiscally conservative with respect to debt, buying on time, use of credit cards, or spending on tangibles such as art, gold, or gems rather than more usual forms of investment. No doubt this conservatism is to a degree involuntary.

The data on various forms of investments reveal the expected: Survivors are, with the sole exception of the arena of mutual/money market funds, the least likely to be active. Although 45 percent own their own homes, only 8 percent would clear over $50,000 following its sale. The data on household assets confirm the low net worth of Survivors. Only 8 percent show total household assets in the $50,000-to-$100,000 range, compared with the sample average of 54 percent and 80 percent for Achievers. Fortunately, debts or liabilities are commensurately small.

Activity Patterns

The daily activity patterns of Survivors are heavily influenced by their high age, low education, and, above all by the drastic limitations of their resources. These factors combine to make their activities more different from national norms than those of any other VALS group—even those of the intentionally out-of-step I-Am-Me group. Survivors, generally because of their age, are strikingly absent from pursuits requiring high levels of physical energy, such as active (and even spectator) sports, outdoor life, or vigorous forms of entertainment. They are not an educated or intellectual group, hence participate infrequently in activities like chess and backgammon, attendance at cultural events, adult education, and reading. Because so many are retired and education and income levels are low, Survivors score lowest in most travel categories, in credit card use, and in insurance coverage. Some of the areas in which Survivors score high are cigarette smoking, TV watching, and the many health concerns associated with age. Survivors are more likely to eat meatless meals than any other group—no doubt a reflection of their limited economic means.

Pursuits in which Survivors score ten or more percentage points above or below national activity averages are listed in Table 3. (Ten percentage points, on the average, corresponds to about a 33-percent deviation from the norm.) Survivors deviate this much from national norms in 130 of the 257 activities covered in the VALS 1980 survey—by far the most of any lifestyle group. A plus (+) indicates that Survivors participate in the activity more than ten percentage points above the average of all the VALS groups; a minus (−) indicates participation ten or more percentage points under average.

Consumption Patterns

Consumption patterns of this demographically older and severely income-restricted group reflect its emphasis on basics and the necessity to satisfy immediate needs. It is no surprise that Survivors underspend the average consumer on a large majority of the products surveyed. Where they show up as above-average spenders, the reason is usually evident. For example, they are high in purchases of used cars and meatless meals, reflecting low incomes; tastes geared to earlier times seem to emerge from preferences for such items as dresses, hot cereal, gelatin desserts, and well-known brand names such as Planters; concern with health is evident in purchases of pain relievers, decaffeinated coffee, and margarine; finally, above-average sales of various household cleaners and personal deodorants possibly suggest less-than-sanitary living conditions, probably mostly in city slums. Perhaps the most telling statistics are the plusses for purchases of canned dog and cat food despite low indices of pet ownership. The explanation is that the pet food is purchased as the cheapest way to buy meat for their own consumption.

Products that Survivors purchase ten or more percentage points above or below the national average are listed below. Because of their extreme economic circumstances it is not surprising to find that Survivors have the least typical consumption pattern of any VALS group. They are atypical in 100 of the 170 consumption areas covered. This contrasts with the next least typical group, Sustainers, at 59, and the most typical group, Belongers, at 20. In the listing in Table 4 a plus indicates above-average and a minus below-average consumption.

SUSTAINERS

Portrait: The Flame

To himself Carlos called it *La Llama*, the Flame, because of the intricate tracery of blue and white and green and red flames painted on the hood and front fenders, flaring back over the polished black body to lick at

TABLE 3
Activities of Survivors

Active sports		Eating out	
Baseball/basketball/football/softball	−	Eat fast food out or take it home	−
Bicycling	−	Eat out on weekends	+
Jogging	−	Eat out on both equally	−
Squash/handball/racquetball	−	Drink cocktail before dinner at restaurant	−
Swimming	−	Health-related food concerns	
Tennis	−	Store brands considered of highest quality	+
Exercise in gym	−	National brands considered of highest quality	−
Golf	−	Collect recipes	+
Snow skiing	−	Nutrition label information is extremely important	+
Water skiing	−	A lot of concern with amount of salt in foods	+
Spectator sports		A lot of concern with amount of vitamins	+
Professional sports events	−	A lot of concern with amount of caffeine consumed	+
College/high school sports events	−	Cigarette smoking	
X-rated movies	−	Have smoked for over 10 years	+
Bowling	−	Stopped smoking over 10 years ago	+
Pool/billiards	−	Smoke less than ½ pack daily	+
Chess	−	Smoke regular cigarettes	+
Backgammon	−	Smoke filter, low-tar and -nicotine	−
Outdoor life		Off-hours work	
Motorboating	−	Work at second job/free-lance	−
Hunting	−	Type personal letters at home	−
Camping overnight	−	Learning	
Trips in recreational vehicle	−	Have spent over $50 for self-instruction	−
Backpacking	−	Have enrolled in correspondence course	−
The arts		Have attended night school	−
Engage in crafts	−	Pleasure travel	
Attendance at cultural events		Travel by air	−
Theatre	−	Stay at hotels/motels	−
Opera/ballet/dance	−	Use rental cars	−
Art galleries/museums	−	Use travel agency	−
Youth entertainment		Business travel	
Pop/rock concerts	−	Travel by air	−
Night clubs/discos	−	Stay at hotels/motels	−
Theme/amusement parks	−	Shopping in stores	
Arcades/video games	−	Major department stores	−
Cards		Drugs from discount drug stores	+
Bridge	−	Return an unsatisfactory product	−
Gardening and baking		Credit cards owned	
Bake bread	+	Visa/Bankamericard	−
Bake pastries	+	MasterCard	−
Do-it-yourself (men only)			
Repair/fix-up projects at home	−		
Work on own car or other vehicle	−		
Eating habits			
Cook outdoors	−		
Give dinner parties	−		
Eat dinner while watching TV	−		
Eat between-meal snacks	−		
Eat vegetarian meals	+		

Table 3: Activities of Survivors (continued)

Gasoline/oil	−
Department/specialty store card	−
No credit cards	+
Purchases with credit cards	
Gasoline	−
Department/specialty stores	−
Business travel	−
Pleasure travel	−
Don't use credit cards for purchases	+
Use credit cards less than a year ago	+
Household credit card balance over $500	−
Personal communications	
Phone friends/relatives locally	+
Phone friends/relatives long distance	−
Visit phone company offices	+
Life and health insurance	
Have individual life insurance	−
Have group life insurance	−
Have health/major medical insurance	−
Have disability insurance	−
Have permanent/whole life/cash value insurance	−
Have term insurance	−
Purchased insurance from agent for one company	−
Individual life insurance security is extremely important	+
Life insurance for women especially needed if	
She is single with no children	+
She is a full-time housewife with children 13-18 living at home	+
Visited doctor	+
Attended movie theatre	−
Would prefer to watch same movie at home on TV	+
Commercial or educational TV watching*	
Watch 7-10 A.M. weekdays	+
Watch 10 A.M.-1 P.M. weekdays	+
Watch 1-4:30 P.M. weekdays	+
Watch 8-11 P.M. weekdays	+
Watch 11 P.M.-2 A.M. weekdays	+
Watch 7-10 A.M. weekends	+
Watch 4:30-8 P.M. weekends	+
Watch 8-11 P.M. weekends	+
Watch 11 P.M.-2 A.M. weekends	+
Type of TV program watched	
Variety shows	+
Game shows	+
Soap operas	+
Morning news	+
Afternoon news	+
Early evening news	+
Think commercial TV is:	
Interesting	−
Educational	+
Exciting	+
Radio listening	
Noon-5 P.M. weekdays	+
Newspaper reading	
Read Sunday newspaper	−
Read comics	−
Read entertainment	−
Read food/cooking section	+
Read sports section	−
Magazine reading	
Read general sports magazines	−
Read specific sports magazines	−
Read human interest magazines	−
Read automotive magazines	−
Book reading	
Belong to book club	−
Housing	
Previously lived in same city/town	+
Live in detached, single-family dwelling	−
Own home	−
Have added room or remodeled in past year	−

*Hours shown are for Eastern and Pacific time. Times are an hour earlier for Central and Mountain time.

TABLE 4
Consumption Patterns of Survivors

Motor Vehicles		Miscellaneous products (ownership)	
Type of car purchased*		Home encyclopedia set	−
Subcompact	−	Manual typewriter	−
Small specialty	−	String grass trimmer‡	−
Compact	−	Chain saw‡	−
Midsize	−	Photographic equipment	
Large	−	Cameras (ownership)	
Luxury	−	Instamatic-type	−
Importance of selected features in		Instant-process	−
purchase consideration†		35mm	−
Convenient dealer location	+	Movie camera	−
Price or deal offered	+	Film (purchases)	
Cost of service/repairs	+	National brand	−
Power and pickup	+	Take photos once a month or more	−
Safety features	+	Clothing	
Value for money	+	Women's clothing (use)	
Purchased foreign-made cars	−	Dresses	+
Own no cars	+	Slacks	−
Own two or more cars	−	Jeans	−
Purchased last car new	−	Men's clothing (use)	
Purchased last car used	+	Suits	−
Durables		Sport/casual shirts	−
Appliances (ownership)		Jeans	−
Clothes washer (separate from		Personal-care products	
dryer)	−	Reasons women buy personal care	
Clothes dryer (separate from		products:	
washer)	−	To maintain personal appearance	−
Dishwasher	−	Women's products (use)	
Electric cooking range	+	Eye makeup	−
Gas cooking range	+	Shampoo	−
Garbage disposal	−	Aerosol underarm deodorant	+
Microwave oven	−	Feminine hygiene spray	+
Freezer (separate from		Facial moisturizer	−
refrigerator)	−	Men's products (use)	
Recreational equipment (ownership)		After-shave lotion	−
Camping/backpacking	−	Shampoo	−
Exercise (at home)	−	Aerosol underarm deodorant	−
Rifle	−	Stick underarm deodorant	−
Racing bicycle	−	Other personal-care products (use)	
Home electronic products (ownership)		Pain relievers/headache remedies	+
Color TV	−	Pets	
Video games	−	Any	−
Hi-fi stereo components	−	Dogs	−
Blank recording tapes/cassettes	−	Cats	−
Prerecorded tapes/cassettes	−	Pet foods and services	
Pocket calculator	−	Dog food (purchase)	
Smoke/fire alarm	−	Canned	+
Decorator telephone	−	Dry	−
Telephone extension for home	−	Moist	−

Table 4: Consumption Patterns of Survivors (continued)

Cat food (purchase)		Other beverages (use)	
Canned	+	Fruit drinks	+
Moist	−	Decaffeinated coffee	+
Selected specialized cleaning products§		Foods (use)	
(use)		Breakfast foods	
Carpet cleaner	+	Hot cereal	+
Drainpipe cleaner	+	Dry-roasted peanuts	−
Toilet bowl cleaner	+	Nut brands purchased	
Beverages and foods		Planters	+
Alcoholic beverages (use)		Switch brands	−
Wine		Confections	
California wine	−	Sugarless gum	−
Any champagne	−	Prepared ethnic foods	
Domestic champagne	−	Prepared, canned or frozen Italian	−
Liquor		Margarine and butter§	
Any liquor	−	Use	
Vodka	−	Margarine	−
Tequila	−	Butter	−
Beer		Reasons for buying margarine	
Any beer	−	Health	+
Domestic beer	−	Taste	+
Imported beer	−	Miscellaneous foods§	
Carbonated beverages (use)		Frozen vegetables	−
Sugar-free soft drinks	−	Gelatin desserts	+

*Data are for last car purchased 1975-1980.
†If respondents were to purchase a motor vehicle in 1980.
‡Homeowners only.
§For women only.

the taillights. But that wasn't all. The powerful car sat low to the road, almost as if it had no wheels. The Flame, if ever there was one, was a super low rider. Upholstery was done in a fur dyed to look like zebra. The engine was chrome-plated, the trunk lined with crushed red velvet. Miniature boxing gloves and a soccer ball dangled from the rear-view mirror. A bar was built into the back seat, and the knob of the stick shift was plated gold. Most important of all, it was loaded with hydraulics.

To Carlos the vehicle was almost alive. He was so proud to have Big Ric's car in his garage that he called his wife Angela to bring young Carlos down to see it. Young Carlos, squalling in his mother's arms, heard The Flame's giant motor throb under his father's skilled hand, its loudness released by the muffler Carlos had so carefully perforated. The little boy watched how his father, with gears in neutral, brakes set, and hydraulics purring made the massive body rock forward and backward to pulses of the motor. It was hard to make a car rock like that—it took both a fine touch and the spongy shocks Carlos had installed. Satisfied with his work, Carlos merely laughed when his son fell asleep. "Wait till he gets a little bit older," he told Angela.

The garage that Carlos owned and ran with his brother was his livelihood. The brothers had a contract with the School District to repair and maintain school buses. So for much of the year, one at a time, the huge yellow buses pulled into Carlos's garage and body shop for overhauls. This contract provided the brothers with a steady business; it also constituted almost their entire official business, recorded, billed, and taxed.

The profits, when there were any, lay elsewhere. In good times lots of the Low Riders brought their cars to Carlos and his brother. Agreements were sealed with a handslap, and payment was in cash. Now that Big Ric, known everywhere as king of the houses, had picked the brothers to work on The Flame, Carlos could figure on even more business from the Low Riders. With luck, this might be a turning point. It might mean Carlos could go on paying off the new refrigerator and color TV even if things got tough. It might mean Angela wouldn't have to return to work, and Carlos would be very proud if he could swing that. It might mean they could save the down payment and qualify to buy the little stucco house with white picket fence and roses growing on it that Angela so loved. Above all, it might mean they never would have to face the poverty, the foreclosures, the repossessions, and the women's tears that Carlos and his brother remembered so well from a decade ago. And right now, to celebrate the money Big Ric had paid them, Carlos and his brother figured they would shoot the works and buy family tickets to the championship soccer game: the hometown Volcanoes against the perennial champs from the big city.

Soccer was Carlos's game. He'd watched it, played it, dreamt about it ever since he could remember. He knew half the guys on the Volcano team. The coach was a good family friend. So the game—Volcs against the champs—was something special for Carlos as well as for the town. It was the little guy against the big. And when it turned out to be no contest, the Volcs scoring early and often to win 5–1, the town went wild.

In the evening the celebrating Low Riders turned out in force. Down the main drag they came, moving slowly as in a parade, their cars filled with family and kids. And in the lead was Big Ric, The Flame loaded with a bevy of good-lookers who worked for him. At the heart of town Big Ric stopped The Flame. And he began to rock. The crowd took up the rhythm joyously. "Rock Volcs! Rock Volcs!" became the chant.

And, engine throbbing, Big Ric rocked The Flame till front and back smashed against the highway. That was the ultimate. "Rock, Volcs, Rock!" came the chant, and every Low Rider in the long line rocked, hydraulics in unison.

Then through the chant came the yelp of police sirens. "Move it," they told Big Ric, "move it fast." And so Big Ric put The Flame in gear and began to move. Delicately he played the pulsing engine against the hydraulics, and slowly, ever so slowly, The Flame rocked out of the intersection. And Carlos watched it all, choked with happiness for his part in The Flame and full of admiration for Big Ric's handling of the car.

And so when, the following morning, the tow truck hauled the smashed Flame into the brothers' garage and body shop, it was like the end of a love affair for Carlos. Big Ric, it seemed, had been stopped by the cops for a search. The girls had gotten out and, foolishly, Big Ric, gunning The Flame into a giant roar, had taken off. That was it. The crash had smashed the engine and stripped away the right side of the car. Miraculously, the left side was unscathed. Big Ric had been arrested, but it wasn't the first time, and Carlos didn't worry about Big Ric and the law. It was the car that got to him. Carlos stood there for a long time gazing at the unmarked side of The Flame, his eyes following the delicate colored traceries leaping from fender to taillight until the blur of tears forced him to look away.

Portrait: Lucia, Joe, and Joey

The dark Italian eyes flashed, and the words came volubly. "You are so"—Lucia was searching for the right word—"so bad, so *wasteful*, Joey. I buy you this and I buy you that, and all you do is break, break, break them. Wait 'til I tell big Joe." That was the ultimate threat. Joey could cope with his mother, but big Joe was something else. Especially in bad times like these, when Joe and most of his friends in the machine shop had been laid off.

The noise from the street four floors below suddenly grew loud. Joey crossed to the window without the fire escape, carefully stepping over his sleeping baby sister. In the twilight it was hard to see, but it was plain that traffic was snarled by some kind of commotion. "Come, Mom, quick," said Joey. Lucia surveyed the confusion, and then it dawned on her. "My god," she said, "that's Joe." Joey already had headed down the four flights of stairs.

It was obvious that Joe was the center of attention. He stood there in the middle of the sidewalk, swaying slightly, red eyes squinting, ready to take on anyone who wanted a fight. Joe was drunk and in one of those moods. "Get away, kid," he said to Joey when Joey rushed to his side. "This ain't no business of yours." But Joe seemed to be fighting no one except some inner enemy. He kept turning, ducking and weaving, with fists raised, but there was no one there. The neighbors, passersby, none of them knew what it was all about. Lucia watched and waited. When the time came, she took Joe by the arm and whispered to him, "C'mon, Joe, let's go home." And she led him off as if he were a child.

But Joe's temper was like the moods of the sea, changing, deep, tempestuous. To the crying baby he said, "Shut up"; to Joey he said, "Get away"; to Lucia he said, "Come 'ere," and when she remonstrated that this wasn't the time or place, he reached out and very easily struck her in the face with his work-hardened fist. And then he lay down on the couch and fell asleep.

Lucia changed the baby, fixed some supper for the three of them, and after a while put Joey to bed. Joey looked up at her and touched her swollen eye. "Hurt?" he asked. Lucia nodded, for the eye was almost closed by now. She leaned over and kissed her little son tenderly.

That was one episode in Lucia's battered life. Her wage as a part-time sales clerk in a gift shop was so low that she and her children qualified for a full allotment of food stamps. Big Joe comes and goes—mostly goes. Of course, he and Lucia are not married, and big Joe, even when he is working and making good money, doesn't help out much. Not even after Lucia got pregnant again and lost the baby at five months. Not even after Lucia was let go at her sales job because, her employer said, she didn't dress well enough.

But even so Lucia and Joey are making it. Joey, it turns out, is smart at school, and his mother is proud of that. Father Calandra has taken an interest in Joey and promises to help him get a good education. Lucia is still attractive to men, and this means an occasional windfall—a good secondhand color TV set one time, a new dress another time. Lucia figures she is smart about money—she knows how to stretch a dollar, although she is a spender rather than a saver. Unlike many people with her background Lucia believes in the virtues of hard work, education, and self-reliance. She has seen many of her friends—kids of folks from the old country—get ahead through work and even schooling. No longer does Lucia expect to make it big herself. Her chance went down the tubes when she had to quit school at age fourteen. Pregnant. Caught with guys on the stuff. Her mother, from the old school, would never speak to her again. So, for better than half her life, she's been on her own. At thirty she is beginning to put on weight, and pretty soon the kind of jobs available to her will be more and more limited. But Joey—he's something else. She'll see to it that Joey gets a real chance, just as her mother had made the same silent promise about her so very long ago.

Demographics

Sustainers are a youngish group who are having a tough time making it. Signs of problems are everywhere. At the time of our survey in early 1980 about 15 percent—five times as many as any other group—were looking for work; 11 percent worked only part time, although the evidence is strong that most want fulltime jobs. For example, only half as many Sustainers as Emulators work full time, although the two groups share many demographic and attitudinal traits. Sustainers are heavy readers of classified newspaper ads, which suggests that they're checking the want ads. The average Sustainer household income in 1979 was about $11,000—on the edge of poverty even for small families, and beyond the edge for the 29 percent of Sustainers who have two or more children under eighteen living at home.

Medium to low educational attainment appears to limit the kinds of jobs Sustainers can get. Only about 8 percent hold white-collar jobs, whereas 30 percent are craft workers or machine operators. The ratio of minorities is high—21 percent black and 13 percent Hispanic.

Two other features of Sustainer demographics suggest they find the going rough. An astonishing 46 percent see themselves as members of the lower or lower-middle classes—markedly the most negative assessment of any VALS group, even higher than the 35 percent of Survivors who so rate themselves. The other indicator is their marital status. They display the highest indices of divorce and separation of any of the lifestyle groups and have the fewest couples still in their first marriage of any group of comparable age.

In view of this background of economic and personal problems it perhaps is not surprising that Sustainers are not likely to be Republicans or conservatives but, rather, middle-of-the road Democrats or liberal Independents. Also in keeping is their absence from suburbia and their preference for city life. Regionally, Sustainers are rather evenly spread, although especially numerous in New England and scarce in the Pacific states.

Attitudes

The attitudes of Sustainers resemble those of Survivors in many matters, but they differ sharply when it comes to moral and contemporary social issues. Resentment of hard times emerges in many ways. Second only to Survivors, Sustainers are likely to mistrust people and to be rebelling against the general state of affairs. They are among the least happy of the lifestyle groups and among those most likely to feel left out of things and to feel things are changing too fast. They have a high need to be part of a group, and they place much value on social status. They are not widely supportive of working women. They get little satisfaction from job or friends and show up distinctly negative on a long list of quasi-political issues, including issues of air pollution, confidence in elected officials and corporate leaders, and consumer issues. Over 60 percent of Sustainers view TV as their main form of entertainment. Sustainers are among those least likely to return an unsatisfactory product or to complain to a store.

But Sustainers are more "with it" in some areas. For example, they are more likely than most to feel sex between unmarried people is not wrong, they tend to support legalization of marijuana, they are more willing than most to act on hunches, and—appropriately, it would seem—they are likely to think of themselves as "a bit of a swinger." As we shall see later, Sustainers tend also to engage in exciting and hedonistic activities. In sum, the data suggest that Sustainers lead lives high in resentment toward the mainstream culture, a resentment that many try to abate through the pleasures of the flesh and reliance on Lady Luck for the good things in life.

Financial Status

Although Sustainers are definitely spenders, their actions appear more conservative than their view of themselves. They are not far from sample averages concerning investing in tangibles such as art, gold, or gems or with respect to buying on time or spending in advance to cope with inflation. We have remarked on the fascinating finding that Sustainers view themselves as financial experts. We suspect that many Sustainers regard financial expertise in terms of making it at all, rather than in terms of the sophisticated concepts that Achievers associate with financial expertise.

Sustainers participate in financial institutions far less than the average household, but more than the still poorer Survivor group. Some of the statistics are of particular interest. Credit card balances are exceptionally high in the group, suggesting debt problems. Thirty percent owe over $5,000 on loans, rather a high level for a group with such limited resources. Perhaps the most telling figure relates to home ownership. Fewer Sustainers than any other lifestyle group own their own homes, and it appears that essentially all who do have mortgages, some more than one. Their drastically tight circumstances are revealed by the finding that in over half of Sustainer households total assets are under $10,000. Only 19 percent (compared with the sample average of 54 percent) indicate assets exceeding $50,000.

Activity Patterns

Sustainers and Survivors show similar patterns in many daily activities but are quite different in social activities, especially those correlating with age. They share with Survivors avoidance of activities associated with large incomes, advanced education, or intellectual and managerial occupations. But being generally much younger and less despairing than Survivors, they show some spectacularly different habits. Sustainers, for example, attend horse races more than any other group. They are also extremely interested in life insurance with coverage that adjusts to life-cycle changes. Many Sustainers tend to be feisty and outdoorsy: they watch a lot of nature and wildlife TV shows and they go fishing frequently more than any other type. They see a lot of X-rated movies, attend discos, drive power cars, drink hard liquor, are active in youth entertainments, are most likely of any type to smoke cigarettes, and are the heaviest readers of tabloids. They shop a good deal at secondhand stores. Curiously, they eat breakfast out more than any other group.

Pursuits in which Sustainers participate at least ten percentage points more or less than the national average are indicated in Table 5. Sustainers deviate from national activity norms by this amount or more in 89 of the 257 activities covered in the 1980 lifestyle survey. This is the third highest "deviation index" of the VALS groups, behind Survivors and the I-Am-Mes.

Consumption Patterns

Consumption patterns of Sustainers reflect their somewhat higher incomes relative to Survivors and hence their ability to spend relatively more on items such as cars, appliances, and home electronic products. Sustainer households rank substantially higher than average in their purchase of small specialty and compact cars, but an above-average fraction are purchased used. They buy predominantly American-made cars.

Their level of consumption of alcoholic beverages is above average,

TABLE 5
Activities of Sustainers

Active sports	Shopping in stores	
Baseball/basketball/football/baseball +	Convenience food stores	+
Spectator sports	Drugs from discount drug stores	+
Pro sports events –	Secondhand stores	+
Horse racing +	Credit card owned	
X-rated movies +	Visa/Bankamericard	–
Bowling +	MasterCard	–
Youth entertainment	Gasoline/oil	–
Night clubs/discos +	Department/specialty store card	–
Theme/amusement parks +	No credit cards	+
Listen to records/tapes +	Purchases with credit cards	
Gardening and baking	Gasoline	–
Vegetable gardening –	Mail order/phone purchases	–
Needlework (women only)	Department/specialty stores	–
Knit/crochet/needlework –	Business travel	–
Eating habits	Pleasure travel	–
Eat dinner while watching TV +	Don't use credit cards for purchases	+
Eat desserts –	Life and health insurance	
Eating out	Have individual life insurance	–
Eat breakfast out +	Have group life insurance	–
Eat dinner out –	Have health/major medical	
Eat at informal restaurant –	insurance	–
Health-related food concerns	Have disability insurance	–
National brands considered of	Have permanent/whole life/cash	
highest quality –	value insurance	–
A lot of concern with amount of	Purchased insurance from agent for	
vitamins +	one company	–
A lot of concern with nutritional	Individual life insurance security is	
quality of food +	extremely important	+
Cigarette smoking	Extremely interested in life	
Have smoked in past month +	insurance with varying	
Have smoked for over 10 years –	coverage	+
Stopped smoking over 10 years ago –	Life insurance for women especially	
Smoke filter, high-tar and -nicotine +	needed if:	
Smoke filter, low-tar and -nicotine –	She is the sole support of the	
Off-hours work	family	–
Type personal letters at home –	She contributes half the family	
Personal communications	income	–
Send greeting cards –	Would prefer to watch same movie at	
Phone friends/relatives	home on TV	+
internationally +	Commercial or educational TV watching*	
Learning	Watch 10-1 P.M. weekdays	+
Have spent over $50 for self-	Watch 1-4:30 P.M. weekdays	+
instruction –	Watch 4:30-8 P.M. weekdays	+
Pleasure travel	Watch 8-11 P.M. weekdays	+
Travel by air –	Watch 11 P.M.-2 A.M. weekdays	+
Stay at hotels/motels –	Watch 7-10 A.M. weekends	+
Use travel agency –	Watch 10 A.M.-1 P.M. weekends	+
Business travel	Watch 11 P.M.-2 A.M. weekends	+
Travel by air –	Type of TV program watched	
Stay at hotels/motels –	Mystery or crime dramas	+

Table 5: Activities of Sustainers (continued)

Comedies	+	Read classified ads	+
Game shows	+	Magazine reading	
Soap operas	+	Read major news magazines	−
Movies	+	Read tabloids	+
Nature or wildlife shows	+	Book reading	
Think commercial TV is:		Heavy readers	−
Educational	+	Read condensed versions	+
Exciting	+	Housing	
Believe commercial TV is getting		Lived in current residence over 10	
better	+	years	−
Radio listening		Previously lived in same city/town	+
Listen 5-8 P.M.	+	Live in detached, single-family	
Listen after 11 P.M.	+	dwelling	−
Newspaper reading		Own home	−
Read daily newspaper	−	Have added room or remodeled in	
Read Sunday newspaper	−	past year	+
Read business/finance section	−		

*Hours shown are for Eastern and Pacific time. Times are an hour earlier for Central and Mountain time.

but a lower-than-average percentage drink wine, and a higher-than-average percentage drink hard liquor (bourbon, gin, and vodka) and domestic beer. A higher-than-average percentage drink regular carbonated soft drinks and fruit drinks. In foods they are disproportionately high consumers of hot cereal and of pancake mix and syrup, and they have the highest level of consumption of breakfast meal-replacement bars. They are also disproportionately high consumers of potato/corn chips, pretzels, gum, candy, canned soups, and frozen TV dinners.

Sustainers deviate ten percentage points from average consumption patterns in 59 of the 170 areas covered. In terms of deviation from national norms this makes them second to Survivors—but dramatically second, since Survivors deviate by this amount in 100 areas. Again, one can presume that the consumption aberrations of Sustainers reflect their low incomes. The areas listed in Table 6 are those in which Sustainer purchases are ten percentage points higher or lower than the national norm.

TABLE 6
Consumption Patterns of Sustainers

Motor vehicles		To maintain personal appearance	−
Types of cars purchased*		Women's products (use)	
Subcompact	−	Pump hair spray	−
Small specialty	+	Aerosol underarm deodorant	+
Importance of selected features in		Stick underarm deodorant	−
purchase consideration†		Feminine hygiene spray	+
Gas mileage	+	Facial moisturizer	−
Prestige	+	Cleansing cream	−
Power and pickup	+	Men's products (use)	
Own no cars	+	Shampoo	+
Own two or more cars	−	Pet foods and services	
Purchased last car new	−	Visits to veterinarians	−
Purchased last car used	+	Selected specialized cleaning products§	
Durables		(use)	
Appliances (ownership)		Air freshener	−
Dishwasher	−	Carpet cleaner	+
Electric cooking range	−	Furniture polish	+
Gas cooking range	+	All-purpose household cleaner	+
Garbage disposal	−	Aerosol bathroom cleaner	+
Home electronic products (ownership)		Drainpipe cleaner	+
Prerecorded tapes/cassettes	−	Beverages and foods	
Pocket calculator	−	Alcoholic beverages (use)	
Telephone extension for home	−	Wine	
Miscellaneous products (ownership)		Any wine	−
Electric typewriter	−	California wine	−
Manual typewriter	−	Other beverages (use)	
String grass trimmer‡	−	Fruit juices	−
Chain saw‡	−	Fruit drinks	+
Expressed any interest in new products		Breakfast foods	
Home computer	+	Cold cereal	−
Service to pay bills by telephone	+	Breakfast meal-replacement bars	+
Complete home controller	+	Snack foods	
Photographic equipment		Potato/corn chips	+
Instant-process cameras	+	Pretzels	+
Film (purchases)		Confections	
National brand	−	Regular gum	+
Clothing		Soups§	
Women's clothing (use)		Canned	+
Dresses	−	Margarine and butter§	
Jeans	+	Butter use	−
Men's clothing (use)		Brands purchased	
Suits	−	Other national/regional brands	−
Sport coats	−	Miscellaneous foods§	
Dress shirts	−	Frozen vegetables	−
Sport/casual shirts	+	Frozen TV dinners (men and	
Personal-care products		women)	+
Reasons women buy personal-care			
products:			

*Data are for last car purchased 1975-1980.
†If respondents were to purchase a motor vehicle in 1980.
‡Homeowners only.
§For women only.

6

Dreaming
the American Dream:
The Outer-Directed Groups

BELONGERS

Portrait: The Stories of Spunk Clarenden

To the best of my recollection, this is what Spunk Clarenden told me as we waited for the doctor to see us in his waiting room in Belfast, Maine.

"Well, I was born down the road a piece. Funny thing is my dad owned the local telephone company in 1910. Sold it to John McNamara in 'eighteen, when I was two. Funny because I worked for Ma Bell for thirty-five years. Fine, fine outfit. People say they're always gobblin' up the little guys, but it ain't that way. Why up north aways—I guess this was in the fifties—Sam Elliott had this little telephone outfit, hardly bigger'n the palm of your hand. Well, the company sent me up there plenty a times to do some trouble shootin'. Sam didn't know nothing' about a lotta technical type things, but he was a nice fella, and the company never charged him a cent for all the times I was up there using company equipment and workin' on company time. Never got any credit for that though. All you hear about is the gobblin' stuff.

"Yea. Thirty-five years with Ma Bell. Been secretary to the Masons here in town for twenty-nine goin' on thirty years. Keep all kindsa records. If I die tomorrow, my wife could tell you everything that's happened. August fifth and my wife and me, we'll be married forty-three years. Never did have any kids, though. Real pity. Yea. I been in

84

the choir at the Congregational Church for fifty years. Third longest. Fifty years, and I'm only sixty-five. Mrs. Coombs, she's been there sixty years, and Mac—that's Joe MacPherson—been there fifty-six years. Mrs. Coombs, she's gettin' on. Better'n eighty. But still sings like a bird, I'll tell you.

"You know, all that singin' came in handy in the war and the sergeant wanted somebody to take over the bugle corps. I could read music. So I whipped 'em into shape, I'll tell you. Me a Pfc—a one-striper, with a little bugle right here on my arm. Made it to Sergeant later after taking some of that communications stuff. You know, they wouldn't let me outa the country because I knew about that communications stuff? So we hung around a lot. I remember the time we got orders to march to—god, I forget the name, but anyway it was twenty-eight miles. Pack up, march there, everybody, no gettin' out of it. Well, there was this Frenchie. He was cook of the outfit and didn't know a thing about soldiering. So he asked some of his pals to load his pack. Dumbest thing he ever did. Those guys, they loaded him up with the usual, and they stuck in a piece of iron this big by this big, and thick. Musta weighed a ton. Boy you shoulda seen that Frenchie sweat, and his pals were walkin' along trying to keep their faces on straight. The funniest thing, though, was the officers. Hell, none of 'em could march five miles. They was achin' and bellyachin' and cussin' like nothin' you ever heard.

"Lemme know if ya gotta move on. I was inoculated with a phonograph needle, ya know. But anyway, after the war a lot of the vets went to work for the company. A lotta them were good—real good—but, god, there sure were others. I remember one old guy who knew the business up and down. He pointed to one of these young vets, and he told me: 'Ya see that guy over there? Not worth a damn. Why, I taught him everything I know and he *still* don't know a thing.' We sure had a laugh over that.

"Funny thing about how if you don't ring your bell, no one's going to ring it for you. There was quite a spell there when I had the cleanest phone booths in the county. Used to stop on the way to a job, spend five, ten minutes cleanin' up a booth. God, you wouldn't believe what people would do to those booths. Go to the bathroom in 'em, use 'em as a trash can—you name it. Got awards for having the cleanest booths in the county. Saved the company money, too. Could charge the time to the booth instead of travel to the job. You wouldn't care about that unless you was a stockholder. My wife an' me, we used to put every nickel we had into the company stock—buy Ma Bell, not the Boston outfit. Got better'n a thousand shares, and that feels good. These young guys these days don't do that. I can't figure out what they figure. But they better take care of themselves because no one else is going to do it for 'em. Seem to figure they know everything. Why, I remember one time the pole crews down in New Jersey were sinkin' forty, fifty holes a day and up here we was hittin' maybe ten, fifteen. So these young kids were sent up to show us how. Well, that was somethin'. We sat back and watched. Very first hole they hit a rock this big. Had to dig 'er out by hand. Next thing they hit another. Well, we were really enjoyin' this, watchin' how those young guys were showin' us how to do it . . ."

The door to the doctor's office opened and Spunk was called in for an examination.

Portrait: Myra: Old Stock

Myra lives the simple life outside a small Southern town. Her husband Bill farms parttime, is a parttime mechanic, and is known for the beer he brews at home. As a family they have what they need. They have three kids, aged seven, ten, and thirteen. They are healthy, outgoing, happy kids, as yet unaffected by the "funny ideas" of high schoolers. They all live in a white clapboard house, with a barn no longer used for livestock, on better than sixty acres, half of it set to pulp pine. Myra and Bill are old stock in the area, known to be reliable, good folk, and it looks as if their kids will grow up to be the same.

The weekly schedule is almost unvarying. There is the weekday hustle to get the kids off to the school bus in time. Almost every evening has its special TV show. Myra's favorites are "Walt Disney," "The Waltons," and "Happy Days." The focus of her life is as mother, housewife, and cook. Myra is an excellent cook, and she loves it. She is teaching her daughter, now seven, to bake because she feels it is important for girls to know how to bake—it shows a woman cares about her family. Wednesday evenings Myra usually attends the club meeting, where community affairs are discussed and Edna Walso gives a book review; occasionally a guest lecturer holds forth. But generally neither Myra nor her family are much interested in world affairs. Friday is grocery day. Saturday she and Bill go to the movies or attend some social gathering. Only on birthdays are they likely to invite people to their home. Sunday, of course, is for church. Bill and their daughter sing in the choir. The sermon is often discussed later at home. Nightly prayers and family grace before meals are required. Further, each of the children must say a Bible verse before eating—and no repeats. And then comes Monday and the hustle to get the kids off to the school bus on time.

The big days of the year are likely to be family days: Christmas, Thanksgiving, Memorial Day (because Myra's eldest brother was killed in Korea), birthdays (except for hers!). In the fall Myra takes each of her children, one by one, to do school shopping at Sears, in a town twenty-five miles distant. While there she often buys records of country and western music, which she and Bill both love. She stocks up on magazines—*Family Circle*, a scattering of romance magazines, and anything that has headlines about the love affairs of the famous. Myra knows what Bill will say about these, but she also notices that he doesn't let them go unread.

In a way the world has passed Myra by. Women's liberation means nothing to her; she deeply opposes the kind of thing that goes on nowadays between girls and boys in the high school. It wasn't that way when she and Bill were classmates and sweethearts there. And she worries about her daughter and the boys, although that's still a long way off. Although she takes good care of her husband and children, Myra does not spend much time on her own looks and dress. For her family she shops thriftily; for herself, miserly. Still and all, Myra considers that she lives the good life—content, tranquil, relaxed, and full of the pleasures and rewards of a happy family.

Demographics

Belongers tend to be above middle age, female, white, middle-income, and middle-class. More of them have been married than any other lifestyle group, and fewer (other than the very youthful I-Am-Mes) have been divorced or separated. They tend to live in the South, with fewer in the more sophisticated census regions such as the Mid-Atlantic, the Pacific, and New England. They overwhelmingly prefer living in towns and the open country to big-city or suburban life. The majority have graduated from high school, but only 7 percent are college graduates. A higher percentage of them view themselves as middle-class than any other lifestyle group.

They are more Democratic than Republican or Independent, yet more conservative and middle-of-the-road than liberal. Indeed, only 10 percent rate themselves as liberal, a figure second only to the 8 percent of Achievers who are liberal.

Only about 40 percent work—34 percent full time and 7 percent parttime—and 28 percent are homemakers, the highest percentage of any values group. They are drastically underrepresented in technical, professional, managerial, and administrative occupations but come out about average in clerical, crafts, and operator and laborer categories. In terms of household income in 1979, 52 percent were between $10,000 and $25,000. Average household income was $17,300—not far from the 1979 national average. About 10 percent had incomes over $30,000, and as we shall see later, many Belongers hold considerable assets. The rapid increase in value of agricultural land in recent years undoubtedly has benefitted many rural Belongers.

The overall picture is of a large, aging group a bit removed from the center of action, tending strongly toward traditional attitudes.

Attitudes

Belongers show up as highest or lowest among the lifestyle groups in ten of the attitudinal items listed in Table A-2 in the Appendix. The items reveal a great deal about the Belonger style of life.

○ Belongers are least likely to think their greatest achievements lie ahead; they appear content with the way things are rather than feeling passed by.

○ Practically all Belongers feel "my family is the single most important thing to me." This powerful family orientation is reflected in many attitudes of Belongers.

○ Belongers are more likely than any other group to feel it is wrong for an unmarried man or an unmarried woman to have sexual relations. Fifty-eight percent feel that way, versus only 10 percent for the Experiential group.

○ Belongers are tied with a very different group, the Experientials, in feeling "it's more important to understand my inner self than to be famous, powerful, or wealthy." Apparently Belongers' faith in people and the family find expression here, along with their relative indifference to showy forms of Outer-Direction.

○ More Belongers than any other group see themselves as conventional rather than experimental. This is in keeping with their traditional orientation.

○ Belongers are tied for high with the Experientials in their rating of: "Overall, I'd say I'm very happy." This high score suggests that Belongers are comfortable with their personal situations despite having a variety of complaints about social trends.

○ Belongers, most emphatically, do not consider themselves swingers!

○ Neither do Belongers tend to act on hunches. However, the data on this item are remarkably similar across the lifestyle groups, suggesting this is a difficult question to answer.

○ Belongers have the highest confidence index of any VALS group with respect to both elected officials and military leaders, pointing to general patriotism and support of tradition.

The hallmark of Belongers is a powerful attachment to the status quo, if not to the ways of yesterday. Belongers are likely to think things are changing too fast. Second only to Survivors, they feel that the place of women is in the home. Only a handful support legalization of marijuana. A sense of group—of being part of a larger entity—is very important to most Belongers. It is probably because of this need that Belongers tend to get a lot of satisfaction from their jobs and from friends.

Belongers are very much middle-of-the-road on consumer and broad social issues such as limiting industrial growth, spending on the environment or armaments, or sentiments concerning the energy situation. We know from our data that Belongers are deeply patriotic, loving the pomp and ceremony of tradition, and also strong America-firsters. This is a group whose roots go deep and hold fast.

Financial Status

The outstanding feature of Belonger finances is the combination of general financial contentedness and marked financial conservatism. More than twice as many Belongers as Emulators (70 to 32 percent) express satisfaction with their current incomes, even though Belonger incomes are about $1,000 a year less. Further, fewer Belongers than Emulators expect to be able to maintain their standard of living in the coming five years, and fewer had improving incomes in the recent past.

Fiscal conservatism, apparently, is what enables Belongers to feel so secure financially. Again comparisons with Emulators are revealing. Only 38 percent of Belongers regard themselves as spenders, compared with 60 percent of Emulators. Belongers are less likely to buy on time, go into debt to cope with inflation, or to invest in tangibles such as art, gold, or gems. Far more Belongers than Emulators keep credit card balances under $100. Three times as many have no debts or liabilities, and only about half as many have debts exceeding $10,000.

The upshot is that Belongers have accumulated considerable assets over the years. A high 82 percent of Belongers own their own homes, a figure second only to 87 percent for Achievers. Mortgages appear to have been paid off on about 30 percent of these—substantially the highest fraction in the lifestyle groups. Over half Belonger households have assets exceeding $50,000. Belongers are active—although much less so than Achievers—in essentially all financial activities, such as credit cards, checking accounts, mutual and money market funds, savings instruments, stocks and bonds, and real estate.

Activity Patterns

Because the group is so numerous, Belongers make up the largest single market for many of the activities examined in the lifestyle survey, even when Belonger participation rates are low. For example, the data show that the percentage of I-Am-Mes who sometimes go bowling (78 percent) is more than twice that of the Belongers (34 percent). Nonetheless, the number of Belongers who sometimes bowl (19 million) is three times the number of I-Am-Me bowlers (just over 6 million).

In terms of participation rates Belongers tend to be low in vigorous activities, cultural pursuits, inner-growth activities, adult education, use of libraries, pleasure and business travel, use of credit cards, and reading of most types of magazines.

It is clear that Belongers watch their spending and are not given to the more faddish activities. Perhaps because so many Belongers are traditional housewives, they seem to prefer home and family activities and such pursuits as gardening and baking, needlework, collecting recipes, writing letters, sending greeting cards, and watching TV (especially during daylight hours). Belongers are heavy readers of food/cooking sections of newspapers and like to read domestic and tabloid magazines. They use trading stamps and coupons more than any other VALS type. Reflecting the profound stability of this kind of personality, Belongers are more likely than any other type to have lived in their current residence for over ten years and (along with Achievers) to live in a detached, single-family dwelling that they own. These housing patterns help explain why do-it-yourself activities loom so large in Belonger families.

TABLE 7
Activities of Belongers

Active sports		**Learning**	
Baseball/basketball/football/softball	–	Have spent over $50 for self-instruction	–
Squash/handball/racquetball	–	Have attended night school	–
Swimming	–	**Business travel**	
Tennis	–	Travel by air	–
Spectator sports		**Credit cards owned**	
X-rated movies	–	Department/specialty store card	–
Youth entertainment		**Life and health insurance**	
Pop/rock concerts	–	Have group life insurance	–
Night clubs/discos	–	Have disability insurance	–
Arcades/video games	–	Attended movie theatre	–
Pool/billiards	–	**Commercial or educational TV watching***	
Attendance at cultural events		Watch 10 A.M.-1 P.M. weekdays	+
Theatre	–	Watch 1-4:30 P.M. weekdays	+
Gardening and baking		**Type of TV program watched**	
Flower gardening	+	Sports programs	–
Vegetable gardening	+	Morning news	+
Bake pastries	+	Early evening news	+
Health-related food concerns		**Newspaper reading**	
Collect recipes	+	Read food/cooking section	+
Cigarette smoking		**Housing**	
Have smoked for over 10 years	+	Lived in current residence over 10 years	+
Off-hours work		Own home	+
Work at second job/free-lance	–	House over 25 years old	+

*Hours shown are for Eastern and Pacific time. Times are an hour earlier for Central and Mountain time.

Activities in which Belongers differ by ten percentage points or more from national participation averages are listed in Table 7. Only thirty-two items are listed—by far the fewest of any lifestyle group. This finding reveals the lack of extremes in the Belonger lifestyle and their deep-seated desire to fit in rather than stand out.

Consumption Patterns

The Belonger characteristics of needing to fit in and of preferring the traditional or conventional over "new and improved" products are reflected in their patterns of consumption. Again, because of the large size of this group in absolute numbers (57 million adults), Belongers constitute a substantial share of most markets, even though the percentage of them using any particular product may be well below the average.

Belonger households are major buyers of both large and compact

American-made autos. Important current purchase considerations to them are convenient dealer location, cost of repairs and servicing, and safety features, the last probably reflecting concerns for the family. Exterior styling is relatively unimportant. They prefer American-made cars to imports.

In appliances Belonger households show a higher-than-average level of ownership of freezers and lower ownership levels for dishwashers, garbage disposals, food processors, and microwave ovens. These patterns possibly reflect their preference for doing things in the traditional way, as well as their older homes and rural living habits. In general they exhibit average levels of ownership of recreational equipment, home electronic products, and photographic equipment, and they appear to have below-average interest in new high-technology products such as home computers.

In clothing Belonger women are particularly frequent wearers of slacks. Slacks appear to be sufficiently ingrained in their lifestyles that employment status has little effect. Fewer Belonger men than average tend to wear suits, dress shirts, and jeans.

Belongers are substantially below average in consumption of all types of alcoholic beverages and regular carbonated soft drinks. A higher-than-average percentage consume fruit juices as well as regular and decaffeinated coffee. They are disproportionately high consumers of traditional breakfast foods, with the highest level of use of cold cereal; a lower-than-average percentage eat snack foods such as potato/corn chips and pretzels. Their use of canned soups, butter, and margarine is higher than average, and their use of gelatin desserts is substantially above average.

Belonger consumption patterns are much the closest to national norms of any VALS group. In only 20 of the 170 areas covered do they deviate from the national norm by more than ten percentage points. This contrasts with 100 for Survivors, 59 for Sustainers, 51 for I-Am-Mes, 47 for Experientials, and 28 or 29 for Emulators, Achievers, and the Societally Conscious. Areas in which Belongers vary most from averages are listed in Table 8.

EMULATORS

Portrait: Roger and the Big Time

It was a fabulous feeling to close the deal. It called for celebrations at the office and with his girlfriend, Debbie. It meant boastful calls to his

TABLE 8
Consumption Patterns of Belongers

Durables			Pet foods and services		
Appliances (ownership)			Cat food (purchase)		
Dishwasher	–		Canned		–
Garbage disposal	–		Dry		+
Recreational equipment (ownership)			Beverages and foods		
Exercise (at home)	–		Alcoholic beverages (use)		
Racing bicycle	–		Any alcohol		–
Home electronic products			Wine		
(ownership)			Any wine		–
Hi-fi stereo components	–		Liquor		
Pocket calculator	–		Any liquor		–
Patio furniture	–		Beer		
Clothing			Any beer		–
Men's clothing (use)			Domestic beer		–
Suits	–		Foods (use)		
Dress shirts	–		Margarine and butter*		
Personal-care products			Reasons for buying margarine		
Women's products (use)			Taste		+
Eye makeup	–		Miscellaneous foods*		
Men's products (use)			Gelatin desserts		+
Shampoo	–				

*For women only.

mom and even to his ex. This was the high point thus far—the start of better things to come—the first wave of the big time—the edge of the dream—the first sniff of bucks with a capital B.

Roger had come a long way from the little railway town in Arkansas. He was the first of his family to make it to college, though he lasted only two years. He was the first to hold "a three-piece-suit job," as he put it. He was the first to wind up working in a big city—Chicago. He was the first to move in the circles of big business. And now he was the first to make a killing—a $1.5-million sale and $100,000 commission, half of it his, clear.

He had worked for it, God knows. There were the countless price estimates, shaved a hundred times by driving special bargains with suppliers. There were the long, heavy-drinking evenings with the client. There were the not-so-subtle special favors for his client and half of his friends, too, it seemed. There were the presentations and the endless questions, technical and otherwise. There was the paper work—page after page of specifications of every conceivable type. There were the sudden trips out of town to meet contacts of the client to make sure all their needs were met. There were the contracts revised and footnoted over and over until he knew every detail by heart. And, finally, the envelope arrived. It contained the signed contract and a letter saying, in full: "Dear Roger: Here is the contract. Please move the delivery date from June to May. Sincerely, Bill."

That triggered it. First came the car. Small, foreign, road-hugger, stick shift, muscled, red, expensive. Then there were the presents for Debbie. Sets of black lingerie, a long weekend skiing in the Alps, three days in Acapulco, a one-nighter to San Francisco, a down payment on a fur-lined suede coat. Then the tailor-made suits and shirts for himself, Gucci shoes, Pierre Cardin ties, cashmere sweaters, a secondhand college ring he found in a pawn shop, with a stone that looked like a ruby, an all-leather imported attaché case, English raincoat—the works. And then the parties, one after the other. To one of them Roger invited his boss. This was a mistake. His boss knew something of the lifestyle of young up-and-comers like Roger, but his wife did not. She was shocked by the raucousness, the drinking, the wild dancing, the mysterious communal pipe, and the general abandon. Debbie, alert to her reactions, tried to converse calmly with her, but Debbie was deep into the party and didn't make a lot of sense. It was a good six months before Roger's boss stopped hearing from his wife about that awful party.

So it was that Roger's fifty thou went down the pipes fast. He awoke one morning to realize he was in debt and, worse, that there were taxes and alimony still to pay. Roger went to his boss to ask for an advance on the "sure-thing" sale he was working on. But his boss was tough. "Son," he told Roger, "you never have a sure thing. You ought to know, too, you're not going to make it here in this firm living the way you do. There're plenty of salesmen here making twice what you do and they aren't throwing it away. They have better sense. They're looking ahead. They're developing contacts for the long haul. I'm telling you something important, Roger. I hope you're hearing."

But he wasn't. When he ran across a sale of waistcoats, he forgot his debts and bought three. When he had lunch with friends, he arranged in advance to have it charged to him. The pleasure he got from the careless sweep of the hand and the words "forget it" was worth the cost many times over. But then Roger ran into bad luck, breaking his ankle trying to take some steps three at a time. This was catastrophic because obviously he couldn't get around to make his calls. His boss came to visit while he was stuck at home. The boss had two bits of news. First, the "sure-thing" sale had gone to another firm. And second, one of his creditors had moved to attach the next $10,000 Roger earned, if and when that came to pass. His boss wished him luck and asked if there was anything he could do. Roger said no.

That evening Roger fixed himself a couple of extra drinks. He moved over to where he could catch a sliver of a glimpse of the towers of Chicago past the dull bricks of the deep, narrow air shaft of his building. What surprised Roger was that his mind was back in his hometown in Arkansas, and the slim towers of Chicago somehow put him in mind of the skyline of Little Rock, where, Roger knew, there were sales jobs if you knew your stuff.

Portrait: Flash from the Past: Sheila

Looking back on it, the amazing thing was that she'd made it at all. There were so many embarrassing moments, and a few that were closer to terror. The embarrassing ones she could almost smile at now—like using the wrong fork at Mrs. Markham's dinner party. Then there was the time during the annual meeting when she was called on and couldn't get a word out and just sat there and cried. That was one of those moments of terror.

Was it really ten years ago now that she'd arrived in San Francisco—the big time—looking for a job? Her two years at a community college at home in the Central Valley qualified her for nothing, it seemed. When she was offered a trainee spot in the sales department of a well-known food company, she took it, hardly noticing what was expected of her or what she got paid. No company with such fabulous offices on the twenty-second floor of a modern building with a spectacular view of San Francisco Bay could be other than the perfect place to work. Luckily, she was right.

In the beginning it was people who made it right. She and four other trainees did "the eleventh," as her sales district was called, under the stern, watchful eye of Mr. Markham, an exceptional salesman and exceptional human being. Almost at once he took Sheila under his wing, tutoring her in the subtleties, for Sheila had an instinctive gift for selling and needed only to see how professionals did it to copy them almost flawlessly. Sales was a gift her mother had, too, although it showed up only rarely, in local politics or the PTA. Sheila thought of this at length during one trip when the trainee group visited outlets not far from her hometown. But Sheila could not bring herself to show her new associates the messy farm where she grew up or introduce them to her gruff, unshaven father or her aproned mother with her quick, intelligent eyes. To her family she could boast of her new life; to the new she could not reveal the old.

And what boasting she did, especially to her little brother Jeb. She boasted of colossal corporate deals, of the big money to be made in sales, of the parties she attended, of closets full of clothes, of rumored executive ocean voyages to Hawaii, of life on Russian Hill, of a hundred other things that hardly pertained to her at all. The funny thing was that in telling Jeb she began to believe these things too—to think this was the way she should live.

A subtle change came over Sheila. She became louder, more aggressive, more demanding, more competitive, more conspicuous in what she did and how she did it. She took to tightly tailored pants suits, black stockings, and eye shadow. In meetings she learned the trick of the surprise remark and the undermining silence. She learned to threaten invisibly. Smart, adroit, efficient, she found out how to look good at the expense of others. For the first time she developed enemies, partly because she was moving ahead, gaining new responsibilities, and building a reputation as a woman who "thinks like a man." And so it was for six or seven years of driving growth and professional advancement—hard work but good times, leading where she wanted to go. It was no longer other people who made the company right for her; it was she, Sheila herself, who made it right.

The invitation to the Markhams' dinner party came almost as a shock—certainly a surprise. Mr. Markham was retired now, but he came into the office periodically and kept track of things in the department. Sheila had almost forgotten him. Nevertheless, she accepted the invitation with pleasure.

The Markhams lived down the Peninsula in a large, gracious home full of family memories and memorabilia. Cocktails were served on the side porch overlooking the coastal hills, dinner in the chandeliered dining room with its arabesqued rug, after-dinner drinks in the paneled library lined with books of many kinds—most, it turned out, of Mrs. Markham's choice. It was at this dinner that Sheila used the wrong fork for her shrimp. Clandestinely she tried to change to the right one, but she knew Mrs. Markham had noticed. Sheila, unaccustomedly these days, blushed.

Most of the guests had left when Mrs. Markham asked Sheila to come with her into the library. There Mrs. Markham told her that she and Mr. Markham had happened to be driving in the Valley and found themselves in Sheila's hometown. They had asked for directions and made their way out to the farm where Sheila was raised. Mrs. Markham looked at Sheila keenly, but Sheila's head was down. She was studying the grain of the oaken floor. "I thought your mother was a remarkable and lovely lady," Mrs. Markham said. And Sheila looked up into those gray-blue, gentle eyes of Mrs. Markham's, and suddenly she was in tears, uncontrollably in tears. "She reminded me so very much of you," said Mrs. Markham.

And so it was that Sheila, in a flash from the past, rediscovered her mother and with her all the warm family memories of childhood. And, too, she learned something that was to guide her future: that people like the Markhams—wealthy, established, respected—live by more than the glitter of success.

Demographics

Key demographic attributes of Emulators include their youthfulness (median age, twenty-seven years), the fact that there are more men than women, with many singles and considerable minority-group representation, and a low self-assessment of their social standing. Almost all Emulators are high school graduates, and about a fourth have attended college. Politically Emulators take a middle to liberal position; only 13 percent are Republicans.

A higher percentage of Emulators work full time than any other lifestyle group, and fewer work parttime. They are severely underrepresented in the intellectual, highly trained domains of professional, technical, managerial, and administrative jobs to which many doubtless aspire. They far exceed national norms in sales, clerical, crafts work, and machine-operator occupations. Half of Emulator households had incomes in 1979 between $15,000 and $25,000, and 17 percent, probably including many two-worker households, made more.

This financially ambitious and hard-working group prefers city life because that is where the good jobs are and the big life is to be found. They are the most urbanized of the lifestyle groups, the least likely to live in towns and the open country. In terms of census regions they are quite evenly distributed, being most overrepresented in the South Atlantic and most underrepresented in the East South Central area. (See page 278 for a map of census regions.)

Attitudes

Considering their youthfulness the attitudes of Emulators are surprisingly middle-ground. They rank at the extremes in only 3 of the 41 items listed in Table A-2. Belongers, on the other hand—famed for not being extravagant—show ten extremes, and Sustainers—who resemble Emulators in many respects—display no fewer than twenty extremes.

Perhaps the outstanding feature of the attitudes of Emulators is their vehemence concerning social situations involving individual action. This seems to be the principal area in which their personal feelings are vented. Emulators would rather go to a party than stay home. They are emphatic in their belief that sex between unmarried people is not wrong. They support the right of women to work. They definitely see themselves as "something of a swinger." And they are second only to the Experientials in feeling that marijuana should be legalized.

They deeply mistrust both people and institutions. Job satisfaction is low. Confidence in elected officials and company leaders is minimal. Many doubt that the energy crisis is real, and they have little faith in government, public utilities, or oil companies as sources of information about energy.

Financial Status

Emulators, despite average household incomes exceeding $18,000 in 1979, rank second only to Sustainers in wanting to get ahead financially. Only about a third are not dissatisfied with their present finances. They are definitely spenders, not savers. Although most feel it is unwise to buy on time or to go into debt to combat inflation, Emulators are clearly living on the edge of insolvency. While the percentage of Emulators with loans outstanding is very close to those for the more affluent Achievers and Societally Conscious, the motivations behind the loans are vastly different. The Achievers and Societally Conscious often go into debt voluntarily, for tax purposes. The Emulators are in debt because their income is insufficient to support their purchasing habits. To complete the picture of fiscal instability, Emulators hold relatively small balances in checking accounts, in savings instruments, and in stocks and bonds. Finally, only 10 percent of them would have $50,000 or more left from the sale of their home, a percentage that is lower than all groups other than the poverty-ridden Survivors. The Emulators' financial habits, it appears, fully justify the group's concern about money.

Activity Patterns

Emulators surprised us by showing so few deviations from national activity norms. They turn out to be second in conformity to Belongers and essentially tied with Achievers. We take this to mean that Emulators, as the name implies, tend to copy the patterns of others rather than express individual drives. This is in dramatic contrast to I-Am-Me patterns. The remarkable activity differences illuminate the huge contrasts between transitions into the Outer-Directed and Inner-Directed paths of the double hierarchy. We regard this as a major confirmation of the theory underlying the VALS typology.

The activity patterns of Emulators bespeak a young group, neither intellectual nor artistic, not oriented to people or the home, socially inclined but without the financial resources required for extensive use of credit cards, pleasure travel, or fashionable dining out.

Other activities that Emulators favor fill out the picture of their direct, not especially elegant lifestyle: bowling and pool/billiards, visits to night clubs or discos and to arcades for video games, poker, eating dinner while watching TV, eating at fast-food restaurants, cigarette smoking, dependence on group life and health insurance, preference for comedies and movies on TV, belief that TV is getting better, readership of classified ads, and likelihood of moving recently into a house over twenty-five years old. Even though Emulators rate low in having and using credit cards, they are more likely than most to have household credit card balances exceeding $500. Since their incomes are not high, this suggests that many Emulators are in debt.

The 43 activities (out of 257 studied) in which Emulators deviate from national norms by ten percentage points or more are listed in Table 9.

Consumption Patterns

Patterns of product ownership and use among Emulators are closer in some ways to those of the I-Am-Mes than to those of the Achievers they seek to emulate. Undoubtedly this reflects in part the shared demographic attributes of Emulators and I-Am-Mes. Interestingly, this similarity is strikingly not reflected in the area of activities, where the two groups tend to display quite different patterns.

Emulator households are disproportionately high purchasers of subcompact and small specialty cars, and relatively more of them than the national average buy foreign-made cars. An above-average percentage purchase used cars. Their current purchase considerations show a higher-than-average preference for an interesting combination of features: exterior/interior styling, prestige, price or deal offered, durability/reliability, and value for the money.

Incidence of ownership of home electronic products among Emulator households is above average—substantially so for hi-fi stereo sets and prerecorded tapes or cassettes. In the area of women's clothing no

TABLE 9
Activities of Emulators

Bowling	+	Personal communications	
Pool/billiards	+	Write letters to friends/relatives	−
Youth entertainment		Send greeting cards	−
Pop/rock	+	Phone friends/relatives long	
Night clubs/discos	+	distance	−
Theme/amusement parks	+	Business travel	
Arcades/video games	+	Stay at hotels/motels	−
Cards		Credit cards owned	
Poker	+	Gasoline/oil	−
Gardening and baking		Purchases with credit cards	
Flower gardening	−	Gasoline	
Vegetable gardening	−	Life and health insurance	
Needlework (women only)		Have individual life insurance	
Knit/crochet/needlework	−	Have group life insurance	+
Design clothes	−	Have disability insurance	+
Sew to make something	−	Commercial or educational TV watching*	
Eating habits		Watch 10 A.M.-1 P.M. weekends	+
Eat dinner while watching TV	+	Type of TV program watched	
Eating out		Comedies	+
Eat lunch out	+	Movies	+
Eat dinner out	−	Early-evening news	−
Eat at fast-food restaurant	+	Believe commercial TV is	
Health-related food concerns		getting better	+
Collect recipes	−	Newspaper reading	
A lot of concern with amount of		Read daily newspaper	−
sugar in foods	−	Read business/finance section	−
A lot of concern with nutritional		Read classified ads	+
quality of food	−	Read food/cooking section	−
Cigarette smoking		Housing	
Have smoked in past month	+	Lived in current residence over 10	
Have smoked for over 10 years	−	years	−
Stopped smoking over 10 years ago	−	Own home	−
		House over 25 years old	+

*Hours shown are for Eastern and Pacific time. Times are an hour earlier for Central and Mountain time.

distinct pattern or variance from the norm emerges. Emulator men prefer more informal attire, wearing suits, sport coats, slacks, and dress shirts less frequently than the other VALS types and jeans more often. Emulators are disproportionately high consumers of alcoholic beverages, preferring beer, vodka, rum, and tequila. They also have an affinity for champagne and for imported wines. They have among the highest consumption of high-sugar and high-carbohydrate products such as regular carbonated soft drinks and snack foods (except nuts), gum, and candy.

As with activities, the Emulators are surprisingly close to national consumption norms. Indeed, only the traditional Belongers are more

TABLE 10
Consumption Patterns of Emulators

Durables		Men's products (use)	
Appliances (ownership)		After-shave lotion	−
Dishwasher	−	Pet ownership	
Electric cooking range	−	Fish	+
Gas cooking range	+	Pet foods and services	
Home electronic products		Cat food (purchase)	
(ownership)		Moist	+
Hi-fi stereo components	+	Beverages and foods	
Prerecorded tapes/cassettes	+	Alcoholic beverages (use)	
Miscellaneous products (ownership)		Any alcohol	+
Home encyclopedia set	−	Liquor consumption	
Manual typewriter	−	Any liquor	+
Expressed any interest in new		Beer	
products		Any beer	+
Home computer	+	Domestic beer	+
Clothing		Carbonated beverages (use)	
Women's clothing (use)		Regular soft drinks	+
Jeans	+	Other beverages (use)	
Men's clothing (use)		Fruit juices	−
Suits	−	Decaffeinated coffee	−
Sport coats	−	Margarine and butter*	
Slacks	−	Reasons for buying margarine	
Jeans	+	Health	−
Personal-care products		Taste	+
Women's products (use)		Miscellaneous foods*	
Eye makeup	+	Frozen vegetables	−
Shampoo	+	Gelatin desserts	−

*For women only.

typical of national patterns, although Achievers and Societally Conscious rank about the same. Table 10 shows the twenty-nine areas where Emulators differ from the average by ten percentage points or more.

ACHIEVERS

Portrait: D.J.

Donnelly Jowett White, universally known as D.J., was holding forth in his corner office. "Know how I got here?" he asked with an expansive gesture toward the towers of Houston, spectacularly visible through the floor-to-ceiling glass. "Well, it all started here." D.J. plucked two worn slips of paper from his wallet, stubs from paychecks he'd earned selling vacuum cleaners to housewives some thirty years before. Squinting, he read off the faded figures: $954 and $1,326. "Not bad for a kid in college," he observed. "Man," he added, waving again at the Houston skyline, "it's a goddam long way from Wheeling, West Virginia." D.J. always gave both town and state as though no one had ever heard of either.

Wheeling, of course, was D.J.'s hometown. D.J.'s father had been sheriff there through the thirties and forties, until the new politicians forced him from office. Within a year he was dead. From his father D.J. had inherited a powerful physique, a commanding manner, and a determination to get ahead. He bitterly resented what had been done to his father. He figured, if ever he could, he'd go back to West Virginia and maybe run for governor and in some obscure way even things up.

Again D.J. addressed the little group of reporters in his office. "Guess you fellas know some of the history," he said. "Came down here in 1956 to make my fortune." He laughed, and the reporters laughed with him. "Right off got myself a piece of the action at the Snow Flake. We had exactly one outlet then, down at the corner where the Sewell Building is now. Smartest thing I ever did. Especially my partner." D.J. always was careful to pay due respects to his partner of the early years. Unfortunately, his partner was dead now, killed in an auto accident. "My partner, Mac—you know who Mac was, of course—was the best ice cream man there ever was. Knew how to make it good and how to make it cheap. I handled the sales. When the Sewell people came along and wanted to take over our location, that was our chance. We owned close onto half the block. With that money we really got going. Opened up outlets in Houston, then Dallas, then Fort Worth. Got better than seventeen hundred Snow Flakes now, pretty much all over the country. Next Monday we open number seventeen hundred and forty-two in San Diego." D.J. always did know the company statistics. He grew reflective. "I'll tell you, these have been good years. It's not only the bucks—of course, I have no objection to them—but it's helping the system. Making it work. Putting things together so they hum. Having a part in what's going on. You know, really running the show." The reporters nodded and scribbled at their pads.

The occasion for interviewing D.J. was the sale of the Snow Flake chain. It was going lock, stock, and barrel to World Foods for $312 million. D.J.'s share would be 10 percent, but that of course by no means constituted his total resources. D.J. was selling because he sensed it was time, for the business and for him personally. For the business because D.J.'s instincts—and the falling growth rate of Snow Flake—

told him the ice cream business was not what it used to be. For him personally because he felt a need for change, for something new. He'd shown himself and others that he could make it. He noticed that lately he thought more of the past. He thought it would be fun to get into sports—buy a piece of a franchise if he could. Pro football was his choice because he'd been first-string halfback at West Virginia and they'd had a helluva team.

"You know," he said almost to himself, "it would be kinda nice to go back to Wheeling, West Virginia, for a bit." There was his habit again of giving both town and state. "Expect things have changed more than a mite. And there are a couple of loose ends from long ago I'd like to look into."

What he was referring to was the circumstances surrounding his father's dismissal as sheriff so long ago. But D.J. did not speak of his reasons for selling Snow Flake, of his ambitions in pro ball, of his thoughts about running for governor in his home state, and most of all he was silent about his father.

"Well, boys," D.J. asked, "any more questions?" There were none. "Okay, then, how about a little of the best ice cream there ever was to close the deal while it's still hot?" D.J. laughed softly at his little joke.

Portrait: Elizabeth the Artist

"I will not have you calling me Elizabeth," Elizabeth was saying to her thirteen-year-old son. "I am your mother, and that's what I wish to be called. Not Mom, not Elizabeth, but Mother." "Yes, Mother," said her son.

Elizabeth was on edge because the Pleasanton Art Club was meeting at her home that afternoon. She was president, and the occasion was the annual election of officers; would her efforts be successful in beating out Mrs. Stametz? Then, too, she was cross because her daughter Joan had just arrived from school with a note about not having done her homework. Elizabeth had sent her up to her room with the threat she'd have her father speak to her. "Not that that would help much," she thought to herself: "He's the one that's easy on the children, I'm the one who has to see that things get done."

Elizabeth had arranged for her friend Cathy to nominate her for reelection, and she'd written out in detail what she deemed to be her qualifications. College graduate; a year of law school—stopped to have a child; married to a lawyer; two children; sometime book reviewer for the Pleasanton *Times;* member of Pleasanton Congregational church;

member of PTA, one year as president (you were allowed to be president for only one year, the notes to Cathy pointed out); organizer of the women's investment club; sponsor of the Waldo County Hospital and the Pleasanton High School orchestra; member of the state Historical Society—the list went on. At the end came her qualifications in the field of art: graduate of Hopewell Art Institute; lessons from watercolorist Caroline Owens and portraitist Jay Kawalik; one-woman show in the Pleasanton Gallery; three-year member of the Pleasanton Art Club, one year as secretary, one year as president.

It was an impressive dossier, and Cathy did it justice in nominating Elizabeth. Mrs. Stametz didn't stand a chance, although everyone, including Elizabeth, said the secret balloting must have been very close. Business over, the members of the art club enjoyed the sunny weather, the view of hills from the back patio, and the delicious, catered tea. Elizabeth confided to several that her ambition for the coming year was to enlarge the roster of membership by "luring," as she put it with a smile, some men into joining.

The gentility of her mood was gone by the time her husband got home. The need for action was again upon her. What about seeing to it that Joan did her homework? How could she avoid the embarrassment of being called "Elizabeth" by a thirteen-year-old? Could they arrange a party for all the men in the area who might join the Art Club? Where should they have it? What had he—her husband—done about inviting Judge and Mrs. Laplam for dinner? And how about the golf tournament? What flight would they be in? Who was seeded where? What about getting the Millers to play with them in Scotch foursomes? Finally she told her husband about being re-elected to the presidency of the art club. His congratulations were immediate and enthusiastic.

For a minute Elizabeth basked in the unaccustomed warmth of her feeling for her husband. It took her back to earlier times—to her childhood, to a high school dance, to her days in law school when she quit because she wanted so much to marry, to have a child, to be a mother. And then the day's events swarmed back into the forefront, and she thought about how much there was for her to do and how few hours there were in the day.

Demographics

Achievers are the heart of upper-middle-class America. There are about 37 million Achievers, 15 million women and 22 million men, making them the most male-dominated of the lifestyle groups. Their median age is forty-three—some four years older than the Societally Conscious, nine years younger than Belongers, and more than twenty years younger than Survivors.

One of the most interesting things about Achievers is their marital status. Their age is such that we would expect them to show the highest proportion of marrieds, and they do. But they also show exceptionally low fractions of divorced or separated individuals and of singles and "living togethers." The overall pattern suggests that Achievers generally have solid marriages. Over 80 percent have children living at home; most of the children are over twelve, and many are of college age.

Achievers are by far the most prosperous of the lifestyle groups. In 1979, 60 percent had household incomes between $25,000 and $50,000, and 5 percent had incomes exceeding $75,000. Their average income of $31,400 exceeded that of the next most affluent group by over $4,000. Half of all Achievers live in the suburbs; only 30 percent live in medium or large cities, the second lowest percentage (to Belongers) of the values types. Achievers are quite evenly distributed among the census regions, although they are underrepresented in the South Atlantic and overrepresented in the Pacific region.

Ninety-five percent of Achievers are Caucasians; 2 percent are black, 1 percent Hispanic, and 2 percent "other." They are a well-educated group: 27 percent have some college, a further 18 percent are college graduates, and an additional 15 percent attended graduate school. Almost half hold jobs that are professional, technical, managerial, or administrative. They have the highest percentage of self-employed people (21 percent) and the lowest fraction of those looking for work (1 percent).

This background of success and prosperity no doubt contributes to the Achievers' high self-rating in terms of social class. No less than 41 percent regard themselves as upper-class—about double the national average. Further, Achievers have more than twice the percentage of Republicans as any other lifestyle group and the fewest who regard themselves as Democrats or Independents. Similarly, they are the most politically conservative of any group; only 8 percent say they are political liberals.

Attitudes

The attitudes of Achievers reveal them as a well-adjusted, self-confident group, with a sense of clearly being in control, strongly supportive of the economic system, doubtful about "modern" social movements.

Only 20 percent often feel left out of things going on around them. This is the lowest fraction of any lifestyle group and contrasts with 63 percent for Sustainers. They rank highest in feeling people are generally honest and trustworthy; they rank lowest in feeling rebellious. Achievers are less likely than most to feel "everything is changing too fast today." These attitudes express the assurance and sense of command characteristic of Achievers. It therefore is no surprise to learn that 84 percent of Achievers feel they have more self-confidence than others.

Their support of the economic system emerges in many attitudes. Achievers, for example, are the most supportive of any group of U.S. involvement in world affairs. They are far more likely than other lifestyle types to oppose limits on industrial growth and to support spending on military armaments. Achievers are the least alarmed about air pollution. Overall, they have more confidence than other groups in organizational leaders, especially corporate leaders. They are especially apt to think products are getting better and safer. They get more satisfaction from their work than any other group. Clearly, Achievers find life rewarding.

Personal conservatism is a powerful force among Achievers: 77 percent (second highest to Belongers) say they are more conventional than experimental. They also rank second to Belongers in feeling that "my family is the single most important thing to me." They don't see themselves as swingers; they strongly oppose legalization of marijuana. They are a good deal less likely than the average person to approve of sex between unmarried people or to believe a woman with small children can work and still be a good mother. The overall picture here is that Achievers really prefer the social standards of the 1930s, '40s, and '50s, the decades when most Achievers were growing up. The emergent values of the 1960s and '70s are not those of Achievers, but largely those of the children of Achievers.

It nonetheless seems clear that most Achievers are able to live with—if not approve of—contemporary values, for 94 percent declare themselves to be overall "very happy." Achievers, despite the rebellious attitudes of some of their children, seem quite able to lead lives of their own liking.

Financial Status

Achievers lead the lifestyle groups in almost all financial activities. We have already seen that their average incomes exceed those of other groups by a considerable margin. The same holds for most forms of financial resources. For example, more Achievers than any other life-style group:

- Have one or more credit cards (87 percent)

- Have checking accounts (97 percent)

- Have checking account balances of over $1,000 (30 percent)

- Have mutual or money market funds (25 percent)

- Have mutual or money market fund balances of over $50,000 (12 percent)

- Have savings accounts, certificates, etc. (91 percent—only 1 percent less than the Societally Conscious group)

- Have savings balances of over $50,000 (4 percent)

- Have stocks or bonds (50 percent)

- Have stocks or bonds worth over $50,000 (16 percent)

- Have investment real estate (35 percent)

- Would clear over $50,000 from sale of investment real estate (38 percent—4 percent less than the Experiential group)

- Use services of a stockbroker (25 percent)

In addition more Achievers (87 percent) than any other group own their own home—83 percent single-family dwellings, 4 percent townhouses, 9 percent apartments or condominiums, and 4 percent mobile homes. Money remaining from the hypothetical sale of their homes was estimated at between $50,000 and $100,000 per dwelling in a third of the cases and over $100,000 in 11 percent.

Forty-two percent of Achievers have debts or liabilities exceeding $25,000, but commitments are over $100,000 in only 5 percent of the situations. There is evidence that the debts of many Achievers are in the form of tax shelters, in contrast to the debts of Emulators.

Total estimated household assets far outstrip debts, as 90 percent of Achievers place the total value of their assets at over $25,000, 48 percent over $100,000, 7 percent over $500,000, and 3 percent over $1,000,000.

Against this background of affluence it could be anticipated that

Achievers are no longer especially ambitious financially. This is in keeping with the high level of satisfaction with their current financial position and the fact that over half felt in 1980 that their finances had improved in the previous three years. As in the area of attitudes, it appears that Achievers are conservative. Less than half see themselves as spenders, and most think it unwise to buy on time; at the same time, however, they rank highest among the lifestyle groups in thinking it pays to be in debt as a means of coping with inflation.

One final note. Thirty percent of Achievers regard themselves as financial experts. Only Sustainers, at 42 percent, exceed this level (as explained earlier, Sustainers probably interpreted the question to mean something very different from the more sophisticated interpretation of Achievers).

Activity Patterns

Achievers, easily the most affluent of the VALS types, are of an age to have reached positions of leadership in business, politics, and the professions. Their activity patterns clearly reveal this background: Achievers score high in such activities as playing golf, attending cultural events, drinking cocktails before dinner, adult education, traveling for pleasure and business, owning and using credit cards, having life and health insurance, and reading newspapers (especially business and sports sections) and business magazines. Achievers who smoke tend to be heavy smokers—a characteristic especially prominent among young Achievers, perhaps indicating high pressure and stress. Along with Belongers, Achievers are most likely to consider national brands to be the highest quality.

The evidence is that many I-Am-Mes are the children of Achievers and still live at home. As a result, Achievers are probably the buyers of much equipment whose use shows up more in I-Am-Me activities than in Achiever patterns. Thus, for example, it seems likely that Achievers are the core market for such capital-intensive sports as motorboating, sailing, flying, gliding, and possibly a variety of other active sports in which many participants are I-Am-Mes.

Achievers tend not to be involved in the arts and are surprisingly indifferent to health-related food concerns. They are not big TV watchers and rank above average only in viewing sports programs. Achievers' interest in sports—perhaps reflecting competitive drives—shows up not only in TV watching, but in newspaper and magazine reading and in attendance at professional, college, and high school sports events.

In forty-two activities, listed in Table 11, Achievers deviate from national norm by ten percentage points or more. In terms of overall conformity this places them behind Belongers and essentially tied with Emulators.

Consumption Patterns

The product-ownership and use patterns of Achievers reflect their traditionalism as consumers coupled with their willingness to experiment with technologically based products and their leadership in establishing norms and fashion. In a number of ways their product-ownership and use patterns are similar to those of the Societally Conscious. This is not surprising since both are successful, confident, mature groups.

In their auto purchases Achiever households show above-average ownership of luxury and midsize cars. As expected, they have the highest levels of ownership of two and three cars and of buying new rather than used cars. They own more appliances than average, substantially so for dishwashers, food processors, garbage disposals, and microwave ovens. They rank above average in ownership of all types of recreational equipment (except motorcycles), home electronic products, and photographic equipment.

Achievers show a traditional and conservative approach to clothing. Achiever women are above average in frequent use of skirts and dresses, and Achiever men in use of suits, dress shirts, sport coats, and slacks.

In their alcoholic beverage consumption Achievers show a disproportionately high use of wines and champagne, most kinds of liquor, and domestic beer.

In terms of aberrations from national consumption norms Achievers are essentially tied with Emulators and the Societally Conscious at a bit below average. Only Belongers conform more closely to average patterns. Achievers differ from national averages by ten percentage points or more in the twenty-nine areas listed in Table 12. The affluence of Achievers is revealed by the fact that they consume more than average in every category shown except one. In contrast, three-fourths of the consumption deviations for Survivors are on the low side.

TABLE 11
Activities of Achievers

Active sports		Department/specialty stores	+
Golf	+	Business travel	+
Spectator sports		Pleasure travel	+
College/high school sports events	+	Personal entertainment	+
Cards		Don't use credit cards for purchases	−
Bridge	−	Life and health insurance	
Eating out		Have individual life insurance	+
Drink cocktail before dinner at		Have group life insurance	+
restaurant	+	Have disability insurance	+
Cigarette smoking		Have permanent/whole life/cash	
Have smoked for over 10 years	+	value insurance	+
Stopped smoking over 10 years ago	+	Purchased insurance from agent for	
Learning		one company	+
Have spent over $50 for self-		Commercial or educational TV watching*	
instruction	+	Watch 1-4:30 P.M. weekdays	−
Have attended night school	+	Type of TV program watched	
Pleasure travel		Soap operas	−
Stay at hotels/motels	+	Newspaper reading	
Use rental car	+	Read daily newspaper	+
Use travel agency	+	Read Sunday newspaper	+
Business travel		Read business/finance section	+
Travel by air	+	Read food/cooking section	−
Stay at hotels/motels	+	Read sports section	+
Use rental cars	+	Magazine reading	
Use travel agency	+	Read business magazines	+
Credit cards owned		Housing	
Visa/Bankamericard	+	Live in detached, single-family	
American Express	+	dwelling	+
Gasoline/oil	+	Own home	+
Department/specialty store card	+	House over 25 years old	−
No credit cards	−		
Purchases with credit cards			
Gasoline	+		

*Hours shown are for Eastern and Pacific time. Times are an hour earlier for Central and Mountain time.

TABLE 12
Consumption Patterns of Achievers

Motor Vehicles		Sport coats	+
Purchased last car new	+	Dress shirts	+
Three or more vehicles owned	+	Jeans	−
Durables		Personal-care products	
Appliances (ownership)		Women's products (use)	
Clothes dryer (separate from		Cologne and perfume	+
washer)	+	Eye makeup	+
Dishwasher	+	Aerosol hair spray	+
Food processor	+	Facial moisturizer	+
Garbage disposal	+	Men's products (use)	
Microwave oven	+	After-shave lotion	+
Recreational equipment (ownership)		Pet foods and services	
Exercise (at home)	+	Visits to veterinarians	+
Racing bicycle	+	Beverages and foods	
Home electronic products		Alcoholic beverages (use)	
(ownership)		Wine	
Hi-fi stereo components	+	California wine	+
Pocket calculator	+	Any champagne	+
Telephone extension for home	+	Foods (use)	
Miscellaneous products (ownership)		Margarine and butter*	
Home encyclopedia set	+	Reasons for buying margarine	
Electric typewriter	+	Taste	+
Patio furniture (homeowners only)	+	Miscellaneous foods*	
Clothing		Frozen vegetables	+
Men's clothing (use)			
Suits	+		

*For women only.

7

In Search of Self:
The Inner-Directed Groups

I-AM-MES

Portrait: Red "Softy" Stevenson

There was, so to speak, a heavy pane of glass slicing through the Stevenson family, separating Red from his parents. They could see each other but not hear, touch, smell, or communicate.

In the evening Mr. Stevenson sat in his library, fire ablaze, reading his beloved accounts of the Civil War. His collections of Lincolniana and papers concerning cavalry battles were famous. Almost daily he got word of rare items coming on the market. His greatest pleasure, other than running the family business, lay in sudden trips to small towns or auction houses to examine potential additions to his library. And while Mr. Stevenson lived in the chivalrous world of 120 years ago, Mrs. Stevenson sat engrossed in the tight, perfect world of detective stories. These evenings together were precious to them both, although neither mentioned nor often even recognized that happiness.

In the evening Red staggered across the stage, guitar throbbing, throat mike catching and making audible the gurglings and retchings of his larynx, even above the racket of a thousand teenagers screaming their approval. Then came the silence like the night, for they knew what was to come. Reaching center stage, Red's skilled fingers plucked out the tune, suddenly hauntingly fragile. His voice went gentle, echoed, played games with the tune. The drums beat slowly, and the background humming of the troupe brought it all together into superb soft punk. That was Red's thing. His invention. What the critics called "a major advance."

They gave him forty-five, maybe sixty seconds for his thing. And then the chanting began. "Softy," they chanted, "Softy, Softy, Softy," again and again in cadences. And to compete with the noise the gentleness went from Red's voice and the tune struck hard.

Four hours later, costume torn, sweat not yet dried, exhausted, half-drunk, smoked out, the same skilled fingers groped for the crevices of his girlfriend's body. The evening, indeed the night, was done.

Of a Sunday morning Mr. Stevenson offered his wife his arm as they closed the front door behind them and started the pleasant walk to church. The edgeless fresh air, snow-white cumulus clouds, and hint of color in the wisteria suggested an early spring. They talked about it. As they walked past well-kept yard after well-kept yard, they felt the world was on their side. And they could be sure that Reverend Snowden would preach an edifying sermon, that they would return home for a prelunch Sunday glass of wine for Mrs. Stevenson and a Sunday Scotch for Mr. Stevenson, who would spend a long afternoon watching the ball games on TV. It was the good life.

Of a Sunday morning Red joined his girlfriend and his pal Tom in the Porsche and headed for the country. Blue sky and white clouds and a land about to burst with youth made the day beautiful. And they carried with them the precious packet of baby blue pills. The plan was to stop at an open meadow, preferably one where the hills ran away in echoing folds, and see what happened. And this they did. For Red it turned out to be a day like none he had known before.

It started with him walking behind his parents on the way to church, as he had so many Sundays of his childhood. But as the world of fantasy turns, the scene transformed. Red saw his mother settled on the meadow like a giant warmer of teapots. And as he watched, she grew and grew to enormous size becoming soft and languid and horribly without seams. And still she grew until, to his gaze, she exploded, sending coruscating streamers of putrescence filling the sky in every direction. The sweet meadow air was suddenly stinking with the foulest stench of the universe. And then the tea cosy that was his mother collapsed in a lifeless, colorless, scentless pool on the slope of the meadow.

The blue stuff works in waves, sometimes close-folded and then galaxy-long. When Red came back, his father was there smiling that damned Civil War smile of his. Revenge was short. The bottle of Scotch was in his hand. It was a simple matter to smash the neck and thrust the jagged edges into his father's throat so that the blood ran red and blue and green and his father was no more. There was no grief, for in a flash of lucidity Red knew that his father, for him, had long ceased to live.

And so the pane of glass remained, whitening with time.

Portrait: Sally and the Dolphins

You could practically hear everyone suck in their breaths when Sally entered. From top to toe she was something to behold. One side of her hair—or was it a wig?—was dyed green, the other side deep purple. Neatly, her sandals matched except, of course, the colors were on opposite sides. For the party she wore an opalescent sari of her own making, put together from yards and yards of diaphanous silk material her mother had brought home from India. Around her waist, firmly keeping the folds and wraps of the sari in place, was a thick leather belt bedecked with brass eyelets and a massive brass buckle showing a cowboy riding a bucking bronco. This was an authentic buckle from the rodeo circuit, given to Sally by an admirer. Her beads were made of South Seas shells, her purse of woven grass.

Sally was also wearing a scowl, for she did not wish to appear to be pleased with her getup. As she advanced into the crowd, she acknowledged the appreciative nods and glances of her friends. Rod was the first to speak to her: "Ya got it, Sal," he said. And for the first time Sally smiled. She knew she had it.

In point of fact Sally had "had it" all the eighteen years of her life. "It," of course, was money and suburban life and good looks and private schooling and a horse and tennis lessons and a swimming pool and doting, permissive parents. On Christmas vacations she worked as a salesclerk in a local specialty shop owned by one of her father's best friends; this passed for the "real world." The money Sally earned there she hoarded, in spectacular contrast to her handling of the allowance her parents gave her.

As the party wore on, the appropriateness of the grass purse became apparent. In the corner a thin, dark lad was weeping silently and alone. No one inquired why. A thickset, redheaded chap with heavy glasses was holding forth, mostly to himself, on how old-style liberalism was passé. For emphasis his powerful arms poked great holes in the smoky air. A girl, tall, slim, and graceful as a blade of timothy, was reciting dark poetry to anyone who would listen. Her soft voice was perfect for the melancholy lines she chose: "Full many a time have I been half in love with easeful death, called him sweet names in many a mused rhyme . . ." But Sally was at the center of things. Under the influence of the sweet weed, as she called it, she was riding silver dolphins through sapphire seas. Animatedly she shared it. How slippery, she said. How dreamy. How wild. "Cowboys stay on longer" said one of the boys, evoking a gust of laughter. As it faded, the voice of the tall, slim girl came through: ". . . the foam of perilous seas in faery lands for-lorn . . ."

In the morning the sight of her green and purple wig perched atop her dresser brought a distant smile to Sally's face. The party had been all that she'd hoped—her dress more than that, despite the tear it suffered and the sarcasm of that weepy kid about wearing a belt with a sari—it made her mad how much he knew about Indian dress.

Her mother had almost gone wild when Sally returned from the party. She was up watching TV in a drowsy state, but the sight of her daughter in that "outlandish garb," as she called it, changed things in a hurry. Her hair—"those lovely blonde curls of my baby"—came in for the worst denunciation as Sally coldly declined to remove the wig, letting her mother rave on. And then came a fusillade about being "embarrassed," "chagrined," "mortified," and the "failure" she felt for having a daughter who would act like Sally. This was not the first nor would it be the last such scene. Both of them knew that.

Sally's mind drifted back to the leaping dolphins of the night before. They are the graceful ones; they are the lovely ones; they are the steeds of the mind. She remembered how in a rash moment she had tried to tell her father of them. "What dolphins?" he asked, "I don't see any." The recollection faded. And quickly, almost unaware, with her hand she drew in the air the repeated curves of dolphins leaping endlessly in the sapphire seas. They were her dolphins, her creation.

Demographics

More than any other lifestyle group, I-Am-Mes are defined by their demographics. Their four most distinctive traits are age, marital status, occupation, and background.

Dramatically the youngest group in the VALS typology, I-Am-Mes have a median age of twenty-one; 91 percent are under twenty-five, and only 2 percent are over thirty. The group is so young that only 1 percent is married—the same number as those divorced. To our surprise, none in the sample indicated they have a "living-together" arrangement.

Forty-four percent are students. This compares with 7 percent for the next highest student group, the Experientials. Obviously many I-Am-Mes have still to complete their education; large numbers have some college, but relatively few have graduated or attended graduate school.

Most I-Am-Mes were raised in comfortable if not affluent settings. There are many indicators of this. For example, 30 percent of the fathers of I-Am-Mes graduated from college or went to graduate school. This compares with 14 percent for Achievers and only 4 percent for Belongers.

The biggest surprise about I-Am-Mes is their extraordinary imbalance along sex lines. We had expected a roughly fifty-fifty male-female ratio, but our data show 64 percent male and 36 percent female, making them even more male-dominated than the Achiever group, which is 60 percent male. This ratio is all the more extraordinary in that the Experientials, most of whom were I-Am-Mes five to fifteen years ago, show a skew in the other direction: they are 55 percent female and 45 percent male. If these data are more than statistical aberrations, they seem to suggest that it is easier for men to adopt (and to admit) Inner-Direction today than it was in the 1960s and much of the 1970s. This switch removes one significant block to growth in this lifestyle.

I-Am-Mes are 91 percent Caucasian—less white than Belongers and Achievers but much more than Emulators or the two Need-Driven groups. Interestingly, I-Am-Mes contain a considerably higher fraction of Hispanics than the older Inner-Directeds, suggesting long-term trends in the composition of the inner-directed groups.

The self-assessed social class of I-Am-Mes exactly matches the sample average. This is unexpected because I-Am-Mes clearly come from favored backgrounds. The evidence is that both I-Am-Mes and Experientials tend to downplay their social standing. One speculative explanation is that these groups tend to reject affluent Achiever values through a kind of perverse downward emulation of the urban underclass.

Politically, as one would anticipate, I-Am-Mes tend to be liberal and Independents.

About 38 percent of I-Am-Mes work full time and 9 percent part-time. Occupations appear to reflect starting levels: clerical, crafts, and sales are the most common. As far as we can judge, the average annual income of I-Am-Mes is about $9,000.

The picture of I-Am-Me finances is confused for two reasons. Many I-Am-Mes have answered our survey questions in terms of their parents, not themselves. For example, although the group averages only twenty-one years of age and only 1 percent are married, 34 percent say they have children over eighteen living at home! The system error is especially evident in responses to financial questions; in the case of income, for example, 10 percent of I-Am-Mes claim levels of over $40,000 in 1979—a figure that is far from consonant with their occupational distribution and age. The other problem is that the income figures we report are for households, not individuals. Since 98 percent of I-Am-Mes are single, this fact alone would make their income estimate noncomparable with the other groups.

As one might expect of a youthful and flamboyant group, I-Am-Mes tend to live in cities and to avoid small towns and the open country. They are very unevenly distributed among the census regions, being strikingly overrepresented in the Mid-Atlantic, South Atlantic, and East North Central, strikingly underrepresented in the East South Central, West South Central, and Pacific areas.

Attitudes

The attitudes of the I-Am-Me group present rather a mixed picture. They emerge, as one would expect, as socially active. But they are curiously unsupportive of many social trends and less eager for change than one might expect.

Social activity is revealed by high ratings on such items as liking to think of oneself as a bit of a swinger and preference for going to a party rather than staying at home.

Personal ambivalence accompanying a transitional phase of life is suggested by the implied contradictions in many of their responses. For example, 99 percent think their greatest achievements are ahead, yet they tend to feel left out of things; they have the highest percentage of people who consider themselves experimental rather than conventional, yet they are highest or next highest in thinking it important to be part of a group and to have social status; they are least likely to feel the U.S. should be active in world affairs, yet 90 percent think air pollution is a major world danger; 90 percent say they get a great deal of satisfaction from friends, yet they are considerably below the average in thinking people are trustworthy and honest. A final interesting contrast: I-Am-Mes rank highest in saying they act on their hunches, yet they are below average in considering the inner self more important than power or influence.

The most significant aspect of I-Am-Me attitudes, however, is the contrast of their opinions on social issues with those of the other inner-directed groups, the Experientials and Societally Conscious. It is striking that the I-Am-Mes are more conservative than the older Inner-

Directeds, although by no means as conservative as the Outer-Directeds. As a result, they rather consistently represent a middle ground between Belongers and Achievers (prototypical Outer-Directeds) and Experientials and Societally Conscious (prototypical Inner-Directeds). The accompanying tabulation compares these groups on ten key items.

ITEM	AVERAGE POSITION OF BELONGERS/ ACHIEVERS	POSITION OF I-AM-ME	AVERAGE POSITION OF EXPERIENTIAL/ SOCIETALLY CONSCIOUS
Believe unmarried sex is wrong	51%	20%	13%
Believe woman's place is in the home	37	19	4
Agree working women can be good mothers	45	52	75
Believe marijuana should be legalized	15	47	50
Agree too much is spent protecting the environment	42	20	12
Believe industrial growth should be limited	40	53	58
Agree too much is spent on military	19	32	44
Have good deal of confidence in elected officials	36	28	23
Have good deal of confidence in company leaders	40	23	19
Have good deal of confidence in military leaders	59	50	28

We shall leave the interpretation of these findings to Part IV.

Financial Status

As explained a few paragraphs earlier, financial data for the I-Am-Me group are rendered suspect by the clear fact that many I-Am-Me respondents in our survey answered in terms of their parental families, not in terms of themselves as individuals. We therefore have restricted our presentation of I-Am-Me financial data in Table A-3 to the first ten items, which relate to financial opinions and not explicitly to financial status.

The available data show the I-Am-Me group to have several strong opinions. First, they definitely see themselves as spenders, not savers. This is accompanied by the lowest self-ranking of any group as financial experts, the conviction that it's wise to buy on time, and a relative preference for spending on tangibles (art, gold, gems) rather than on more usual investments. Generally, I-Am-Mes are dissatisfied with their current financial condition, but they take a middle stance regarding financial ambition and the importance of financial security. However, they expect to do all right: They rank second only to the Experientials in expecting to be able to maintain current standards of living over the coming five years.

Activity Patterns

In many ways this young, vigorous, inventive segment of the population displays the most distinctive activity patterns of any VALS type. In 45 of the 257 activities covered, the I-Am-Mes are twenty percentage points or more removed from the national average (corresponding, on the average, to at least 50 percent higher or lower than the norm). This is more than twice as many as for any group other than the out-of-it Survivor group, and compares with no more than two for any Outer-Directed group. When the measure of deviance is ten percentage points or more from the norm, the I-Am-Mes show a score of 101, again second only to Survivors. It is clear that what the I-Am-Mes do and don't do is related to their youthfulness; nevertheless, there is no doubt that the I-Am-Mes possess a unique, highly self-expressive lifestyle— almost surely originating in uninhibited individualism, facilitated by favored economic and social circumstances.

Areas in which the I-Am-Mes lead other VALS types by a wide margin include many of the active sports, bowling, pool/billiards, chess, backpacking, painting/drawing/sculpting, creative writing, several youth entertainments, poker, smoking of medium-tar filter cigarettes, movie attendance, and readership of specialized sports magazines. Although not so far ahead of the average, I-Am-Mes also exceed all other groups in motorboating, hunting, work on their own cars, snacking between meals, traveling abroad, reading comics, and reading general sports, human-interest, automotive, and news magazines.

If I-Am-Mes enthusiastically engage in some activities, they are almost equally decisive about shunning others. Thus they are dramatically low participants in gardening and baking, needlework, health-related food concerns, use of trading stamps and coupons, use of credit cards, life and health insurance, TV watching (especially during prime evening time), newspaper reading, and home ownership (although they score high in adding rooms and remodeling).

Listed in Table 13 are the 101 activities in which the I-Am-Mes differ from the average pattern by ten percentage points or more.

Consumption Patterns

The I-Am-Mes show some unique consumption patterns, even differing substantially from those of the other Inner-Directed types.

More I-Am-Me households than average own small specialty and subcompact cars, but fewer than average buy their cars new. I-Am-Mes rank exterior styling and power and pickup as important features in their current car-purchase decisions.

The I-Am-Mes are very much involved with recreational activities, and I-Am-Me households are among the highest in ownership of recreational gear, particularly camping/backpacking equipment, exercise equipment, motorcycles, and racing bicycles. In home electronic products they reveal the highest incidence of ownership of black-and-white television sets; they are also substantially above average in ownership of hi-fi stereo equipment (including prerecorded and blank recording tapes).

I-Am-Me women and men dress more informally than other VALS types and are disproportionately high wearers of jeans.

Their drinking and eating patterns are also distinct. They are among the highest in frequent consumption of alcoholic beverages. They prefer domestic and imported beer and tequila and rum drinks. They also are among the highest in frequent consumption of high-sugar, high-carbohydrate, high-calorie foods such as regular carbonated soft drinks, snack foods (particularly potato/corn chips, pretzels, and nuts), gum, and butter. Frequently on the run, they appear to favor convenience foods such as instant soups, prepared ethnic foods, instant coffee, and frozen TV dinners.

I-Am-Me consumption patterns are distinctly aberrant, differing from the national norm by ten percentage points or more in 51 of the 170 areas studied. Only Survivors at 100 and Sustainers at 59 are more aberrant. The areas in which I-Am-Mes differ most from the average are listed in Table 14.

TABLE 13
Activities of I-Am-Mes

Active sports		Eat at fast-food restaurant	+
Baseball/basketball/football/softball	+	Drink cocktail before dinner at	
Bicycling	+	restaurant	−
Jogging	+	Health-related food concerns	
Squash/handball/raquetball	+	Collect recipes	−
Swimming	+	A lot of concern with amount of salt	
Tennis	+	in foods	−
Exercise in gym	+	Cigarette smoking	
Sailing	+	Have smoked for over 10 years	−
Snow skiing	+	Stopped smoking over 10 years ago	−
Water skiing	+	Smoke filter, high-tar and -nicotine	+
Spectator sports		Smoke filter, low-tar and -nicotine	−
Professional sports events	+	Off-hours work	
College/high school sports events	+	Work at second job/free-lance	+
X-rated movies	+	Library users	
Bowling	+	Use audiovisual materials	+
Pool/billiards	+	Learning	
Chess	+	Have spent over $50 for self-	
Backgammon	+	instruction	−
Outdoor life		Have enrolled in correspondence	
Motorboating	+	course	−
Hunting	+	Pleasure travel	
Camping overnight	+	Travel abroad	+
Backpacking	+	Shopping in stores	
The arts		Large discount stores	−
Paint/draw/sculpt	+	Use trading stamps	−
Write poetry/fiction/nonfiction	+	Use coupons	−
Youth entertainment		Credit cards owned	
Pop/rock concerts	+	Visa/Bankamericard	−
Night clubs/discos	+	Department/specialty store card	−
Theme/amusement parks	+	Purchases with credit cards	
Arcades/video games	+	Mail order/phone purchases	−
Listen to records/tapes	+	Department/specialty stores	−
Cards		Business travel	−
Poker	+	Pleasure travel	−
Gardening and baking		Don't use credit cards for purchases	+
Flower gardening	−	Household credit card balance	
Vegetable gardening	−	over $500	−
Bake bread	−	Life and health insurance	
Bake pastries	−	Have individual life insurance	−
Preserve food at home	−	Have permanent/whole life/cash	
Needlework (women only)		value insurance	−
Sew to make something	−	Have term insurance	−
Sew to repair/mend something	−	Don't know	+
Do-it-yourself (men only)		Purchased insurance from agent for	
Work on own car or other vehicle	+	one company	−
Eating habits		Extremely interested in life	
Eat dinner while watching TV	+	insurance with varying	
Eat between-meal snacks	+	coverage	+
Eating out		Attended movie theatre	+
Eat lunch out	+		

Table 13: Activities of I-Am-Mes (continued)

Commercial or educational TV watching*		Read feature writers' columns	–
Watch 7-10 A.M. weekdays	–	Read food/cooking section	–
Watch 8-11 P.M. weekdays	–	Read main news section	–
Watch 8-11 P.M. weekends	–	Read sports section	+
Watch 11 P.M.-2 A.M. weekends	+	Read travel section	–
Type of TV program watched		Magazine reading	
Comedies	+	Read general sports magazines	+
Movies	+	Read specialized sports magazines	+
Morning news	–	Read human interest magazines	+
Early evening news	–	Read automotive magazines	+
Late evening news	–	Read men's magazines	+
Radio listening		Book reading	
Listen 5-8 P.M.	+	Read condensed versions	–
Listen 8-11 P.M.	+	Housing	
Listen after 11 P.M.	+	Live in detached, single-family	
Newspaper reading		dwelling	–
Read daily newspaper	–	Own home	–
Read Sunday newspaper	–	Have added room or remodeled in	
Read business/finance section	–	past year	+
Read comics	+		

*Hours shown are for Eastern and Pacific time. Times are an hour earlier for Central and Mountain time.

EXPERIENTIALS

Portrait: The Road to Forever: Mary

Mary is tall, lean, and dark, with wild gray eyes that somehow give the impression of a bird about to take wing.

Mary is only twenty-nine but already has put a lot of living behind her. Her upbringing was unspectacular. She was raised in the southern part of California, had the usual pains and misfortunes in public schools, went to the university, where she majored in physics and, in fact, took an M.S. in mathematics—something that seems astonishing now. She was the only girl, and the youngest child, in a middle-class family. Her mother was a housewife, her father a minor executive in a department store. She married right after college, but the marriage lasted only three years and produced no children. The main thing Mary got out of her marriage was the realization that one could be loved for oneself—a cornerstone of what was to come.

At no time did Mary participate extensively in campus politics, the Vietnam rebellion, or demonstration for other causes. During those years she lived a routine life, doing the things expected of her, and doing them well.

TABLE 14
Consumption Patterns of I-Am-Mes

Motor vehicles		**Personal-care products**	
Types of cars purchased*		Women's products (use)	
Small specialty	+	Cologne/perfume	+
Importance of selected features in		Eye makeup	+
purchase consideration†		Shampoo	+
Exterior/interior styling	+	Facial moisturizer	−
Power and pickup	+	Men's products (use)	
Purchased last car used	+	After-shave lotion	−
Durables		Cologne/perfume	+
Appliances (ownership)		Shampoo	+
Clothes washer (separate from		Aerosol underarm deodorant	+
dryer)	−	Other personal-care products (use)	
Clothes dryer (separate from		Pain relievers/headache remedies	−
washer)	−	**Beverages and foods**	
Dishwasher	−	Alcoholic beverages (use)	
Garbage disposal	−	Any alcohol	+
Refrigerator/freezer combination	+	Beer	
Recreational equipment (ownership)		Any beer	+
Camping/backpacking	+	Domestic beer	+
Exercise (at home)	+	Carbonated beverages (use)	
Swimming pool‡	+	Regular soft drinks	+
Motorcycle	+	Other beverages (use)	
Racing bicycle	+	Fruit juices	−
Home electronic products		Regular coffee	−
(ownership)		Decaffeinated coffee	−
Black-and-white TV	+	Foods (use)	
Color TV	−	Snack foods	
Hi-fi stereo components	+	Potato/corn chips	+
Blank recording tapes/cassettes	+	Pretzels	+
Prerecorded tapes/cassettes	+	Cashews	+
Miscellaneous products (ownership)		Confections	
Chain saw**	+	Regular gum	+
Clothing		Prepared ethnic foods	
Women's clothing (use)		Prepared, canned or frozen	
Slacks	−	Italian	+
Jeans	+	Reasons for buying margarine††	
Men's clothing (use)		Health	−
Suits	−	Miscellaneous foods††	
Sport coats	−	Frozen vegetables	−
Dress shirts	−	Gelatin desserts	−
Slacks	−		
Jeans	+		

*Data are for last car purchased 1975-1980.
†If respondents were to purchase a motor vehicle in 1980.
‡Homeowners only.
**Homeowners only.
††For women only.

With the dissolution of her marriage when Mary was twenty-four, she changed. The first thing she did was to retake her maiden name. For the first time in her life she felt—and was—free. She took a four-month motorcycle trip with a male friend down through Mexico and Central America. This was her way of declaring her independence. It was an act that shocked her parents and friends, as she very well knew it would, and left them asking: "What in the world has happened to our Mary?" What had happened was that Mary had very suddenly discovered the excitement of living vividly, independently, and with abandon. The burst of the moment became more important than the life-long plan. For the first time Mary was living a life of inner discovery.

As a result, long-suppressed memories began to echo through Mary's consciousness. She remembered a strange incident during her marriage. In a depressed period she got a call from an old friend she had known and dated in college. He told her he sensed from afar she was depressed (how did he know?) and things would get better. They did. She recalled how one of her colleagues in the library where she worked then gave her a book on the Sufis. She read it with a mixture of puzzlement and awe. Now, suddenly, it all made sense.

With such memories surging within her, Mary started doing things and reading things she never would have earlier. She moved away from her home area to northern California. She took a job with a high-technology company, where her training in physics and mathematics—although no longer of real intellectual interest to her—enabled her to make excellent money. She was successful, for Mary understood people well and was easily able to capitalize on her knowledge.

She bought a house of her own with a huge live oak in the back yard. Later she was to find that a tree was one of her most potent symbols. She became a gourmet cook, often using only vegetables she grew in her garden. She learned about nutrition and stopped eating certain processed foods. She went on special diets to combat negative inner feelings. She had a series of living partners, each different, each fun, each transitory. And once she fell deeply in love with an intense, demanding man who offered her only sex and an opportunity to be totally absorbed in him. The breakup of that relationship brought Mary her deepest depression in years and taught her something of the costs of freedom.

But the big events of Mary's life lay not in external matters but in her gathering sense of being part of a larger scheme of things. She read—absorbed may be a better word—*A Course in Miracles* and found in this holistic philosophy so strangely dictated to its author by an unbidden voice a kind of perfection and wisdom she had never encountered before. Research on ESP and the hemispheres of the brain engaged her deepest interest. She learned how to consult the *I-Ching* and soon would take no major step without checking its wisdom through those coins. Astrology suddenly took on new meaning, and Mary, who is a Gemini, became an expert in reading the astrological signs. She learned Rolfing. She made a point of meeting psychics and talked endlessly with them about the nature of things. Like the Eskimo sculptor who listens to the hunk of soapstone to hear what shape it wants to be, Mary was finding dozens of new ways to learn about herself.

And all of these she shared. And thus new, deeper friendships were formed. She left her high-tech job to work—at less than half her former salary—as a roving promotion expert for a group of small communally run business co-ops. She sold her home with the big tree and with several others bought a large old home, where they all live.

Today Mary feels that her world has finally taken a shape of its own, formed partly by her and partly by the mysterious force whose ebbs and flows shape all there is. She is, she believes, walking the road to forever.

Portrait: Michael the Poet

Michael is a poet. His writing is somber, subtle, complex, and (to many) obscure. He has not had much luck in publishing. A few of the small magazines have accepted some of his work. An uncle paid for the private printing of a slender volume of his poems, a volume Michael called *Mounds of Tears* after an American Indian description of a grave. But mostly he and friends used to read their stuff aloud at small literary wine parties, which sometimes turned into orgies. Today Michael's life—at age twenty-six—is more isolated and lonely, and his poetry is even more a cry in his inner stillness.

Michael was born in the heart of Buffalo County, South Dakota. His father was postmaster in the town where Michael grew up; his mother, a wispy, colorless, rigid woman, was a devoted wife and mother—she could have been the model for Grant Wood's painting, *American Gothic*. Michael enjoyed his small-town upbringing. He played football well enough to get a mention in his senior year for All-State end. He led an active, proper social life.

Things began to change when Michael went away to college at State. He was lucky enough to encounter two professors who sparked his interest. One was an aging, disappointed scholar of eighteenth-century literature—a man who declared himself a "humanist." Despite the forty years between them, Michael and this man struck up a real friendship. Years later what Michael remembered best about college were his visits to the professor's home with its lovely, mellow, book-lined living room. The old humanist died when Michael was in graduate school. One of the first poems that Michael wrote tried to express the ineffable sense of loss he felt when he got the news. Michael wanted further to repay his debt by dedicating a book to this man. Countless times he wrote and rewrote the dedication in his mind.

The other professor who influenced Michael was very different. He was a youthful, ambitious, brilliant teacher of economics. In Michael he saw a younger version of himself and, unbidden, he undertook the task of being Michael's mentor. So it was that Michael, responding both to praise and to prods, majored in economics, won a prestigious fellowship, and went to graduate school in the East to continue his studies in economics.

It was in graduate school that Michael met and fell in love with Jane, a gentle, loving Southern girl whose passion in life was classical music. They were married in the university chapel. For two years, before their first child came, they lived an idyllic, simple life together. Their home was full of music and flowers that Jane grew in the summer on a little plot of land a neighbor let them use.

Michael's inner metamorphosis began during this halcyon period. The study of economics increasingly became a burden and a bore. More important was the time spent with his wife and, later, with their first-born. He began to write poetry and short stories, hesitantly at first, then more boldly after his old friend the humanist died. Michael began to attend courses in poetry, go to literary lectures, seek out writers on campus, neglecting his studies in economics. One evening one of a small group they had to their home remarked to Michael: "Well, if you're going to be a poet you got to live it, not just talk it. You've got to give it a one-hundred-percent shot."

The comment struck Michael like a thunderbolt. It changed his life radically. He and Jane and their two children (one just born) moved to Vermont, talked his uncle into buying them a ramshackle farm, and now are trying to live off the land. Michael attended Zen centers where for weeks no words were allowed. His poems became more somber and obscure, but far more meaningful to him. Michael always had an affinity for paradox, and now his studies in Eastern religions deepened his sense of the continuities in his life. He wrote in his poetry how each person should contribute to "the lamilar flow of the universe" and of how insensitivity to the naturalness of things produces turbulences in the universal flow. He wrote of his "entry point" in South Dakota and of how he surely would return there in the fullness of time for his "exit."

Michael's world, it is clear, is now altogether removed from that of his childhood or of his university years. It is a world inside him—a world of giant, mysterious flows and heaving currents, of intricate passages and stygian caves, of sinuous rivers and deserts of many hues. It is a world that taxes his powers of expression to convey to others; thus far at least, Michael has been able to explain this world to very few others.

Luckily for him, Michael's marriage has remained firm and full of love. The reason, mostly, is Jane's capacity for change and growth— that and the gentleness of her Southern heritage, which enables her, for now at least, to subjugate much of herself to her husband. But the winters of Vermont are bitter and the snow is deep, and it remains to be seen how things will go for them.

Demographics

The Experientials are a relatively prosperous postwar group (median age twenty-seven) of excellent education, liberal tendencies, and a pronounced preference for living in the West. Their demographics show few extremes, but those that do occur are revealing.

Nine percent of Experientials have "living-together" arrangements, the highest fraction of any lifestyle group. An exceptional number of "other" minorities—probably mostly Orientals—are Experiential, but relatively few blacks or Hispanics are. Thirty-eight percent are college graduates, second only to 58 percent for the Societally Conscious. The fewest of any group regard themselves as conservative. Thirteen percent work parttime vs. a sample average of 8 percent; there is a lot of evidence that Experientials prefer parttime work, presumably to be free to pursue activities that bring them pleasure. Although many earn $25,000–30,000 a year, almost 30 percent earn less than $15,000, so that the average household income among Experientials in 1979 was $23,800. Finally, Experientials are dramatically overrepresented in the Pacific states: almost a fourth of them live there, in contrast to 14 percent of the adult population as a whole.

Areas in which Experientials are unusual but not unique include their high percentage of singles (28 percent), the fact that over half regard themselves as Independents in politics, the unusually high fraction (27 percent) who hold professional or technical jobs, and their preference for city living over small towns or the country.

Attitudes

Attitudes reveal a good deal more about the Experiential lifestyle than do demographics. These are powerfully inner-directed people—happy, permissive in personal living, but full of doubts about the way the system works. Ninety-six percent rate themselves as very happy, a score that ties them with Belongers as the happiest of the lifestyle groups. The Experientials feel very much involved with what's going on, and they expect the future will bring them success and accomplishment. Again, 96 percent believe the inner self is more important than outward signs. Hence, unlike the less confident I-Am-Mes, the Experientials don't rely much on being part of a group, nor is social status of prime importance. Belief in the value of the inner self undoubtedly reinforces their conviction that marijuana should be legalized (61 percent so believe vs. 28 percent for the sample average) and their approval of sexual relations between unmarried people (only 10 percent think it wrong). This permissiveness dovetails further with the Experientials' overwhelming support of women participating in world affairs, whether or not they have small children. It also is not surprising to find that their confidence in organizational leaders is consistently less than the sample average. In view of these sentiments it is little wonder that Experientials are prone to act on their hunches, see themselves as experimental, get a great deal of satisfaction from nonwork activities, and place little reliance on TV for entertainment.

In the domain of social trends the liberalism of the Experiential group emerges clearly. Among the lifestyle groups they are high or the highest in agreement with the following statements:

○ Industrial growth should be limited.

○ Air pollution is a major worldwide danger.

○ Not enough is spent on protecting the environment.

○ Too much is spent on military armaments.

○ The energy crisis is real, not imaginary.

On consumer issues the Experientials take a middle position. They are less likely than most to feel the consumer movement has resulted in increased prices.

Financial Status

People living experientially are not centrally concerned with money. Yet money, most people admit, is a wonderfully useful lubricant between inner and outer worlds, and even those not driven by it pay it due respect. So it is with the Experientials. About half of those in the group agree strongly that financial security is important and that they want to get ahead financially. These people are optimistic, even though they tend to be spenders rather than savers. More than most they are satisfied with their present finances. Although less than a fourth regard themselves as financial experts, over half expect to be able to maintain current standards of living in the years ahead. They seem not to have any particularly aberrant financial habits—they come out about average on such matters as the desirability of being in debt, buying on time, or investing in tangibles.

Because the Experientials are a well-educated group and relatively prosperous despite being predominantly in their twenties, it is not surprising to find that they are vigorous participants in financial markets. Eighty-three percent have credit cards, and balances are exceptionally high—18 percent exceed $1,500, for example. Ninety-one percent have checking accounts, 90 percent savings accounts, 29 percent have stocks and bonds, 23 percent invest in real estate, and 17 percent have money in mutual or money market funds. Relative to other lifestyle groups, the Experientials are particularly involved in real estate investment, where over 40 percent of those active would clear better than $50,000 were they to dispose of holdings.

A few Experientials appear to be dabblers in stocks and bonds. Only 11 percent have stockbrokers (compared with 25 percent for Achievers), and only 6 percent own stocks and bonds valued at over $10,000. Yet 3 percent appear to have annual transactions through their brokers of over $10,000—and half of these of over $50,000. It seems reasonable to assume that the latter include the 6 percent of Experientials with household assets of over half a million dollars—no doubt the result of inheritances in many cases. The dabbler phenomenon in investments is often associated with young, bright people engaged in professional or technical work, which 27 percent of the Experientials are.

Homeownership among Experientials is low—53 percent vs. a national average around 73 percent—no doubt reflecting the large singles component in the group. Almost all homeowners hold mortgages. Estimates of money left from the hypothetical sale of the home are between $10,000 and $50,000 for 54 percent and over $50,000 for 28 percent. These figures are almost exactly on the sample average.

The debt pattern of Experientials is in keeping with young people in the process of establishing themselves. Relatively few are free from debt, but only 12 percent have debts of over $50,000. The debt pattern and the assets pattern, discussed below, suggest there is a small group of Experientials of very substantial means.

Estimates of the total value of all assets run from 6 percent for over $500,000, to 24 percent for $50,000 to $100,000, to 26 percent for under $10,000; 1 percent place assets at over $1 million. Compared with sample averages, more Experientials appear at the extremes: under $10,000 and over $500,000.

Activity Patterns

This group is in many ways a more mature, less extreme version of the I-Am-Mes. Although more Experientials work, have families, and have less free time, they retain many of their earlier patterns while developing new ones. As a result, where I-Am-Mes score very high in an activity, Experientials also tend to score high but not as high. The same is true for areas of low participation. This characteristic is useful to marketers trying to project future trends.

But the diminution effect is by no means universal. Although the greater maturity of the Experientials seems to mean that they slowly abandon some of their more youthful pursuits, it also means that they take up other activities probably deemed unsuitable (or out of financial reach) in earlier years. For example, Experientials see fewer college and high school sports than I-Am-Mes but just as many professional sports events. They see fewer X-rated movies; bowl less; play less pool/billiards, chess, and backgammon; and do less motorboating and backpacking. Although they paint/draw/sculpt less, they engage more in crafts and play musical instruments more. In the do-it-yourself area Experientials do more home-repair work than I-Am-Mes, but less tinkering with cars. This pattern of extensive involvement continues strongly in health-related food concerns, self-learning, business travel, and most financial activities. It would appear from these shifts that the Experientials are the most involved of any VALS group with pure inner-directedness; they are the most active in meditative and spiritual pursuits, and their concern with cultural and educational activities seems to be on the increase. They seem to have moved in these directions while simultaneously tempering their involvement with more physical activities. At the same time they are more engaged with the practical world of work than they were in their I-Am-Me years, and this is reflected in many financial and work-related activities.

TABLE 15
Activities of Experientials

Active sports	
Baseball/basketball/football/softball	+
Bicycling	+
Jogging	+
Squash/handball/racquetball	+
Swimming	+
Tennis	+
Exercise in gym	+
Sailing	+
Snow skiing	+
Water skiing	+
Spectator sports	
Professional sports events	+
Bowling	+
Pool/billiards	+
Chess	+
Backgammon	+
Outdoor life	
Camping overnight	+
Backpacking	+
The arts	
Write poetry/fiction/nonfiction	+
Attendance at cultural events	
Theatre	+
Opera/ballet/dance	+
Art galleries/museums	+
Youth entertainment	
Pop/rock concerts	+
Night clubs/discos	+
Theme/amusement parks	+
Arcades/video games	+
Listen to records/tapes	+
Inner Life	
Yoga or meditation at home	+
Cards	
Poker	+
Needlework (women only)	
Knit/crochet/needlework	−
Sew to repair/mend something	+
Do-it-yourself (men only)	
Repair/fix-up projects at home	−
Eating habits	
Eat dinner while watching TV	+
Health-related food concerns	
National brands considered of highest quality	−
No difference in quality of brands	+
A lot of concern with amount of sugar in foods	+
A lot of concern with possible effects of additives	+
A lot of concern with nutritional quality of food	+
Cigarette smoking	
Have smoked for over 10 yrs	−
Stopped smoking over 10 yrs ago	−
Off-hours work	
Work at second job/free-lance	+
Personal communications	
Phone friends/relatives long distance	+
Library users	
Use audiovisual materials	+
Learning	
Have spent over $50 for self-instruction	+
Have attended night school	+
Pleasure travel	
Travel by air	+
Business travel	
Stay at hotels/motels	+
Shopping in stores	
Secondhand stores	+
Specialty stores	+
Health and life insurance	
Very interested in insurance that varies with lifestyle	+
Use trading stamps	−
Purchases with credit cards	
Personal entertainment	+
Know and understand term "holistic health"	+
Attended movie theatre	+
Commercial or educational TV watching*	
Watch 8-11 P.M. weekdays	−
Watch 8-11 P.M. weekends	−
Types of TV program watched	
Afternoon news	−
Early evening news	−
Think commercial TV is:	
Unimaginative	+
Newspaper reading	
Read entertainment section	+
Book reading	
Heavy readers	+
Read condensed versions	−
Housing	
Lived in current residence over 10 years	−
Lived in detached, single-family dwelling	−
Own home	−

*Hours shown are for Eastern and Pacific time. Times are an hour earlier for Central and Mountain time.

Areas in which the Experientials are notably active include swimming, racquet sports, and snow skiing. They engage more in yoga and home meditation than any other group and are distinctly concerned with the health aspects of food. They are more likely than any other group to work at a second job or to free-lance.

The Experientials remain highly social. Many of their sports activities are in this direction; they attend a lot of movies (and watch little TV), read entertainment sections in newspapers, use credit cards especially for personal entertainment, fly a good deal on pleasure trips, and—more than any other VALS type—tend to telephone friends and relatives long distance. Their deep self-confidence seems to us to show up in their somewhat curious shopping habits: they lead or are among the highest in using secondhand stores *and* specialty shops; further, along with the Societally Conscious, they are particularly likely to return unsatisfactory products.

Experientials deviate from national activity norms by ten percentage points or more in 64 of the 257 areas studied. The areas in which the Experientials differ most from norms are listed in Table 15.

Consumption Patterns

Key characteristics of the Experientials—such as the search for direct and pleasurable experiences, their try-anything-once attitude, preference for process over product, and active outdoor orientation—are evidenced in their pattern of product ownership and use.

Experiential households have among the highest incidence of ownership of compact, subcompact, and small specialty cars, but like the I-Am-Mes, fewer of them purchase their vehicles new. They are highest in ownership of, and preference for, foreign cars, and they show the highest ownership of European cars of any VALS type.

Ownership of dishwashers and garbage disposals is among the highest in the typology. Ownership of recreational equipment is also high—Experiential households are substantially above average in owning camping/backpacking equipment and racing bicycles. In home electronic products higher-than-average ownership levels prevail for video games and prerecorded and blank recording tapes.

Experiential women show an interesting pattern in their clothing preferences. Disproportionately more wear jeans, skirts, and dresses. They wear bras less frequently than any of the other VALS types, perhaps reflecting their "free spirits." Experiential men are among the most frequent wearers of jeans and sport and casual shirts, but they also wear suits more often than average. The patterns for Experiential men and women suggest a preference for more informal attire tempered by a certain conformity to the demands of the world.

Wines, including champagnes, and domestic and imported beers are the favored alcoholic beverages. Overall, the consumption of liquor by Experientials is about average, except for tequila, for which they are tied with Emulators for the highest usage.

Their above-average consumption of sugar-free soft drinks, sparkling mineral water, and sugarless gum, and lower-than-average use of coffee, candy, margarine, and butter probably reveal dietary and health concerns. Their experiential nature appears in their above-average use of prepared ethnic foods, such as Mexican or Chinese frozen entrees.

Compared with national "deviation consumption patterns" the Experientials are on the high side. There are 47 areas out of 170 in which their usage is ten percentage points higher or lower than the norm—a figure far below the Survivors' 100 but considerably higher than 20 for Belongers and 28 or 29 for Emulators, Achievers, and the Societally Conscious. Areas where Experiential consumption is ten percentage points above or below national average are listed in Table 16.

SOCIETALLY CONSCIOUS

Portrait: The Sisters

They were born in the twenties in the comfortable old home on the corner lot in a town on Long Island. In the thirties they came and went daily from house to school while their father commuted to the big city, returning quietly to the house, almost unobserved. As a family they listened to Lowell Thomas, took summer vacations, climbed the big beech on the side lot, and heard as if from far away that terrible things were happening in the world. In the forties they went away to colleges of their choice—fine New England schools—returning during holidays and beginning to wonder what to do with their lives.

Jennifer, the eldest, had a complex, intellectual turn of mind, a gift for the written word, and a surprising interest in science. Her mother was always puzzled that her daughter had chosen to major in chemistry. Margaret, two years younger, inclined more to the arts and people. She was the one who struck up acquaintances with strangers and the one people asked after first. One would not say that either was exactly pretty, but their directness and honesty made them attractive.

The war touched the family little. Their father, whose business was in

TABLE 16
Consumption Patterns of Experientials

Motor vehicles		Men's products (use)	
Types of cars purchased*		After-shave lotion	−
Compact	+	Shampoo	+
Large	−	Aerosol underarm deodorant	−
Purchased foreign-made cars	+	Stick underarm deodorant	+
Durables		Pet foods and services	
Appliances (ownership)		Dog food (purchase)	
Clothes dryer (separate from		Canned	−
washer)	+	Use of veterinarians	+
Dishwasher	+	Selected specialized cleaning products‡	
Garbage disposal	+	Air freshener	−
Refrigerator/freezer combination	+	Beverages and foods	
Freezer (separate from		Alcoholic beverages (use)	
refrigerator)	−	Any alcohol	+
Recreational equipment (ownership)		Wine	
Camping/backpacking	+	Any wine	+
Motorcycle	+	California wine	+
Racing bicycle	+	Any champagne	+
Home electronic products (ownership)		Domestic champagne	+
Video games†	+	Beer	
Hi-fi stereo components	+	Any beer	+
Prerecorded tapes/cassettes	+	Domestic beer	+
Photographic equipment (ownership)		Imported beer	+
35-mm camera	+	Other beverages (use)	
Clothing		Regular coffee	−
Women's clothing (use)		Decaffeinated coffee	−
Skirts	+	Foods (use)	
Slacks	−	Snack foods	
Jeans	+	Nut brands purchased	
Bras	−	Planters	−
Men's clothing (use)		Switch brands	+
Sport/casual shirts	+	Confections	
Jeans	+	Sugarless gum	+
Personal-care products		Margarine and butter‡	
Women's products (use)		Reasons for buying margarine	
Eye makeup	+	Health	−
Shampoo	+	Miscellaneous	
Aerosol underarm deodorant	−	Gelatin desserts	−
Feminine hygiene spray	−		

*Data are for last car purchased 1975–1980.
†TV owners only.
‡For women only.

meat brokerage, had things easier than before. There were no brothers to go off to war, no real boyfriends they worried about; the little privations of gasoline rationing, occasional food shortages, and the like they could easily handle. Most difficult was the cigarette shortage.

What you could get, even from the New Jersey underground sources their father seemed to know about, hardly passed for a decent smoke.

It was after the war that the first break came in the family living pattern. Jennifer moved to an apartment in New York. She had landed a job as writer for a chemical trade magazine—a high-powered job where she was the only woman and in competition with men who had ten and twenty years of experience. But Jennifer cared. She put in long hours. She did her homework. And she did well. It was not the way of the publisher to use kind words. Lack of criticism was his sign of praise. And the city life was exciting and invigorating.

Margaret moved differently. She became executive secretary to a man powerful in the entertainment world. Every workday she would catch the 7:43, change at Jamaica, and be at her desk on time. Every evening—almost—she caught the 5:31, changed at Jamaica, and was at home, usually with a sheaf of papers, in plenty of time for the seven-o'clock news and dinner with her parents.

For almost fifteen years this was the pattern. Then two things happened that made a difference. First, their father died, swiftly and unexpectedly, of heart failure. Although he had moved through life almost noiselessly, his death resounded in the family. The worst were the voids that loomed when family routines were upset by his absence. Their mother was never again quite the same. But he had provided well; the house was free and clear, and through the years he'd invested so that now his wife and his daughters could, with care, get along.

Second, the town—the lovely treed and sidewalked town made for strolling and summer chatting and neighborhood teas, the town of the sisters' secret passageways and tiny escapades—began to change in composition. At first it was slow. Only "the best" blacks bought in. But momentum gathered, and it became clear that the tide was rushing to engulf the comfortable old home on the corner lot.

The sisters and their mother worried. They worried about property values. They worried what friends would say. They worried about the tidiness of the town. And more than anything they worried about safety, especially because their mother was left alone day after day when the sisters were at work in New York.

One evening Margaret was mugged as she walked home from the train station. Knocked down, her nose smashed by an iron pipe, her purse stolen, beads ripped from her neck, she lay on the sidewalk still clutching her sheaf of papers from the office.

The event triggered major changes in the lives of the sisters. It wasn't long before Margaret quit her job in New York to stay home to help protect their mother, who no longer was well. And Jennifer began to feel ill at ease with her high-pressure, intense work in technical journalism. To a degree she felt it was a disadvantage being a woman in a man's work world, but more than anything she came to feel it was work attuned to industry, not people. The final straw came when their mother died. The shock and sadness was great. There is no preparing for such things.

As a result of her mother's death, Jennifer, as Margaret had before her, almost wholly changed her way of life. She left her job in Manhattan's towers, gave up her apartment in town to move back home, and set about preparing for a new career as a physical therapist in a local hospital. The assignment was to help mostly older people work out the kinks in their muscles and bones. It took strong hands and a strong back, but it was rewarding for the gratitude it evoked and the obvious relief it produced. This was a job as different from high-pressure journalism as one could imagine, and it suited the new Jennifer perfectly.

The sisters talked and talked about selling the old home and moving to a town they fancied would be safer, for now it was Margaret who stayed home all day alone. She dared not work and leave their house empty, for the word would soon be out. Even so, the copper downspouts were ripped from the house one day. Instead, Margaret became a community leader, at first along with several of her white friends, and then, when they moved away, with her new black friends.

She organized district cleanup committees that undertook to prune the overgrown trees and bushes along the streets. They constructed areas for garbage pickup and helped organize weekend teenage groups to sweep up the litter. The town would do none of these things. Margaret tried to convince the city councilmen that the drug pushers should be rounded up and jailed, daily if need be. Everyone knew who they were. They lounged in the city park along the main street, indolently playing pickup basketball while they waited for the young dudes to drop by to do business. Margaret's efforts got nods of approval but no action.

Her neighbors—and, indeed, most of the town—recognized Margaret as concerned, able, and well-intentioned. Many respected her. But the tidal force of social change was stronger than anything she or Jennifer could stem.

Today the sisters are an island. Yet daily Jennifer goes to her job in the hospital. She is the group head now, concerned with what to do when her staff leaves to go to richer, better-equipped hospitals in white neighborhoods. Daily Margaret still goes her rounds, smiling even when a kid makes his getaway across the back of their lot and the police come to ask questions. They are living there right now in the comfortable old home on the corner lot. It seems a world removed from the protected years of their childhood and even farther from their years in the midst of high-powered business in New York. But the sisters persevere, doing what is to them right, happy in their own way, unheroic, and, finally, unafraid.

Portrait: Mort[1]

Across the gray waters came the disembodied voice. Mort cut the motor and listened. It came again. "Two whales at three o'clock." Its source was a tiny figure speaking through a bullhorn atop the seacliff on South Wolf Island, Canada, just north of the Bay of Fundy. Mort reversed his little outboard and put seaward into the long slants of the late-afternoon sun. Soon one of the three people in the boat stood up. "There they are," she called, pointing to starboard. Again Mort cut the motor, and the little boat coasted onward toward the whales.

They lay low in the water, their black forms immobile, occasionally expelling air and water through their blowholes with a whooshing sound. Over the side of the boat went the hydrophone, the tape recorder turned on. Still and movie cameras started working, while two of the researchers in the boat described their observations to the third, who wrote them in a notebook. "There's something wrong," said Mort. "They're too close to shore and too lethargic. Maybe they're sick." But there was nothing wrong. The whales had been sleeping until disturbed by the boat. Then they wheeled downward and disappeared.

The two were northern right whales, third largest of the whale species and considered the most endangered of the whales. Because they are slow-swimming, easy to kill, and float when dead, they have become known as the "right" whale for hunting.

That evening and during the winter months Mort and his colleagues would check the day's data for anything unusual and especially for correlations with vocalizations. Right whales do not sing in the melodious fashion of the humpback. Low-frequency calls are employed in deep-water, long-distance communication, and high frequencies are used for nearby communication. The low frequencies sound like a wolf snarling in a tunnel; the high frequencies are emitted as a warbling note, rising in pitch.

Mort feels that an understanding of right whale vocalizations may help in finding ways to protect them. For the same reason he and his team are exploring more dramatic whale habits such as lob-tailing, in which a whale strikes the water's surface with its giant tail flukes; breaching, in which whales leap from the water to land with a great splash; and spy-hopping, in which whales lift their heads high above the water and seem to peer around. Modes of diving and mating and giving birth are also of interest.

It is a specialized, technical, rigorous, and even dangerous life that Mort lives. This is as he wants it. Long years of academic training as a marine biologist and fieldwork in the Aleutians and off the coast of Patagonia lie behind him. Politics was never his interest, but even so, mostly to please his friends, he has joined in marches to Washington and found himself thrilled to be part of so massive a throng. He has also demonstrated on behalf of wilderness areas, antinuclearism, world forests, and protection of migratory bird flyways.

So Mort is half intellectual, half man of action. When, as a young Ph.D., he had his choice of teaching in a midwestern university or directing a research study of the lives of the northern right whale, he had no trouble making up his mind. There was good and useful work to be done. The teaching could wait, and it would be the better for his time on the gray waters of the Bay of Fundy.

Demographics

Demographic hallmarks of the Societally Conscious include:

- Excellent education: Fifty-eight percent have graduated from college or attended graduate school (sample average: 21 percent). Only 15 percent have not gone beyond high school (sample average: 52 percent).

- Liberal politics: Fifty-seven percent declared themselves Independents (sample: 35 percent) and 53 percent liberals (sample: 23 percent).

- Intellectual jobs: Fifty-nine percent are employed in professional or technical occupations (sample: 18 percent).

- Affluence: Half had household incomes of over $25,000 in 1979 (sample: 36 percent), and their average income was $27,200 (sample: $18,000).

- Census regions: Almost a third of the group lives in New England or the Pacific states (sample: 21 percent). They shun the South (23 percent vs. 32 percent for sample).

The group is the most equally balanced between the sexes of any in the typology. They have an exceptionally large number of children living at home with them, as would be expected of a group with a median age of thirty-nine. Seventy percent are married, 8 percent are single, and 16 percent are divorced or separated. This last figure is second highest among the VALS groups (second to Emulators at 20 percent) and suggests a certain stress and tension to the Societally Conscious lifestyle. It is interesting, too, that 7 percent of the group is black, compared with 2 percent for the Experientials and Achievers and 3 percent for I-Am-Mes and Belongers. In view of their evident prosperity and occupational prestige it is to be expected that only 9 percent of the group characterize themselves as lower-class and 33 percent (second to Achievers' 41 percent) upper-class.

Attitudes

The attitudes of this group are distinctive in that they are more consistent and coherent than those of most. It is generally a self-confident, independent group, persuaded that "the system," both economic and social, needs an overhaul. In keeping with this pattern the Societally Conscious are least likely of any group to think that social status or being part of a group is important. They don't particularly feel left out of things or that things are changing too fast. Indeed, they tend to feel that things aren't changing fast enough. Here are some of the issues on which the Societally Conscious (S.C.) differ strongly from our total sample:

- Believe woman's place is in the home: S.C. 3 percent, sample 30 percent.

- Agree that women with small children can work and still be good mothers: S.C. 72 percent, sample 55 percent.

- Believe marijuana should be legalized: S.C. 39 percent, sample 28 percent.

- Think unmarried sex is wrong: S.C. 15 percent, sample 39 percent.

- Believe air pollution is a major worldwide danger: S.C. 91 percent, sample 81 percent.

- Agree too much is spent on protecting the environment: S.C. 13 percent, sample 34 percent.

- Believe industrial growth should be limited: S.C. 58 percent, sample 48 percent.

- Agree too much is spent on military armaments: S.C. 38 percent, sample 27 percent.

- Have a good deal of confidence in elected officials: S.C. 19 percent, sample 30 percent.

- Have a good deal of confidence in company leaders: S.C. 16 percent, sample 31 percent.

- Have a good deal of confidence in military leaders: S.C. 23 percent, sample 49 percent.

- Agree the energy crisis is real and not the concoction of interested groups: S.C. 66 percent, sample 54 percent.

Despite these differences from the norms the Societally Conscious do not view themselves as rebelling against things. The rebellious groups are those that strikingly mistrust people and feel left out; the Societally Conscious, in contrast, apparently feel they have a say in things, although they may disagree with the majority. Everything suggests that the group is impassioned, knowledgeable, and effective. In Part IV we will suggest something of its probable role in the years to come.

Financial Status

Two things are interesting about the financial situation of the Societally Conscious: first, their incomes and total assets are substantial, and second, they are clearly the least financially motivated of the groups. The latter point is significant because it means that Societally Conscious people are driven by their private convictions more than by financial considerations.

Low economic motivation is revealed by the Societally Conscious group's response to the first two items in Table A-3 in the Appendix: Only 38 percent strongly agree that financial security is important (vs. sample of 53 percent), and only 28 percent strongly desire to get ahead financially (sample is 44 percent). This relative disinterest occurs even though the group exceeds the average only modestly in being satisfied with present finances, in feeling they've improved in the recent past, and in expecting to maintain current living standards in the future. We find it interesting and faintly amusing that the group rates itself as a bit more inclined toward spending than saving. They behave in what many consider a shrewd fashion in being more prone than most to go into debt to cope with inflation, to buy on time, and to prefer tangibles such as art, gold, or gems to the more standard forms of investment.

Societally Conscious people are active in all financial markets. Considering their affluence, however, they are prime customers in relatively few areas. Nine-three percent have checking accounts, but they are just about at the sample average in the fraction keeping balances over $1,000. Forty-one percent have mutual or money market funds, but their holdings appear smaller even than those of Emulators or Belongers. They come out a bit higher relatively in ownership of savings accounts, stocks and bonds, and investment real estate. Like the Experientials, the Societally Conscious dabble in the stock market: although only 16 percent own stocks and bonds valued at over $10,000 (compared with 40 percent of Achievers), 25 percent of these generate annual transactions of over $10,000 (almost identical to 26 percent for Achievers, with their much larger holdings).

Three-fourths of the Societally Conscious own their own home—a bit above the sample average—and 73 percent have mortgages—distinctly higher than average. One-fourth estimate that they would clear over $50,000 if they were to sell their homes.

In terms of indebtedness 40 percent of the Societally Conscious have debts or liabilities exceeding $25,000. This compares with 33 percent for Experientials, 42 percent for Achievers, 15 percent for the risk-averse Belongers, and 0 percent for the poverty-stricken Survivors. The Societally Conscious thus appear to be reasonably risk-taking.

Of the group two-thirds place their total assets at over $50,000 and 31 percent place them at over $100,000. These figures are considerably lower than those for Achievers but materially exceed all other groups, especially in the $100,000-and-up ranges.

Activity Patterns

This is the inner-directed group that has attained positions of influence and status, hence no longer feels the need for the self-display so prominent among I-Am-Mes and, to a lesser degree, among Experientials. The assurance that comes with success and influence perhaps accounts for the many similarities between Achievers and the Societally Conscious. In spite of being ideologically opposed in many areas these two types are on the same side of average (that is, above or below average in participation rates for a given activity) in a large majority of activities in which both deviate appreciably from national norms. It seems clear that maturity and success have a major influence on quantitative activity patterns. Even so, we suspect that qualitatively Achievers differ more from the Societally Conscious than participation numbers show. That is, we surmise that the reasons for engaging in—and the satisfaction the two groups draw from—the various activities are often quite different or even opposed, even though frequency of participation may be identical. An example could be attendance at a major art exhibit. Opening ceremonies would tend to attract Achievers. The Societally Conscious would attend at less hectic times. But additional research is required to determine how extensive are the motivational differences between the two groups.

Societally Conscious people score high in the areas one would expect in a well-educated group of middle years, many of whom hold excellent professional or technical jobs. Areas of high scores include participation in the arts, attendance at cultural events, concern with health aspects of food, work at home, use of library facilities, self-learning, pleasure travel, business travel, ownership and use of credit cards (including many household balances over $500), life and health insurance, understanding of "holistic health," watching educational TV, and reading of books and news magazines.

People holding Societally Conscious values especially tend to engage in healthful outdoor sports such as cycling, jogging, swimming, gym exercise, and sailing. They indulge in intellectual games like chess but don't participate much in such pursuits as bowling, pool/billiards, motorboating, hunting, or card games. Like other Inner-Directeds they patronize both secondhand stores and specialty shops and are not loath to return unsatisfactory products. They display a low incidence of watching commercial TV, although they (like Achievers) watch a good many sports programs. They don't rate commercial TV well on any measure, but they are enthusiastic watchers of educational TV.

The group is probably the most literate of the VALS segments, so it is not surprising to find that the Societally Conscious are above-average readers of many parts of the newspaper, of many types of magazines, and of books.

An interesting final note: The Societally Conscious, along with Sustainers (!), are most likely to have looked into solar heating. One suspects that the motives of the two groups are very different: Sustainers hope they may get subsidized heating; the Societally Conscious are hoping to aid the nation's energy predicament.

The activity patterns of Societally Conscious people are not notably aberrant. In 51 of the 257 areas examined their participation patterns differ by ten percentage points or more from the national norm (corresponding to a total deviation averaging about 33 percent). This places them a bit closer to Achievers than to the Experientials or the I-Am-Mes. The areas in which the Societally Conscious differ most from the norm are listed in Table 17.

TABLE 17
Activities of Societally Conscious

Active sports		Credit cards owned	
Swimming	+	Visa/Bankamericard	+
Sailing	+	MasterCard	+
The arts		Gasoline/oil	+
Write poetry/fiction/nonfiction	+	Department/specialty store card	+
Attendance at cultural events		No credit cards	−
Theatre	+	Purchases with credit cards	
Opera/ballet dance	+	Gasoline	+
Art galleries/museums	+	Business travel	+
Health-related food concerns		Pleasure travel	+
National brands considered of		Personal entertainment	+
highest quality	−	Don't use credit cards for	
No difference in quality of brands	+	purchases	−
A lot of concern with amount of		Household credit card balance over	
sugar in foods	+	$500	+
A lot of concern with amount of		Life and health insurance	
saccharin consumed	+	Have group life insurance	+
Cigarette smoking		Have disability insurance	+
Stopped smoking over 10 years ago	+	Know and understand term "holistic	
Off-hours work		health"	+
Work at second job/free-lance	+	Commercial or educational TV	
Type personal letters at home	+	watching*	
Personal communications		Watch 10 A.M.-1 P.M. weekdays	−
Phone friends/relatives locally	−	Watch 1-4:30 P.M. weekdays	−
Library users		Watch 8-11 P.M. weekdays	−
Use audiovisual materials	+	Educational TV watching	+
Learning		Type of TV program watched	
Have spent over $50 for self-		Soap operas	−
instruction	+	Think commercial TV is:	
Have attended night school	+	Interesting	−
Pleasure travel		Exciting	−
Travel by air	+	Newspaper reading	
Stay at hotels/motels	+	Read business/finance section	+
Use rental cars	+	Magazine reading	
Use travel agency	+	Read major news magazines	+
Business travel		Book reading	
Travel by air	+	Heavy readers	+
Stay at hotels/motels	+	Housing	
Use rental cars	+	Lived in current residence over 10	
Use travel agency	+	years	−
Shopping in stores			
Return an unsatisfactory product	+		

*Hours shown are for Eastern and Pacific time. Times are an hour earlier for Central and Mountain time.

Consumption Patterns

Patterns of consumption among the Societally Conscious reflect their conservationist and ecological concerns as well as their preference for simple living and frugality. Nonetheless, their product-ownership and -use patterns are quite similar to those of Achievers in a number of ways, including ownership of appliances, recreational equipment, and home electronic products, and consumption of alcoholic beverages.

A higher-than-average percentage of Societally Conscious households buy subcompact cars, and fewer than average buy midsize and large cars. A substantially higher-than-average percentage own more than one vehicle and purchased their last vehicle new. Price or deal offered, gas mileage, durability/reliability, and value for the money are important purchase considerations for this type of person.

Societally Conscious households rank high in ownership of dishwashers, garbage disposals, and food processors. A higher-than-average percentage also own camping/backpacking equipment, exercise equipment, and swimming pools. Ownership of home electronic products by this group is higher than average, particularly for color television, video games, hi-fi stereo components, blank recording tapes and cassettes, pocket calculators, and telephone extensions in the home.

In their dress the Societally Conscious appear more traditional and conservative than the other Inner-Directed types. An above-average percentage of Societally Conscious women wear dresses and skirts, and fewer than average wear jeans. Societally Conscious men are among the highest in incidence of wearing suits, dress shirts, sport coats, and slacks.

The beverage and food consumption pattern of the Societally Conscious is slightly different from those of the other two Inner-Directed types. Their incidence of consumption of alcoholic beverages is significantly above average, but their preferences are more varied. More Societally Conscious than I-Am-Mes and Experientials consume wines and liquor, favoring whiskey blends, Scotch, gin, and vodka above the other liquors—somewhat closer to the consumption pattern of Achievers.

Health and diet concerns are reflected in their other food consumption patterns. A substantially lower-than-average percentage of the Societally Conscious use regular carbonated soft drinks, preferring sugar-free carbonated soft drinks, sparkling mineral water, and fruit juices. They also are disproportionately high users of fresh, frozen, and canned seafoods. On the other hand they are above average in consuming regular coffee.

TABLE 18
Consumption Patterns of Societally Conscious

Motor vehicles		Cat food (purchase)	
Own two or more cars	+	Canned	+
Durables		Dry	−
Appliances (ownership)		Selected specialized cleaning	
Dishwasher	+	products*	
Garbage disposal	+	Aerosol bathroom cleaner	−
Freezer (separate from		Toilet bowl cleaner	−
refrigerator)	−	Beverages and foods	
Recreational equipment (ownership)		Alcoholic beverages (use)	
Exercise (at home)	+	Any alcohol	+
Racing bicycle	+	Wine	
Home electronic products (ownership)		Any wine	+
Hi-fi stereo components	+	California wine	+
Pocket calculator	+	Liquor	
Clothing		Any liquor	+
Men's clothing (use)		Carbonated beverages (use)	
Suits	+	Regular soft drinks	−
Sport coats	+	Foods (use)	
Dress shirts	+	Canned soups	−
Personal-care products		Confections	
Women's products (use)		Regular gum	−
Aerosol underarm deodorant	−	Miscellaneous foods*	
Feminine hygiene spray	−	Fresh, frozen, or canned seafood	+
Men's products (use)		Gelatin desserts	−
Shampoo	+		
Pet foods and services			
Dog food (purchase)			
Moist	−		

*For women only.

The Societally Conscious are essentially tied with Achievers and Emulators in terms of differences in consumption patterns relative to the national norm. Only Belongers are more conforming. The 28 areas (out of 170 studied) in which Societally Conscious patterns differ by ten percentage points or more from the national average are listed in Table 18.

8

Putting It Together: The Integrateds

Portrait: Unfolding: The Storalls

They had been good years—twenty-four of them now. Next year it would be a quarter of a century since John and Betsy Storall, bright, ambitious, and in love, had walked together down the aisle of the little white church in the small Minnesota town where Betsy had been raised.

The years had brought their good and their bad moments, but mostly they had been good. The best were the two children—Jeb, now in college, and Lucy, about to graduate from high school. There was John's business, and that had been good, too. He'd gone into printing because he cared about a handsome page and loved the smell of fresh ink. Over the years he'd gone from salesman to pressroom manager to owner. The business had brought in a very comfortable income for the Storall family. The bad part was Betsy's illness—the polio that left her barely able to walk, although her upper body was unimpaired. But she had found her compensations in drawing and recently in pottery, for Betsy's long and flexible hands had a way with clay.

They had been good years, but somehow they had come to an end. It was hard to say just why or how, but their purpose in some sense had been fulfilled. The Storalls had made the marriage work, they had achieved a comfortable financial position, and together they had overcome the quivering fear of being crippled. And they did not worry about their children. It was as if a curtain were being silently and invisibly drawn across the part of their lives that lay behind them.

And so when John had looked across the dinner table and, glass in hand, toasted his wife "to our next lives," Betsy had known instantly what he meant, although not a word about it had been exchanged.

That evening was eight years ago now. Quickly the decision had been reached to sell the printing business, buy some acreage on Lake Seguin—an area Betsy knew well from her childhood—build their home looking out across the calm waters, and move as soon as possible. This, they knew, was what lay on the other side of the curtain.

John is handy. He had built, with a bit of help from town plumbers and electricians, three cabins on far parts of the property. These the Storalls rent for income or use for summertime guests from their former world. From printing John has turned to wood. His shop in the basement is equipped with first-grade hand and some power tools. He has spent many an afternoon cutting and fitting, joining and gluing furniture for their home and the cottages. Desks, tables, chairs, lamps, firescreens, sofas, bed frames, each of Storall design (for the family passes on each), are painstakingly finished, sanded, and oiled.

His love of cabinetry makes John sensitive to wood. He has standing rights for first look at the fine woods delivered to Plimpton's Lumber. When word comes of a new delivery, he and Mac Plimpton turn the hardwood boards one by one, noting the grain, the color, the mix of milk and old wood, and especially for cherry and butternut, how the bark edges the plank. This done, the choices made and the prices agreed on, they load the Storall pickup and then repair to Sally's Saloon for a couple of beers.

These are important occasions. For furniture John favors curly maple, cherry, and black walnut in the hardwoods. In the softwoods it's butternut (hard to find these days), incense cedar, and sometimes white pine. For construction he uses mostly spruce. Sometimes, to surprise Betsy, who on occasion likes to carve, he will buy a chunk of mahogany—African when he can get it because the burls make for pleasant effects. Mac Plimpton keeps an eye out for the unusual, and that keeps things interesting.

Income from the proceeds of the sale of the printing business plus rent from the cottages cover most of the family's expenses. But it was close for a while, and that's one reason why Betsy's skill with wheel and brush made so large a difference. From books she had learned the art of ceramic paintings and now she was almost famous for her work, delicately washed and lined onto clay tablets and fired into ceramic permanence in the kiln John had built for her. Her style has a certain Chinese touch, but her skies are individual and unique, as are those of a watercolorist. Already in Minneapolis, St. Paul, and Chicago her stone art, mounted in stands of red cherry or black walnut built to specifications by John, has brought prices of $500 and up. And she has heard from galleries in Los Angeles and New York. Things, Betsy said, were unfolding as easily as the opening of a flower.

Portrait: Tree Sammath, the Builder

Tree was an able, successful young man, bearded, blond, well educated, and with every social grace, so when the word got out he was undergoing psychoanalysis, his friends and parents wondered aloud what was "the matter" with him. Tree could not have told them. All he knew was that his job, despite his evident success in it, no longer held his interest. Then, too, there was the floating anxiety that all too often arose in him, and the distressing fact that he couldn't put three words together in writing in a fashion that satisfied him. Neither logic nor learning yielded an explanation. When he described his feelings and fears to Dr. Coltart, he was incredibly relieved to hear the doctor thought analysis could be of help—no guarantee, but it might help.

First there were the magnificent open dreams. Night after night images raced through Tree's brain of the bones of mountains, of splendid desert arches that once supported giant caves 100 miles down, of the endlessly stretching ocean that transformed into a sea of tears. Giant combers made of tears crashed on an inner shore.

And then came the dark, complex, intricate, highly fashioned dreams. There were channels lined with shining limestone and rooms filled with clockwork so densely packed it was dangerous to pick one's way across. There were places where oiled pistons throbbed and moved as in the hold of a ship. There were Rousseauesque tropical forests full of fierce faces, the serried dancing girls, and the deep seaweed moving to and fro under the influence of mysterious currents.

There were the dreamy color dreams . . . great gules, lakes of purples, blues, greens, oranges shifting and blending and moving away and flooding and vanishing only to reappear.

There were the eye dreams. Pig eyes, rhino eyes, lidded and naked eyes, blind eyes, fathomless eyes, eyes that stared and eyes that blinked hideously. These were eyes that studied him, measured him, watched and watched and watched. And then came the wonderful dream when he, Tree, was watching, scrutinizing them!

And finally there were the people dreams.

It was in the midst of the people dreams that Joanie came into Tree's life. She was one of those who seemed to have no trouble being what she felt. Pretty, quick, with hazel eyes full of humor, she trusted what she was and found it good. She wouldn't let Tree get too serious. One time he wondered aloud why he got such extravagant pleasure from touching her. "I guess it's because I am a girl," she said. Another time she made him laugh by saying boldly, "You know, if you made love to me, you probably would never get over it." She said this very slowly. She was right, as it turned out. And then there was the day Tree was holding forth on change and how important it was. Joanie agreed. "You know," she said, "without change there would be a lot of wet babies."

But change truly was important for Tree. He was becoming more relaxed, more aware as the moment came and blossomed, more gentle, more loving, more full of the sense that the tide pool and the farthest nebula move to the same forces.

One spring weekend Tree and Joanie took off from town for the country. They drove in silence through the hills and meadows they knew so well. Joanie asked: "Tree, what do you want to do? What do you want to be? Maybe I shouldn't say this," she went on, "but I think there are three parts of you. There is the sensible, logical, efficient part. There is the ambitious part that wants to get ahead. You use those parts now. And then there's the softer, poetic, human part. That's the new part of you. That's the part I love the best."

Tree moved his hand from the steering wheel to hold hers. "I want to build. I want to be a builder," he said. Joanie responded immediately: "You mean you want to become an architect? To build homes and skyscrapers and theaters and parks and everything where people can live and be themselves? Oh, Tree, I think that's perfect."

It was not what Tree had meant, but it was what he should have meant. And it struck him funny how life kept coming cavorting around the bend. He began to laugh. Joanie watched him, puzzled. "What is it, Tree?" she asked. "It's just the way things *move*," he said. The little frown disappeared from Joanie's face as she understood. And she joined in, making his laughter theirs.

Statistics

As explained earlier, we have not yet been successful in defining the Integrateds in statistical terms. As a result we cannot provide treatment parallel to the other lifestyles in terms of demographics, attitudes, financial status, activities, or consumption. In our description of the Integrateds in Part I, however, we have included some surmises on these facets of the Integrated lifestyle. Comments on the changing role of the Integrated lifestyle are contained in Part IV.

PART

III

USING
THE
TYPOLOGY

9

The Typology, People, and Business

ON TYPING YOURSELF

Our way of identifying the dominant lifestyle of an individual involves a complicated system of scoring up to sixty attitudinal and demographic features of a person, as explained in the introductory material to Part II. The details of the system are proprietary and cannot be given here. Even so, readers of this book can get a pretty good notion of their predominant lifestyle types in several ways. The simplest and perhaps the most reliable way is to ask yourself: which of the lifestyles is *most* like me? Which do I *most* identify with? Having selected the primary lifestyle, you can repeat the process for "second most like me" and "third most like me." The chances are the "most like" and "most unlike" styles will be easier to identify than intermediate lifestyles. The reason is that our typology is a nested model, like the layers of an onion. This means that, almost surely, several—possibly all nine—lifestyles are inside you. Those most potent in your present way of life will be outermost and hence easily identified. The more deeply a lifestyle is buried—that is, the further it is behind you—the less sharply you will identify with it. The result is that you'll probably be very certain which styles you definitely are not.

More systematic approaches are possible. For example, a one-by-one comparison of your demographics, attitudes, and finances with the data provided in Tables A-1, A-2, and A-3 in the Appendix will give you a more specific reading of your operative and distant lifestyles. This approach in combination with the intuitive identification approach may be more reliable than either one alone.

A couple of further remarks. Almost nobody is pure 100 percent any lifestyle, so you should expect to find that you differ from your dominant lifestyle pattern in some respects. People who are in transition from one way of life to another may find they are about equally like several lifestyles. Many of our survey respondents showed very similar scores for two lifestyles, usually styles that are adjacent in our typology.

The Integrateds pose a particular problem because to date we have not developed a reliable computational way to identify them. The theory behind the VALS framework says that Integrateds should score high in both of the lifestyles that precede this lofty stage: that is, Achiever and Societally Conscious. If you rate yourself as half Achiever and half Societally Conscious, you are at least a candidate for being Integrated. We find, however, that the temptation to rank oneself at the pinnacle of the typology is remarkably strong! Among audiences we have spoken to over half the people have rated themselves as Integrateds—a most improbable distribution. But, of course, it is good and healthy and probably wise to think well of oneself so the error—if error it be—is harmless enough.

PERSONAL LIFE

Many people find the values perspectives set forth in this book to be helpful in understanding themselves and others. But it should be plain that this kind of use of our work requires that the typology be understood in depth. One of the most important things about people is that they are wonderfully complex, with myriad secret subtleties and invisible drives. Nonetheless, you will find that many of your friends—and nonfriends, too—will fit into our lifestyle typology, some rather completely, some less neatly.

Typing is a fun game to play, but it has its dangers. One is that, very clearly, all 160 million American adults cannot be pigeonholed into nine categories. The splendid truth is that we would need 160 million categories to be truly representative. But our goal lies in the opposite direction. Granting that each person is unique, our inquiry is into commonalities and shared patterns. To reach our present nine lifestyles we have winnowed and sifted and explored and invented all kinds of approaches. We have no illusions that our nine are the only nine (or that only nine exist), but we do think they form a coherent and useful perspective from which to view ourselves, others, and events. The framework, we think, helps one see and understand many things one otherwise might not. So we present our array of lifestyles as a helpful starting point for understanding people and trends—but as nothing more than a starting point.

Love

We have the sense that there is some deep inner matching of values within what we call love. For lucky people perhaps a few times in a life they meet another with whom, mysteriously and invisibly, they somehow merge—become a single entity, as it were—so that trust and understanding and the quick giggle and the start of tears occur almost as if the two were one. Sex and age make no difference, nor to a large degree does background, but we suspect that lifestyle is significant, to the extent that it truly reflects the style and content of a person's values. In terms of the lifestyle typology we think it much less likely that, say Emulators and Experientials (at the poles of the outer-inner spectrum) or Integrateds and Survivors (at the poles of the psychological maturity spectrum) will experience the kind of meshing we mean than will people sharing the same or adjacent lifestyles.

If this concept carries some truth, it may help explain some trends in marriage. There is little doubt that many more people have consciously been changing their lifestyles in the post-World-War-II decades than earlier in our history. When one partner in a relationship changes, the relationship is threatened because the new values may no longer mesh with the old. Hence it would not be surprising to find an increase in divorce rates—a much-documented phenomenon. At the same time one would expect falling-in-love rates also to be high because growing people have a particular need to find partners with whom their values match. Therefore, since love and marriage still go together, rates of trial marriages and remarriages also should be high. And they are.

Distrust and Anger

One of the fundamental properties of the lifestyle hierarchy is that a person very often finds it impossible truly to understand people operating at higher levels, although it often is easy to understand others at the same level or those who have not yet attained that level. This important phenomenon arises because you can't know what it's like until you've been there. Clearly, many actions and conclusions of a person on a high level reflect logics and sensibilities not within the experience of those who have not yet reached that stage. Unhappily, human nature being what it is, the individual who does not understand the thinking of another not infrequently imputes negative motives or assigns various degrees of incompetence to that person. The upshot is at a minimum distrust and at a maximum hate.

The phenomenon is appallingly common. It accounts for an enormous amount of misunderstanding between individuals and between nations. It underlies much antagonism between social classes and between management and employees. This is one reason why rifts sometimes occur between spouses and among longtime friends—one has grown, and the other has not. This is why the social innovator and the global-minded leader so often arouse acute opposition.

It is striking that the lifestyle groups that are high in trust of people are low in rebelliousness or generalized anger and those that are angry are low in trust. The high anger/low trust linkage is especially plain for Sustainers and Emulators and, to a lesser degree, for I-Am-Mes. (The Societally Conscious tend also in this direction, but their success and self-confidence enables them to cope with anger in more constructive ways.) These are the groups marked by the greatest turbulence, the greatest ambition to change their lot. They are, one might say, the interstitial groups sandwiched between more stolid, solid, deeper-rooted groups. In general these are short-lived stages of development from which one either makes it upward or, chances are, slides back. So the trust/anger syndrome seems to be associated with low self-confidence and a feeling of being left out of things, combined with intense upward striving and uncertainty concerning the outcome, manifested by general unhappiness. None of this is surprising, but it does suggest that the transitional phases are the most difficult. Fortunately they are also the briefest and lead to phases with opposite characteristics—those of much trust, much happiness, and a period of either contentedness or achievement of the desired lifestyle.

Ways of Life

There are those who say it's the journey, not the end, that counts. The ambitious ones prize the end, not the way. Few differences more sharply distinguish the lives of outer- from inner-directed people.

For the Outer-Directeds, life tends to be measured in tangibles, often material. For the Inner-Directeds, process is the point. For one, the way is directed, narrow, competitive. For the other, it is like a river rushing in swift, channeled rapids at some times and at other times spreading wide into placid lakes. For one, sacrifice, delay, and effort render the goal all the more precious. For the other, the passing moment is its own reward. For one, control, measurement, things tend to dominate. The other most appreciates nuance, symbolism, surprise, and the personal. For one, the arrival all too often is a dusty disappointment tasting of yesterday's dreams. For the other, static arrival never comes, for each step brings a new land and a new vista ahead.

These differences go deep, accounting for differing views of what confers status and power, what one wants from a job or a book or a marriage, what gives pain and what brings joy. The very meaning of existence is involved because, for one, life's end point—whether one is hurrying toward wealth, or learning, or physical prowess, or admission to heaven—is the leading light, showing the right direction. For the other, the way is full of side lanes, meanderings, and picnics in meadows far away.

Failure

Failure, as we all know, is a personal matter. It occurs when results fail to match expectations. The key question is: *Whose* expectations?

The Outer-Directeds, by definition, tend to accept the standards and expectations of important others—family, associates, and such institutions as school, business, church, or country. The Inner-Directeds, by definition, tend to rely more on their personal reactions and feelings (although it seems clear that no one can wholly disregard the standards of others and still live a sensible or even a legal life).

The perpetual outer-directed failure probably is trying to follow someone else's standard without really comprehending it, or perhaps not being equipped to live up to it. This is the problem of Emulators trying to be like Achievers, whom they neither understand nor resemble. This is the problem of the son, however gifted, trying to be like a father from another generation who developed his way of life to cope with circumstances that no longer exist. This is the problem of countless people who have adopted the most spectacular successes of their times as models—whether in athletics, business, the professions, or the arts. It is obvious that few can match the external accomplishments of their idols. The sad part is that even great achievements are often rendered unsatisfying because the circumstances do not precisely parallel those of the model. A gifted salesperson striving to be a corporate manager will not feel rewarded unless his or her standards are broadened to include success at sales as a mark of distinction. The difficulty is that others may not support such a change of standards, so that the individual is forced into revising personal goals—that is, is forced to become to a degree inner-directed. Without that, no matter how successful the sales effort, a sense of failure will inevitably result.

For the perpetual inner-directed failure the problem is rather different. It is interior, not exterior, standards that establish the unreachable goals. So it is, for example, that many an artist of world renown—such as Vincent van Gogh—continues to seethe with unrest, that the heretic, innovator, or idealist strives ceaselessly to achieve new heights. There are also the people who fail because their inner idealisms are too far removed from outer reality or whose narcissism blocks acceptance by others of the merit of their work.

Of course, this is far from all bad: Without standards, whatever their source, ambition would die. Indeed, many people consider that it is the lack of standards that lies at the source of much failure in schools and, in fact, in all occupations and even in the society as a whole.

OFFICE TYPES

Bosses

There are bosses and bosses, and it makes a lot of difference where they are on the lifestyle hierarchy. There is the indecisive, never-say-no, solicitous, undemanding boss. This type is most likely a Belonger who places getting along above productivity, *we* above *I*, and companionship above work. Such bosses tend to be loyal, hard-working, and conscientious, but not effective from a production standpoint. They fit admirably into positions where personal aspects are critical to success of the work, where rules are clear and unequivocal, where crucial decisions seldom need to be made or can be referred upstairs, and where personal judgments and rankings are seldom needed. In the office Belongers fit in excellently in many clerical operations, reception work, and behind-the-scenes support work.

Some bosses have fists of steel without the benefit of gloves of velvet. They tend to be autocratic, relentless, and unsympathetic. When things go wrong, they resort to craftiness or rage. Such people are often Emulators, possibly Sustainers. Their demands flow from their inner anger and their feeling that the system has it in for them. Anything less than instant absolutist decision is seen as weakness. They expect immediate answers at all times. Because of their own uncertainties they find it hard to praise others. What they understand best is not success but its outer trappings—money, the impressive office, executive perks. Such people often are difficult employees full of negativism and constantly demanding promotions and confirmation of their status. On the other hand these are people who have a powerful drive for upward mobility, hence will move home and family for advancement. They operate best in highly structured jobs, especially where technical or mechanical aspects are more important than human elements. They tend to shine where immediate feedback provides constant measures of how well they are doing; these jobs generally involve production or sales. Being intensely status-conscious, they seem to thrive on the showier kinds of businesses, such as fashion, advertising, or the auto industry.

The Achiever boss typifies the widespread image of the corporate executive—outer-directed, driving, driven, efficient, good at the job, successful. These are the leaders, setting the standards. Because they do, it is not surprising that they show many of the attributes of fist-of-steel Emulator bosses, but with crucial differences. Achiever bosses are decisive without being rigid. They are smart without being crafty, firm without being angry or autocratic. Most are proud of their profession, think of themselves as hard-nosed pragmatists, and find work rewarding, often to the point of being workaholics. Some are people of great human sympathy and personal charisma. As we have seen, almost a fourth are self-employed. Achiever bosses understand well the rules of their jobs, so they tend to develop networks. Their goals are corporate and personal success, usually measured in financial terms. Essentially all the great American business leaders of the past have had a large element of the Achiever in them, and it is they who have developed to a fine degree the arts of efficient production and managerial finesse.

A final type of boss includes the inner-directed executives. We know less about them than the others partly because they represent a relatively recent development, partly because they are a rarer species, and partly because the essence of their style is less visible. These are people (many of them women, we feel sure) who consciously take their most important directions from the right hemisphere of their brains—the intuitive, holistic, nonlinear part of their mind—although they often justify decisions by recasting them in left-brain business school terms. (Incidentally, it is our opinion that many executives who pride themselves on outer-directed "objectivity" reach countless decisions intuitively, often unknown to themselves.) Teamwork and democratic discussion of ideas are common because it is assumed that everyone is interested in company affairs and has something to contribute. At the extreme, inner-directed leaders come close to shunning the financial aspects of success, stressing social and personal aspects—but this remains rare, perhaps because such a posture often blocks the possibility of major corporate growth and not infrequently means business failure.

Inner-directed executives are less entrenched in the system than most and are frequently highly innovative. Their reliance on inner sources yields many imaginative ideas that they tend to chase, sometimes to the detriment of the main line of business. Some gifted directors of advanced technical research and some "creative directors" in advertising agencies are examples of such executives. Driven (and often charmed) by their ideas, they sometimes pursue paths of little interest to their firms, a course that inevitably threatens their jobs. Many, however, inspire great personal allegiance from employees and colleagues. Yet many are easily bored and mercurial in their interests; not a few tend to disdain outer-directed leadership as dull and passé. This reluctance to fit into the standard mold—to "play the game"—has advantages even to traditional firms. Bright, entrepreneurially inclined, inner-directed managers (and there are a lot of them) often make brilliant leaders for developing and introducing new product lines, for updating old lines, for repositioning old products for contemporary consumers, or for combining technical with marketing expertise. But such people may present the traditional company with difficult problems: They are likely to demand rewards (such as sabbaticals) unusual in old-line business practice, they are not likely to "kill themselves" for their work, and they are usually unwilling to move from place to place as a prerequisite for moving up the corporate ladder.

Employees

As employees, the various lifestyle groups ask different things of their jobs. In the discussion below we have tried very briefly to characterize these wants and to indicate the types of jobs that are most suitable.

Survivors. The prime needs here are simple: cash and job security. These people usually work best with things and least well with intellectual tasks. Clerical, crafts, labor, and service jobs are appropriate.

Sustainers. Again, money and job security are prime needs (15 percent are looking for work). These people are ambitious, too; they want to get ahead. For protection Sustainers usually want to be part of a team, often a union. They work well with things and often are mechanically ingenious. Prime occupations: machine operators, laborers, crafts and service workers.

Belongers.   Warmth, security, and inclusion as part of a group are the chief elements Belongers seek. Neither money nor opportunity for advancement rank very high. They work best where the rules are clear, the routine rather invariant, and the atmosphere relaxed. Belongers are especially adept at working with people. In the white-collar domain they do well in clerical and service jobs; many are handy and thrive as mechanics, machine operators, or farmers.

Emulators.   For the Emulator, money, status, and a route to get ahead are the primary job wants. Many are hard-working, intensely competitive, but demanding employees. They are not likely to be union supporters. They probably care relatively little about the kind of work they do, as long as promotions are in view. Both money and perquisites are important aspects of moving up. About a fourth hold technical, professional, managerial, or sales jobs. The less well educated Emulators are found in large numbers in jobs such as clerical, crafts, and machine operators.

Achievers.   Achievers want authority, responsibility, independence, and access to major resources in terms of both personal and financial support. Money is important but not dominant, probably because they already are prospering. A chance to build is often the key attraction of jobs to Achievers. Many work best on problems of output, where progress is easily measured and feedback is prompt. They are, of course, prime prospects for managerial and administrative jobs, and 29 percent work in technical or professional domains.

I-Am-Mes.   Since 90 percent of I-Am-Mes are twenty-five or less, their job requirements are still in the process of formation. Testing of different kinds of jobs and the gaining of experience are often leading concerns. Spending money certainly is wanted, but as yet desire for the longer-term solid salary does not rank high. These people, often bright and innovative, make excellent trainees for almost anything that motivates them. The problem is that their brightness and malleability often lead to flighty enthusiasms and radical shifts in interests.

Experientials.   For most Experientials work, although not unimportant, is secondary to other pursuits. On the job they want freedom to adjust work hours to personal schedules. Parttime work is attractive. As part of benefit packages Experientials favor opportunities for further education and arrangements whereby some form of extended leave is possible. Despite work attitudes that strike some as cavalier, Experientials often become intensely motivated less through loyalty to the firm than through commitment to an idea or desire to support the work of a person they admire. As a result, many prefer the personal atmosphere and independence of small companies to large traditional firms. Over a third of Experientials hold technical or professional jobs, but surprisingly few (7 percent) are managers or administrators. A good many work in clerical or craft occupations; chances are the bearded, college-educated carpenter and the gifted typist in blue jeans and pictured T-shirt are of this ilk.

Societally Conscious.   These are people who tend to take the world seriously. On the job they are often concerned with issues, human and social. They like to work with ideas and concepts. Accomplishment is more important than wordly success per se. Driven and often full of stresses, they fervently seek a voice in corporate policies. Their demands for change—frequently put forth in the name of morality or justice—often are vehement, persistent, and telling. In addition, the Societally Conscious often are gifted and charismatic. They tend to see things in nonconventional modes, hence can be inventive. These people, with their extraordinarily high average level of education, are most attracted to professional and technical occupations. Like the Experientials, many prefer the small, fast-moving firm to larger, more established organizations.

The Integrateds.   The corporate role of the Integrateds we can only speculate about, since we do not yet have a systematic way of identifying them. We know that they are rare. We believe they tend to be fifty-fifty Achiever and Societally Conscious. We think that most are people of middle or upper years, with a few in their twenties. We assume that most are relatively prosperous, happy people most numerous in occupations calling for good educations—notably managers, administrators, technical people, and members of the professions.

What we postulate is that many Integrateds in business have reached that state following years—often decades—as successful Achievers. Having mastered that life pattern, they have felt free to hear and become engaged in the viewpoints of the Inner-Directeds and especially the Societally Conscious. For some this occurred in the context of their job, for others family life and especially their children were the teachers. Having internalized both inner and outer, and having found both valid and valuable, the integrated perspective emerged.

Our sense is that people of this sort probably alter their business style to focus more on global, societal, moral and human issues and less on purely production/competition matters, but we don't wish to overstate the case. We would guess such people become less driven, less stressed, and that some pragmatism gives way to softer measures. If these tendencies are real, such people would probably turn over many managerial duties to concentrate on corporate statesmanship on behalf of the firm, the industry, or of the system itself. Some of these people, we fancy, serve stints in the government.

In Part IV of this book we shall return to the leadership role of Integrateds in social change.

POLITICS

The Common Touch

To get elected one must appeal to many lifestyles. It is this endeavor that produces some of the more spectacular idiocies of politics—sedate lawyers wearing Indian headdresses, for example. It also can call forth the genius of the politician with "the common touch," who can reach other styles without being phony. These are people who can genuinely revert temporarily to an earlier style and actually be there when the need arises. For the national politician this ability is extraordinarily valuable, not only as part of the art of appeal, but as a means of remaining authentic and responsive.

The Activist and the Heretic

We have seen that one of the most fundamental distinctions drawn in our typology of lifestyles is that between Outer- and Inner-Direction. This distinction deals with the cores of people, so it is not surprising to find that it frequently is at the root of activism and the heretical. The inner-directed activist, for example, is more likely to emphasize human concerns over economic ones, aesthetics over efficiency, and meaning over expediency. The qualitative is placed before the quantitative. To many these "quality of life" issues signify soft-headedness, and it therefore comes as a shock to discover how inner-directed activists are often shrewd and effective as well as committed. From the political standpoint the reason such activists wield so much influence is that they are backed up by a large body of supporters. For example, brick-throwing on campuses during the 1960s was engaged in by about 2 percent of college students. But their causes, if not their actions, were supported by around half the student body. Without this tacit support one can be sure the brick-throwers could not have had the extraordinary impact they had. This support phenomenon is what makes single-issue politics so effective. Virginia Hine[1] calls the single-issue network "polycephalic," meaning it has many heads—unlike a hierarchical organization. Having many heads, it is difficult to attack and almost impossible to destroy. Its focus on a single issue means that each network is "pure," relatively free of jurisdictional disputes, and able to emerge and to disappear as the occasion warrants. It is a form of politics superbly adapted to inner-directed activism.

The heretic is the lone activist—the individual fighting for his or her cause without the silent support of others. The cause, of course, need not be political, but not infrequently it is. Somewhere in between the activist and the heretic are countless innovators, some frauds and others genuine, who have not the support of organized networks yet who need not espouse their version of the truth all alone.

Although this picture of the activist and the heretic may sound heroic, it is necessary to remember that issues of virtue or rectitude are not involved. Many an Inquisitor was inner-directed, and countless destructions and brutalities have been performed in the name of the inner light.

Democracy and Revolution

What enables a democracy to function is communication among segments of the society, including lifestyle segments. The great movements of the times have usually involved communication between opposing lifestyle groups. The coherent union movement early in this century emerged from the demands Survivors and Sustainers made upon Achievers. The need to protect Belongers as well as the Need-Drivens from even a weakened Achiever establishment lay behind the revolutionary social legislation of the 1930s. In the 1950s and '60s the Inner-Directeds were the force behind progress in civil rights. In each case communication—whether bloody, vociferous, or chiefly legal—was the essential thing.

When communication does not flow, a dictatorship or a revolution can result. This has been the deepest cause of the overthrow of many a monarchy. It is often said that revolutions do not occur unless the people are above abject poverty. In lifestyle terms this means people are above the Survivor stage—probably at the gutsy, aggressive Sustainer level, possibly led by Emulators.

But, perhaps surprisingly, impassioned Belongers can also lead revolutions. Recently in Iran, for example, the profoundly Belonger legions of the Ayatollah overthrew the Achiever regime of the Shah—a striking illustration of the inability of one level to understand the motives of a higher level, but also a demonstration of the danger of a government losing touch with the lower-level needs of its people. In the United States the Belonger-driven Moral Majority has quite suddenly dropped the posture of the "silent majority" for a more vigorous role.

BUSINESS

In this section we touch briefly on a half-dozen uses of lifestyle thinking for various business functions. The work at SRI International has carried this line of research much, much further than we attempt to do here and has developed elaborate analyses and cross-analyses for many dozens of product lines, specific products, and brand names. Here we are concerned chiefly with the general framework of this application of lifestyle analysis.

Market Segmentation

Perhaps the most fundamental business use of lifestyle research lies in market segmentation. Different values groups tend to buy different products and services for different reasons. The automobile provides a familiar illustration. Our data show that Achievers buy more large and luxury cars; Belongers tend toward "family-sized" cars; the Societally Conscious purchase more gas-savers; muscle cars are bought by Emulators and Experientials; the Need-Drivens are heavy in the secondhand market. Further, there are big differences in how many cars the various lifestyle households are likely to own, their assessment of features desired in a car (style, safety, dealer convenience, price, economy of operation, etc.), the uses to which cars are put, and the country of origin. The Inner-Directeds, for example, are far more likely to buy a foreign-made car than are the patriotic, America-first Belongers. Literally hundreds of market segments can be delineated by running various demographic, attitudinal, and financial cross-tabulations—many more than are worth focusing on from the merchandising standpoint.

But market segmentation by lifestyle is by no means a total solution. Very frequently demographics—especially sex, age, education, and income—are at least as important as lifestyles. With the data in hand it is of course easy to determine the relative influence of each. And there are products that appear intrinsically less values-sensitive than others. Although there are some who will not agree, it seems to us that most consumers are quite indifferent to what brand of gasoline they buy, or which institution stands behind their credit card, what publisher has issued a book, or, other things being equal, what airline they fly. Since the product or service is comparatively values-inert, the promoter is forced to develop special features to gain an edge on the competition. The merchandising trick here is to invest the item with values overtones, which can then become the theme in, say, advertising. It would be interesting to explore this line by lifestyle groups. It could well be, for example, that Belongers respond only minimally on a values level to, say, different brands of wine, an area where values might make all the difference to Emulators and Achievers.

The segmentation approach can be usefully pushed a step or two beyond what we have mentioned. We know, for example, that Emulators lag behind the lifestyle patterns of Achievers by a matter of years—probably decades in some instances. This characteristic could easily be put to good use by a real estate firm that found a certain development or suburb was going "downhill," meaning that Achiever firms and individuals were moving elsewhere. They would be able to pitch to Emulators, especially those from out of town, to find the firms and families attracted to the lingering prestige of the area in transition.

A longer-term aspect of this approach is "following the generations." To illustrate: Entertainment companies with a firm hold on today's I-Am-Me music market well know that the musical taste of current I-Am-Mes will change, probably in predictable directions, in the coming five years. Instead of focusing almost exclusively on seeking to capture emerging I-Am-Me tastes, why not pay more attention to the shifting tastes of today's I-Am-Me market? The approach has the huge advantage of dealing with a marketplace already favorably disposed toward the product, whether it is music, clothes, cosmetics, foods, or some other line. Further, success in following the generation in this fashion should eventually lead to larger (though less intense) markets in the years to come as the rate of change in taste slows and gradually melds to a degree into the more generalized market of ex-I-Am-Mes.

Market Size

Our work clearly is applicable to estimating the sizes of markets influenced substantially by lifestyles. Table 2 in Part II gives our best estimates of the number of adults and the percentage of the adult population by lifestyles for 1980. Parallel information is given in Table 19 in terms of the percent of each lifestyle group. In this case we have omitted the Integrateds because of lack of definitive data on them. This has the effect of increasing the percent of Achievers and Societally Conscious adults in the population by 1 percent each, because we think the 2 percent of Integrateds are drawn equally from these groups.

These tables reveal that the percentage of the market accounted for by a given lifestyle may indicate a high degree of concentration and yet not point to the largest total market. Thus, for example, 80 percent of Survivors may be active in a market, yet they would actually number less than 10 percent of Belongers who also buy these. This comes about, of course, as a result of huge differences in the sizes of the lifestyle groups.

Size estimates can be refined in various ways. For products requiring a very large consumer base, such as many food and household items, the primary lifestyle groups can be enlarged by adding the groups most like them. This approach is probably most required for the smaller groups, and especially the Inner-Directeds. Many users of the VALS material collapse the three inner-directed types into a single entity consisting of some 30 million people who share many lifestyle characteristics.

TABLE 19
Percentage of Total Market by VALS Types

INDICATED PERCENT OF TOTAL MARKET	SURVIVOR	SUSTAINER	BELONGER	EMULATOR	ACHIEVER	I-AM-ME	EXPERIENTIAL	SOCIETALLY CONSCIOUS
10%	0.4%	0.7%	3.5%	1.0%	2.3%	0.5%	0.7%	0.9%
20	0.8	1.4	7.0	2.0	4.6	1.0	1.4	1.8
30	1.2	2.1	10.5	3.0	6.9	1.5	2.1	2.7
40	1.6	2.8	14.0	4.0	9.2	2.0	2.8	3.6
50	2.0	3.5	17.5	5.0	11.5	2.5	3.5	4.5
60	2.4	4.2	21.0	6.0	13.8	3.0	4.2	5.4
70	2.8	4.9	24.5	7.0	16.1	3.5	4.9	6.3
80	3.2	5.6	28.0	8.0	18.4	4.0	5.6	7.2
90	3.6	6.3	31.5	9.0	20.7	4.5	6.3	8.1
100	4.0	7.0	35.0	10.0	23.0	5.0	7.0	9.0

It is even more feasible to move in the other direction. High-profit, low-volume items, including top-of-the-line versions of standard mass products, often benefit from "stiletto" merchandising. Take eye makeup as an example. Using values and lifestyle survey data, one might start by identifying users of eye makeup by lifestyle group. This could be followed by cross-analysis in terms of frequency of use, age of user, occupation of user, household income, and so forth. What you would find is that about 80 percent of the market for eye makeup is accounted for by working Achiever women aged twenty-five to forty-five. For further pinpointing you could easily determine their distribution by marital status, census region, urban/suburban/rural pattern, and many other factors. At this point you would have rather an exact idea of the size and distribution of the eye makeup marketplace as it exists under current conditions of merchandising and consumer preference. The problem then becomes how to extend this market to other types of Achiever women and to other lifestyle groups. This kind of procedure is equally applicable to products and services as diverse as premium liquors, consumer electronics, air travel, cameras, fashion clothing, gourmet foods, automobiles, and scores more.

Advertising

Resuming our eye makeup example: To explore how best to reach this rather sharply defined consumer group, the advertiser or marketer could return to the VALS data and run some further cross-tabulations on the core group. For example, one might explore reasons for buying cosmetics, favored magazines and newspaper sections, when TV is watched, what types of shows are preferred, types of stores frequented, and, of course, attitudes. It would be possible to enrich the descriptive context by working with properly selected focus groups and by administering various psychological tests and inventories to each of the lifestyle groups. All of this is preparation for selecting themes, ambiances, and media best suited for selling eye makeup to working Achiever women aged twenty-five to forty-five.

Attuning the advertisement perfectly to the consumer is a high art which requires the creative leap from the closely defined target to the ensnaring expressive appeal. Successful leaps are often beautifully simple and very effective. Few campaigns have utilized theme symbology more adroitly than the Merrill Lynch series. The bull symbol, of course, is appropriate for an investment firm. But originally it was a thundering herd of bulls (and somehow everyone heard they'd been photographed in Mexico!). Based upon the insight that the key image of investors is that of the Achiever, two things happened. First, the account changed agencies, and with the change came the Achiever image of "a breed apart" to replace the Belonger symbol of the thundering herd. Second, to follow up on the basic symbolism, a whole series of breed-apart bull commercials were designed to reflect different financial predicaments: There was the bull sheltered in a cave from financial storms; the bull pawing through the snow for grass in hard times; the bull in good times crossing a babbling river to reach the rich pastures on the other side; the bull threading a maze, stalking through a china shop, uncovering a needle in a haystack, and many others.

It is fun and interesting to leaf through a magazine asking yourself which lifestyle group each ad appeals to most. Sometimes the message is scrambled, fractionated. There seem to be partial appeals to several groups, and often the appeals are conflicting. This can be subtle: for example, the ad with slick airbrush artwork and homey copy. Sometimes the ad appeals to one lifestyle—say, Emulators—but the product, according to our data, is really more a Belonger item. By and large probably the fewest errors are made in appealing to Emulators and Achievers, because most advertising people and business leaders are themselves Emulators or Achievers. Almost certainly the most errors are made in trying to reach the Inner-Directeds. This is partly because these types tend to be less responsive to external stimuli, but mostly because their psychology is grasped only mechanically by most agency and business people.

On rare occasion there is an ad that seems to span the lifestyle groups—to be a universal. Such ads tend to become famous. Two examples are the celebrated "I can't believe I ate the whole thing" Alka Seltzer ad and the wonderfully appealing Mean Joe Greene accepting a bottle of Coke from a small hero-worshipping boy. Both of these ads are human ads rather than lifestyle ads. One draws its strength from human frailty, the other from human kindness. These are universals.

Product Development, Packaging, and Design

The kind of thinking that goes into matching an advertisement with the consumer can also be applied in product development, packaging, and design. Again the target audience must be defined in the terms important to the product or service. This will differ enormously: For example, a package designed for prescription drugs is radically different from one for mass household use, and the latter is different from one intended for youthful outdoor sports. Similarly, taste patterns vary greatly with lifestyle groups. For Need-Driven consumers the emphasis should be on simplicity, price, and a sense of direct efficacy. The Belongers respond more to human appeals, warmth, and popularity—the item shouldn't be too "different." A sense of prestige, utility, and efficiency has appeal to Achievers and most Emulators. The "new and improved" attracts them. The Inner-Directeds especially incline toward natural materials, muted colors, and soft technology. Where feasible, as in furnishings or home computers, the Inner-Directeds will be attracted to products they can change or interact with.

The work of matching product to consumer should be done systematically, although intuition will inevitably play an important part. One approach is first to select the important dimensions and then identify their poles. For example, poles defining a given product might include conventional/experimental, involved/remote, stripped-down/luxurious, and cheap/expensive. Each target audience is plotted in these terms, of which there may be a dozen or more. A concentrated attempt is then made to match these consumer profiles with product/package/design characteristics. One user of VALS material employs our forecasts of values trends to profile consumer five years ahead. This is helpful because development of the company's products requires at least that much lead time.

Whether the problem is product development, product design, or packaging, the marketer can probably profit from conducting focus-group interviews with sample prototypical consumers as well as utilizing values and lifestyle data.

Personnel and Leadership

There are least three distinct uses of lifestyle information in the area of personnel. The first relates to how employees may be attracted and retained; the second to matching individuals to jobs so that they will be both productive and happy; the third to building teams.

Values data show not only that the various lifestyle groups have distinctive occupational patterns but that they seek different kinds of satisfaction from their jobs and find their rewards in different directions. Some notes on these matters appear in the earlier section, "Employees."

Given distinctive patterns of work preference, it seems clear that recruiting campaigns, indoctrination procedures, and benefit packages should be different for each lifestyle group. One illustration: To attract and hold the gifted Experiential professional or technical person, some sort of a sabbatical arrangement, probably on a shared-cost basis, would be a potent inducement. But to the Emulator this arrangement would be worse than neutral—it would rob him or her of pay and force unwanted free time upon the individual.

It is no easy matter to match people to their jobs, but the lifestyle perspective offers one approach. The first step is to classify the company itself in lifestyle terms. We all know companies we immediately recognize as Achiever firms, others as Belonger firms, and perhaps a few Emulator or Inner-Directed firms. It's an open question whether the truly Integrated firm yet exists. Further, as we all know, one division in a firm may be Achiever and another essentially Belonger, or some other combination. Having established the overall context of the job in question, one needs to classify each category of job as suiting predominantly one lifestyle or another. Important positions should be individually classified. In reaching these decisions management will want to consider the product or service line involved, the prime customers served, and the tradition of the position.

The endeavor is then to pick an individual of the same personality or lifestyle configuration as the job itself. A one-to-one matching should generally produce high efficiency and a minimum of conflicts. "Upstaffing"—for instance, putting an Achiever or a Societally Conscious person into a Belonger slot—will generate boredom, frustration, and dissatisfaction in the employee. However, upstaffing, if done consciously and openly, may be an excellent way of "upgrading" a job category from the Belonger to the Achiever or Societally Conscious orientation. Further, a company seeking to extend its customer line from, say, outer- to inner-directed consumers will certainly want to consider placing leadership of the new endeavor in the hands of an entrepreneurial inner-directed person, whatever tradition has been. "Downstaffing" (the opposite of "upstaffing") is much more dangerous simply because the job will not be effectively handled, and at the same time the employee will soon become angry and perhaps even rebellious.

This brings us to team-building. The lifestyle perspective suggests that effective leadership reflects lifestyle levels. An Achiever, for example, can be an effective leader for the Need-Drivens, Belongers, Emulators, and other Achievers. But, for the reasons discussed in detail in Part I, Achievers less frequently are effective leaders for the Inner-Directeds. Inner-Directeds as leaders sometimes suffer from a lack of pragmatism and undue responsiveness to issues that are peripheral to the business. Belonger or Emulator corporate presidents may have great difficulty attracting the driving, enterprising Achievers or the Inner-Directeds, and thus are robbed of two sources of gifted employees. This sad situation has been spectacularly in evidence in many an old-line family firm. Yet Belonger leaders may lend stability and balance to hard-driving Achievers or starry-eyed Inner-Directeds.

If management can integrate job/lifestyle matching with the lifestyle considerations of team-building, an exceptionally powerful combination should result. To take the further step of adjusting these balances when entering (or withdrawing from) new fields—whether sales, production, or research—should provide a set of managerial insights available to very few.

Planning

Lifestyle research sharpens strategic planning in several dimensions. For some its greatest utility in strategic planning lies in the guidance it provides concerning social and consumer trends. This input is, naturally, only one of many kinds required by the astute planner, but it is by nature difficult to come by.

In our work in this area we have sought to distinguish several areas of values that the planner should consider. First is the general society: Are the number of Belongers, Achievers, Inner-Directeds, etc., rising or falling? What are the qualitative shifts in what defines the various lifestyles? Are new lifestyles being formed? What trends are emerging or vanishing in the lifestyles? What are the leading cultural paradigms and their countercurrents? Considerations of these sorts comprise crucial elements in shaping the corporate and market environment and hence should be incorporated into any scenario for the future.

Less global than societal values are the trends within the firm's industry. Not often, but sometimes, these are crucial. Few, for example, would argue that the failure of the automobile and steel industries to adjust their values to the modern situation has not been central to industry problems. The paralyzing influence of industry tradition is famous for blocking innovation and stultifying growth.

Still closer in is the tradition and the value structure of the individual firm. Few influences are more powerful in determining corporate policies. It is a factor that new managements find difficult indeed to change for, like the sea in a hole in the sand, it seems always to return to where it was before. And this is why "clean sweeps" are so often required if the company is to be set in new directions.

The final source of values to which the planner must pay attention are the likes and dislikes, stylistic and otherwise, of the individual executives who first must approve plans and then implement them. This requirement is hardly ever overlooked, but it frequently is difficult indeed to ascertain top management's values in useful detail. Planners therefore must sometimes resort to blind submission of a spectrum of ideas and programs and learn from management reaction to these what values seem dominant. From the planner's standpoint this is not only inefficient but profoundly discomforting.

10

Other Nations, Other Values

One of the side spurs of research conducted at SRI International as part of the VALS program dealt with the values and lifestyles of five Western European countries: France, Italy, Sweden, United Kingdom, and West Germany. The overall purpose of the research was to probe how applicable the general approach of values and lifestyles was to cultures outside the United States. If the approach provided fresh insights and understandings when applied to advanced Western nations, we would be encouraged in the years ahead to undertake detailed research on Western nations and to extend it to less-developed nations and to countries not part of the Western tradition.

The findings presented here were developed and set forth by Christine A. Ralph MacNulty and published as VALS Report No. 20.[1] Ms. MacNulty, a British mathematician, economic researcher, and futurist, worked closely with members of International Research Institute on Social Change (RISC) in assessing the distribution in European countries of our lifestyle types and how they resemble and how they differ qualitatively from American versions. RISC, founded in 1978 under the aegis of Alain de Vulpian in Paris, is one of the very few (if not the only) organizations able in a systematic way to compare social trends in some seventeen nations around the world. In her research Ms. MacNulty worked especially closely with the RISC national representatives of the countries under study.

Despite drawing upon superior expertise, it must be emphasized that the research reported here is highly preliminary. Definitive results will have to await specific lifestyle surveys for each country along the lines of surveys conducted in the United States.

OVERALL COMPARISONS

Table 20 compares each of the lifestyle types for France, Italy, Sweden, United Kingdom, and West Germany with the U.S. pattern. We see that lifestyles are qualitatively similar in the various countries for some groups but strikingly different in other cases. Very generally, the U.S. and Swedish patterns appear the most similar, the U.S. and West German the most different.

Comparisons of the percentage of each lifestyle group in the U.S. and the five European countries are given in Table 21. Again variations are marked, Sweden most nearly approximates the U.S. pattern, and West Germany is the most different.

FRANCE

Lifestyles in France have been heavily influenced by the French experience. Until the Second World War France was largely agrarian, with a population divided among small farmers and peasants (the majority), the bourgeoisie, and the aristocratic/intellectual upper classes. Following the war the population divided, though not along class boundaries, into two groups: one anticipated and encouraged modernization, and one espoused traditional values and resisted change. In the mid- to late 1950s the first group was in the ascendancy, and France experienced a period of affluence and a dramatic growth in industrialization. This period, however, turned out to be the briefest in Europe as French conservatism led to mistrust of big business. There was widespread concern with issues of pollution and the invasion by industry of agricultural land in northern France. Industrialization, however, led to a larger middle-class population, which tended to be politically middle-of-the-road; peasants and blue-collar workers followed the Socialist and Communist parties, and the intellectuals embraced a form of idealistic socialism.

Survivors and Sustainers. The upshot of these trends is that there are essentially no Survivors in France in the American psychological sense, although a considerable number of widows and peasants are plagued by Survivor-type economic fears. About 18 percent of the French are Sustainers. Concentrated in rural areas and small towns, they tend to be

TABLE 20 Comparison of European and U.S. Lifestyle Types

	UNITED STATES	FRANCE	ITALY	SWEDEN	UNITED KINGDOM	WEST GERMANY
SURVIVORS	Old; intensely poor; fearful; depressed; despairing; far removed from the cultural mainstream; misfits. NUMBER: 6 million; AGE: most over 65; SEX: 77% female; INCOME: 100% under $7,500; EDUCATION: median, 8th-9th grade.	Negligible number, but attributes as in the United States; some older Belongers and Sustainers share characteristics. NUMBER: <1 million.	Similar to U.S. Survivors; live in northern urban slums. NUMBER: <1 million.	Two categories: an older group similar to U.S. Survivors; a very young group of unemployed school dropouts who are alienated, apathetic. NUMBER: 0.3 million.	Two groups similar to those in Sweden: older group is very similar to that in the U.S. The younger, unemployed, are more aggressive than those in Sweden—form cliques. NUMBER: 3.9 million.	Survivors in a psychological sense, not economic or demographic; fearful, envious, and alienated; concerned about social position, physical appearance; antibusiness; many are women. NUMBER: 5.9 million.
SUSTAINERS	Living on the edge of poverty; angry and resentful; streetwise; involved in the underground economy. NUMBER: 11 million; AGE: 58% under 35; SEX: 55% female; INCOME: median, $11,000; EDUCATION: median, 11th grade.	Old peasant women and retireds; poor; little education; fearful; live by habit; unable to cope with change. NUMBER: 6.7 million.	Aging; uneducated; uprooted from agrarian society; dependent; concerned with health and appearance; escapist. NUMBER: 8.8 million.	Wealthier than others; fearful of children's economic future; concerned with own economic security and pensions; afraid of big government and big business. NUMBER: 1 million.	Working-class values; concerned about economic security; family centered; afraid of government and big business; mainly women; the youngest group is 35 years and over. NUMBER: 6 million.	Sustainers in a psychological sense only; negative feelings toward all aspects of life; resigned and apathetic; avoid risks; high level of hypochondria. NUMBER: 22 million.

BELONGERS	Aging; traditional and conventional; contented; intensely patriotic; sentimental; deeply stable. NUMBER: 57 million; AGE: median, 52; SEX: 68% female; INCOME: median, $17,300; EDUCATION: median, high school graduate.	Aging; need family and community; concerned about financial security, appearance, surroundings, health; able to cope with change, but avoid it. NUMBER: 12 million.	Aging; poorly educated; strongly authoritarian; self-sacrificing for family or church; fearful of change; fatalistic; save rather than spend; reject industrial society and its problems. NUMBER: 11 million.	As in the U.S., but more suspicious of government and big business. NUMBER: 1.9 million.	Two groups: one as in the U.S., with addition of wanting more satisfying work; the other, with traditional values, but more active, complaining, wanting improved quality of life; more concerned about education, creativity, emotions; this group is younger, male. NUMBER: 14 million.	As in the U.S., although wealthier and better educated; more concerned about prestige and social standing. NUMBER: 5.9 million.
EMULATORS	Youthful and ambitious; macho; show-off; trying to break into the system, to make it big. NUMBER: 16 million; AGE: median, 27; SEX: 53% male; INCOME: median, $18,000; EDUCATION: high school graduate plus.	Youthful, but older and quieter than in the U.S.; better educated; entertain at home rather than outside; consider ideologies to be dangerous; concerned about health. NUMBER: 4.4 million.	Youthful; mostly male; highly educated; reject family ties; highly materialistic; insensitive to nature; read more than average. NUMBER: 4.8 million.	Slightly older than others; concerned with prestige; want beautiful homes; prefer quieter lifestyles. NUMBER: 1 million.	Older than others; mostly female; more interested in social status than job status; sacrifice comfort and practicality for fashion. NUMBER: 6.9 million.	Fairly young; well educated; mostly male; conscious about job status and social standing; concerned about physical safety. NUMBER: 3.8 million.

Table 20: Comparison of European and U.S. Lifestyle Types (continued)

	UNITED STATES	FRANCE	ITALY	SWEDEN	UNITED KINGDOM	WEST GERMANY
ACHIEVERS	Middle-aged and prosperous; able leaders; self-assured; materialistic; builders of the "American dream." NUMBER: 37 million; AGE: median, 43; SEX: 60% male; INCOME: median, $31,400; EDUCATION: 32% college graduates or more.	Two groups: older, more mature, similar to U.S.; younger are more intuitive; both groups less materialistic than U.S. Achievers; both concerned about ecology, environment, etc. NUMBER: 7.4 million.	Middle-aged; predominantly female; links to family and religion; indifferent to self-fulfillment from work; want success and prestige, but otherwise escapist. NUMBER: 6.6 million.	As interested in status as in money; save more than U.S. Achievers; buy valuables for their children to inherit; this group is the most middle-class of all. NUMBER: 1.4 million.	Too few to be statistically significant; status is geared not to wealth, but social status; wealthy are heavily taxed, so more become Inner-Directed; older people are unwilling to change and keep up. NUMBER: <1 million.	As in the U.S., although more are politically active and more concerned about the environment. NUMBER: 9.2 million.
I-AM-ME	Transition state; exhibitionist and narcissistic; young; impulsive; dramatic; experimental; active; inventive. NUMBER: 8 million; AGE: 91% under 25; SEX: 64% male; INCOME: median, $8,800; EDUCATION: some college.	Older (20-30); well-educated; contemplative; little concern for financial security, social success, or materialism; enjoy their work. NUMBER: 4 million.	Highly educated; middle- to upper-class; 25-35 age; reject both traditional and consumer/industrial societies; political extremists; live now; bored; take light drugs. NUMBER: 4 million.	Older than in the U.S.; entrepreneurial; self-expressive; concerned about self-improvement; reject drugs and alcohol; seek rich inner and emotional life, warm relationships. NUMBER: <0.1 million.	Too few to be statistically significant; exhibit self-expressive characteristics, but are more Societally Conscious. NUMBER: <1 million.	Older than in the U.S.; find work meaningful and self-fulfilling; want to have an impact on society; have a high level of anxiety; emotional vacuum, looking for ideologies. NUMBER: 7 million.
EXPERIENTIAL	Youthful; seek direct experience; person-centered; artistic; intensely orientated toward inner growth.	Young; predominantly male; highly educated; not fulfilled by work, but by leisure; enjoy the present; hedonistic.	Too few to be statistically significant, although some I-Am-Mes exhibit Experiential characteristics.	Hedonists; risk-takers; crave experience and excitement; enjoy dangerous pursuits.	Highly educated; want excitement and adventure; risk-takers; creative and self-expressive; want meaningful work;	Too few to be statistically significant. NUMBER: <1 million.

NUMBER: 11 million; AGE: median, 27; SEX: 55% female; INCOME: median, $23,800; EDUCATION: 38% college graduates or more.	NUMBER: 1.9 million.	NUMBER: <1 million.	NUMBER: 0.2 million.	want to demonstrate abilities. NUMBER: 5.2 million.	Too few to be statistically significant. NUMBER: <1 million.
SOCIETALLY CONSCIOUS Mission-oriented; leaders of single-issue groups; mature; successful; some live lives of voluntary simplicity. NUMBER: 14 million; AGE: median, 39; SEX: 52% male; INCOME: median, $27,200; EDUCATION: 58% college graduates, 39% some graduate school.	Too few to be statistically significant, although most people have stronger Societally Conscious tendencies than in the U.S. NUMBER: <1 million.	Well-educated; generally fairly young; led by protagonists of 1968 protests; want more education; socially committed. NUMBER: 7.9 million.	Want simpler, more basic ways of life; active in communities; questioning and critical; concerned about physical environment and impersonality of large organizations. NUMBER: 0.5 million.	Family-oriented, young; middle-class; more women; well educated; want personal growth, self-expression, and spontaneity; creative, want meaningful, satisfying work; question authority and technology. NUMBER: 6 million.	
INTEGRATED Psychologically mature; large field of vision; tolerant and understanding; sense of fittingness. NUMBER: 3.2 million.	Psychologically mature; large field of vision; tolerant and understanding; sense of fittingness. NUMBER: <1 million.	Psychologically mature; large field of vision; tolerant and understanding; sense of fittingness. NUMBER: <1 million.	Psychologically mature; large field of vision; tolerant and understanding; sense of fittingness. NUMBER: <0.1 million.	Psychologically mature; large field of vision; tolerant and understanding; sense of fittingness. NUMBER: 1.3 million.	Psychologically mature; large field of vision; tolerant and understanding; sense of fittingness. NUMBER: <0.6 million.

179

TABLE 21
Distribution of the Lifestyle Groups in Europe
(percent of adult population)

	UNITED STATES	FRANCE	ITALY	SWEDEN	UNITED KINGDOM	WEST GERMANY
Survivors	4	0	0	4	9	11
Sustainers	7	18	20	15	14	40
Belongers	35	33	25	30	32	11
Emulators	10	12	11	16	16	7
Achievers	22	20	15	22	0	17
I-Am-Me	5	10	9	1	0	13
Experiential	7	5	0	3	12	0
Societally Conscious	8	0	18	7	14	0
Integrated	2	2	2	2	3	1
TOTAL:	100	100	100	100	100	100

poor, with little education, old, and retired. Women predominate. They tend to be fearful and overwhelmed by change. They live largely by habit, doing the same thing every day and purchasing the same types and brands of goods.

Belongers. In France Belongers constitute a third of the population, distinctly the largest lifestyle group in the country. These people are motivated by the need for financial security, warm relationships, "roots," and a sense of belonging to a family and community. Middle-aged to old, they are often retired blue-collar workers and peasants, with a large population of women, especially widows. Status and prestige are important within their local communities. Most avoid change unless it appears to be to their material benefit, such as making major purchases at supermarkets rather than small shops.

Emulators. Emulators in France make up about 12 percent of the population. The group is a bit older than in the United States and is found among white-collar workers, executives, and professionals. They buy to impress others with their status and are very concerned about personal appearance and health. They are open to new products and technological innovations. Unlike Emulators in other countries, they live in society in a quiet way. They tend to entertain at home rather than spend evenings in restaurants, clubs, and discos, and in this respect they are closer to Achievers than Emulators elsewhere. Nonetheless, they are more spenders than savers, and they regard idealists and ideologies as threatening to their way of life.

Achievers.   French Achievers are similar to the Emulators, though a bit older, more mature, and less focused on pleasure. Driven by the desire for wealth and the need to compete, they also enjoy work and find self-fulfillment in it. Younger Achievers, although still rational and logical in business, tend to be more intuitive than their predecessors of ten years ago. Achievers over forty-five tend to express themselves either through acquisitions rather than through personal relationships, or through scholarly, philosophical interests, again aloof from close relationships. Most French Achievers, who comprise 20 percent of the population, have many Societally Conscious characteristics.

I-Am-Mes.   About 10 percent of the French are I-Am-Mes. The group is older and more mature than the American version. Focused on developing and fulfilling their individual personalities, they tend to be contemplative and keenly aware of their physical and mental well-being. They have little concern for financial security, for social success, or for material goods. Well-educated and hard-working, they are found mainly in Paris and other large cities among students, executives, and professionals.

Experientials.   Presently 5 percent of the population are Experientials. Youthful, well-educated, predominantly male, most are students or young executives bent mainly on improving their bank balances. They enjoy leisure activities and especially hedonistic pursuits, on which they spend much of their money. Their prime aim is to enjoy the moment, taking advantage of all the opportunities that life offers, both emotional and material, without much thought for the future or for financial security.

Societally Conscious.   There is no group of appreciable size in France that much resembles the U.S. Societally Conscious person, although we have pointed out that many French Achievers possess some of these characteristics.

Integrateds. About 2 percent of the French population is Integrated. As in the United States the group is psychologically mature, tolerant, self-actualizing. One segment is relatively young, the other in their middle or later years. Typically, Integrateds have interests that transcend national and cultural boundaries.

ITALY

Italy's centuries-old society, based on deeply held beliefs concerning family, Catholic Church, and the State, began to crack in the 1950s and early 1960s under the onslaught of massive industrialization. People flocked to industrial centers and sought to replace traditional values with political activities, trade unions, and mass entertainment. In the late 1960s a new upheaval brought expectations of faster economic gains together with a new permissiveness and a materialistic way of life. This in turn led to a student revolt against materialism and the Establishment in 1968. Social chaos resulted as three groups—traditionalists, modern materialists, and youthful inner-directed types—all had their moments of political influence, though none could command national consensus. Against this background the lifestyle pattern of 1980 has emerged.

Survivors and Sustainers. As in France, there are very few psychological Survivors in Italy despite widespread poverty. The few that exist are victims of the nation's recent exaggerated industrialization. Most are in southern Italy or are members of minority groups living in the slums of northern cities. These are people whose ties with family and church tend to be weak or broken entirely. In contrast, about 20 percent of Italian society are Sustainers. The group consists largely of middle-aged, relatively uneducated housewives, pensioners, and unemployeds who have lost their links with the traditional agrarian society, including its family and church orientation, through urbanization. They have absorbed only superficially the values of industrial society. Unlike U.S. Sustainers, they are concerned with their health and appearance; they tend to emphasize the romantic aspects of life. In a confused situation, having lost past roots and not yet having developed new ones, these are people who seek to escape through TV fantasy, photo-romance and scandal magazines, and, if they can afford it, alcohol.

Belongers. A fourth of Italians are Belongers. They adhere to the traditional agrarian way of life that was the norm until World War II.

Belongers have strict religious and social beliefs. With a fatalistic approach to life and a belief in Divine Will, they accept social differentiations and hierarchies. Their social interactions are restricted to family (including distant relatives), neighbors, and church communities. They have an ethic of self-sacrifice for the family or church and a strong rejection of hedonism. They believe that women's roles are only as wives, mothers, or in religious orders. This strong need for deep and stable roots causes Belongers to reject industrial society and modern materialism. Most are middle-aged to old, poorly educated, retired workers or farm laborers, and peasants living in small towns or rural areas. They have strong authoritarian values and place much emphasis on ritualistic, repetitive ways of life.

Emulators. Emulators form 11 percent of the Italian population and are a vital part of modern Italian society. They have completely severed their links with traditional society, rejecting family ties and the need for roots, while embracing the values of industrial society. They are insensitive to nature and their own psychological needs to the point of not caring about their health, although they pay much attention to their personal appearance. They are happy to accept sexual liberation but do not accept equality for women. The group is young, predominantly male, highly educated, and middle- to upper-class. Emulators strive for successful careers as a source of money rather than for upward mobility. Nonetheless, their buying patterns tend toward status symbols and leisure goods, including magazines, thrillers, and travel books. They enjoy spending and are not concerned with financial security. Leisure time is spent away from home, with friends, in cafés, discos, and bars.

Achievers. Italy's rapid transition from an agricultural nation to an industrial one has created a class of Achievers with early-industrial values, rather than the late-industrial values characteristic of the U.S. Italian Achievers maintain their links to agricultural, religious, and family traditions, escaping into magic and the irrational through books, soap operas, and films. Even so, they emphasize achievement and material consumption, especially of status goods. Work per se they do not find fulfilling. They tend to be middle-aged, and, surprisingly, women predominate. Education is average. At 15 percent of the population they form a large part of the urban, commercial bourgeoisie.

I-Am-Mes. The group of I-Am-Mes in Italy is close to that in the United States, although older (twenty-five to thirty-five years old); it thus exhibits many of the characteristics of the U.S. Experiential group.

They are from middle- to upper-class backgrounds, very highly educated, and are found mainly in large cities in the north of Italy. Many of the people in this group are divorcees or unmarried couples living together. They seem to be heirs of the upheavals of 1968, rejecting both traditional agricultural and consumer/industrial societies. Politically they are extremists, mainly of the left, but some are right-wing; they like to lead, or to imitate, the life of the intellectual. They hardly ever watch television or listen to the radio, spending leisure time with friends, at the cinema, eating out, or taking part in cultural or political activities. Their attitude is primarily one of immediacy, living solely in the present, ignoring both the past and the future. They are unwilling to take time to develop a job or to develop friendships, with the result that they become dissatisfied with work and people. Boredom seems to be their main enemy, and to combat boredom they use light drugs. Presently 9 percent of the population is in this group.

Experientials.   There is no Experiential group in Italy, although the I-Am-Mes have some Experiential tendencies.

Societally Conscious.   This group is younger than its U.S. counterpart, with many members aged fifteen to twenty-five (in the U.S. this group averages thirty-nine years in age), and is well educated. Some members of the group, particularly the leaders, were protagonists in the student protests of 1968. Although still adhering to many of the criticisms of industrial society made in 1968, they no longer believe in violent methods, but rather in gradual change. They are socially committed and take a very active part in cultural and political activities, particularly those that involve improving the lot of those who are poor, old, and deprived. They are motivated by self-discovery and reject drugs as barriers to that process. Their aims are to be better educated and to travel. Many of this group are teachers, students, and skilled workers; they are satisfied with their lives at work and at home. Many of them have maintained their links with religion and are practicing Catholics. They are modern and rational consumers, tending to reject induced needs but satisfying primary needs and their desire for leisure and culture. Their choice of goods is generally determined by rational criteria, although they can be swayed by advertising that emphasizes nature, genuiness, and youth. Presently 18 percent of the population is in this group.

Integrateds.   An estimated 2 percent of Italians qualify as being Integrated. Their characteristics are essentially the same as Integrated people in the United States and in other European nations.

SWEDEN

During the past 100 years Sweden has developed from a barely self-sufficient agrarian society to an industrial one with the highest standard of living in Europe. To many people it is the ideal combination of capitalism and social welfare, of industrial and postindustrial society. At the start of the last century Sweden's population was mostly self-sufficient, providing for themselves by farming, fishing, and hunting. Then overpopulation, accompanied by shortage of agricultural land and food, resulted in large-scale emigration to the United States. Farming was abandoned to the extent that today only 5 percent of the population works on the land. Entrepreneurs, craftsmen, merchants, and manufacturers have flourished, especially with the growth of urbanization. As people flocked to the urban areas, employment problems became critical, because most of them had abandoned their self-sufficient farming and had no resources to support themselves. At first the wealthy tried to handle the redistribution of wealth themselves, by contributions to charity and various programs for assistance. Although this was beneficial, it could not meet the increasing welfare needs, so the government assumed the function of redistribution of wealth.

The welfare system that has developed in Sweden is one of the most comprehensive in the world. It is this emergence of a welfare state that has led to a fundamental change in attitude toward the individual's responsibility for himself and his and other people's livelihoods. By the 1960s and 1970s incomes and standards of living were regarded as being the highest in Europe, although differences in level of income, social status, and educational achievements did not vary radically from those of other countries. Sweden became renowned for its innovations in new and permissive lifestyles and for the success of its social policies.

In recent years government regulation and legislation have increased in an effort to give everyone equal rights and benefits. The legislation regarding production control, the environment, employee participation in decision-making, increasing taxes, and workers' rights to pensions and other social benefits has reduced the attractiveness of entrepreneurship and has eroded desire for individual growth and development. Young people today are asserting that the maintenance and growth of a high standard of living are part of their rights, but are society's responsibilities, not theirs. At the same time young people seem to be adopting a stricter morality in terms of their attitudes toward treatment of criminals, sexual permissiveness, and use of drugs, alcohol, and tobacco. However, this is not seen as a reversion to traditional Puritan ethics, but as a movement toward new inner-directed values.

Survivors and Sustainers.   There are no Survivors in the economic sense, though about 4 percent of the population are Survivors in a psychological sense. These are divided between young people who have just left school or university and older people, often widows or retired, who can no longer cope with life. They have become alienated by this society, which has taken away responsibility to the point where they have no idea of what personal responsibility is (in the case of the young) or have forgotten what it is (in the case of the old). They are apathetic, showing no interest in, or responsibility for, anyone including themselves. They rely on the State for material welfare and believe that it is the function of society to look after them in all respects.

In Sweden Sustainers constitute 15 percent of the adult population. They have characteristics that are almost identical to those of the same group in the United States. Motivated by economic security, they plan their purchases very carefully and apply for all the social benefits to which they are entitled. A good pension is an important goal for them, one of the main requisites of a job. Sustainers are afraid of the government and big business, believing that they cannot be controlled or trusted. Because of this they believe that their own and, perhaps more importantly, their children's future cannot be anticipated, particularly from an economic point of view.

Belongers.   Belongers form 30 percent of the Swedish adult population. They have almost identical characteristics to their counterparts in the United States. Middle-aged to old and low to average in education, they live in small- to medium-sized towns and rural areas. They have traditional values, not as agrarian or church-centered as in Italy, but still with the need to conform and to belong. They are very family-centered and, like the Sustainers, work to earn money for the family— to save rather than spend. Not as fearful as the Sustainers, nevertheless they regard government and big business with suspicion.

Emulators.   In Sweden Emulators constitute 16 percent of the adult population. They are a little older than their counterparts in Italy and the United States. They are concerned first with prestige and second with appearance. These Emulators are particularly desirous of beautiful homes, and they do not live solely in cities; they have diverse places of residence. Although they enjoy outside activities, they are more like the French in preferring a quieter life with less excitement than the Italians.

Achievers.   Achievers, 22 percent of the population, are the most middle-class and the most successful economically of all the groups in the typology. Unlike their U.S. counterparts, who are concerned about improving their social status along with their wealth, the Swedish group wants only material success and the wealth it brings. Although they spend much of their wealth on consumer goods, their home, and their appearance, they save more than their counterparts elsewhere because they are more concerned about leaving an inheritance for their children. This is reflected also in their purchases, which are sufficiently durable and of long-standing value to be passed on to their children.

I-Am-Mes.   The I-Am-Me group is only 1 percent of the adult population in Sweden and, again, tends to be older and more mature than the same U.S. group. They are entrepreneurial, self-expressive, and are concerned about self-improvement, both intellectual and physical. Seeking a rich inner-directed and emotional life, these people reject drugs and alcohol, believing that they are barriers to an inner life. Contentment is seen as being a requisite for inner growth, and thus there is a new desire for coziness, warm relationships, and a simple, healthy life. These latter desires apply to all the Inner-Directeds and to some Outer-Directeds who are concerned with inner growth.

Experientials.   Experientials constitute 3 percent of the population. In a nation that presently is adopting a more moralistic way of life, these people are the hedonists. They crave experience and excitement and become bored with everyday work and living. They are risk-takers and enjoy dangerous pursuits such as hang gliding.

Societally Conscious.   The Societally Conscious, 7 percent of the population, wish to get away from modern technology and back to a simpler, more basic way of life. This group is the most concerned about pollution and conservation of energy and resources, and it is most actively involved in the everyday life of the community. They are concerned about the size and impersonality of government organizations and business. Questioning and critical, they are skeptical and suspicious of experts. In some respects this group exhibits characteristics similar to the Type 2 Belongers in the United Kingdom, although on balance they are more Inner-Directed. Although the result of the 1980 referendum on nuclear power, endorsing the building of such plants, is seen by many as a swing away from environmental concern and similar issues, this group is attracting new adherents, particularly among young people.

Integrateds.   At 2 percent of the population the Integrateds of Sweden appear very similar to Integrateds in other countries.

THE UNITED KINGDOM

At the beginning of the 1950s the United Kingdom was still coping with the aftermath of the war; rationing continued in force and austerity prevailed. By the end of that decade the country was in the midst of an unprecedented peacetime economic boom that provided economic and social stability for almost everyone. It also led the public to expect continued economic growth, particularly because technological developments were occurring at an unprecedented rate, improving productivity and creating new markets.

By the early 1960s the United Kingdom, along with most European countries, was affected by "a new order" emanating from the United States. What are now called "new values" developed—growth of feminism and individualism and the start of the inner-directed values, which have now become accepted and integrated into British society. The United Kingdom did not experience the same degree of social turmoil as other countries, particularly France, Italy, and the United States. Student protests were hardly in evidence during the 1960s, except for the occasional sit-in at a university, and there were none of the violent riots experienced elsewhere. Britain appeared to be an innovator culturally and socially, a country where trade unionism and welfarism coexisted peacefully with productive industry and entrepreneurial activities. It is still recalled with nostalgia as a golden era—the swinging sixties. Yet the seeds of the social and economic despondency that appeared in the 1970s were already sown. The 1960s was a decade of lost opportunities: failure to enter the European Economic Community; failure to revitalize aging industry; failure to reform the trade-union movement; and failure to defuse the growing conflict in Northern Ireland.

When the oil crisis occurred in 1973, the United Kingdom was already experiencing economic and social malaise; industrial unrest was present as a response to, and a contributing factor to, the increasing rate of inflation. Imported inflation and the simultaneous booms and slumps in many nations throughout the world added to the United Kingdom's economic problems and further slowed economic growth. Having lived through the decade of economic crises, and after the initial shock of adjustment to a stagnant economy, Britain appears to be coping with a society that is no longer economically or socially preeminent. The realism with which the British approach situations is apparent in many areas: wage bargaining; disenchantment with, but cynical acceptance of, political promises; and the ability of the young to cope with the prospect of prolonged unemployment. Surprisingly, at a time when preoccupation with job security and pay might be expected because of rising unemployment and economic decline, there is nevertheless growing emphasis on nonmonetary benefits such as improved working conditions or greater opportunity for advancement. Work is regarded increasingly as a source of satisfaction and fulfillment in itself; paradoxically, however, the absence of work does not necessarily mean a lack of satisfaction, as this is sought also in leisure activities.

People also seem to be finding satisfaction through identifying with, and participating in, small institutions and communities. This is seen in a variety of ways: the association with ethnic groups; re-creation of "village atmospheres" even within major cities; and community and self-help groups. Although the United Kingdom does not seem to have found a role among the nations of the world, within the country itself people are beginning to establish new roles spontaneously as a reaction to, and means of dealing with, the socioeconomic despondency. At the same time political swings seem to be especially rampant, including fractionalization of established groups and the emergence of new parties. Despite broad trends toward noneconomic job benefits, many, especially youths, seem to be expressing dissatisfaction with unemployment and inflation, sometimes in such dramatic ways as urban riots.

Survivors and Sustainers. Survivors form 9 percent of the adult population. As in Sweden, they are divided between the very young and the old. The numbers of young people in this group are increasing, probably as a result of increasing teenage unemployment. Generally they have left school at age sixteen and have either been unable to find jobs or are uninterested in work. As individuals they are apathetic and resigned. Unlike similar people in Sweden, they tend to form cliques or gangs with strong internal cohesion: punks, rockers, and skinheads. Within the "safety" of these cliques and gangs, they exhibit strongly aggressive traits against other cliques and gangs, although not against society in general. For instance, it is not unusual for knife fights to erupt between punks and skinheads; yet one skinhead, already on a police charge of knifing someone from another gang, rescued the driver and several passengers from a crashed underground train.

Older Survivors are motivated by basic financial and security needs. They are antimaterialistic, antitechnology, and have no interest in environmental concerns. They conform to traditional values and are against the "new permissiveness." By U.S. standards they are younger than most, starting at forty-five years, and are equally divided between men and women. They have little education and are generally unemployed, or retired, or nonworking housewives, many of whom are widowed, divorced, or separated.

Sustainers constitute 14 percent of the population and are people who identify most strongly with traditional working-class values. They believe that upward social mobility is impossible for them; that the main problem with their country is social discrimination; and that there should be a more equitable distribution of wealth. In some respects they have characteristics that are closer to U.S. Survivors than Sustainers, including a belief that money is the most important goal in life, followed by security. Another characteristic is that they have limited foresight and live for today. They have a functional or practical approach to purchases, but do not plan their purchases according to a careful budget. As in Sweden, they are family-centered and against government and big business, particularly if it smacks of technology. The most surprising characteristic is their age: at thirty-five plus, it is the youngest group of Sustainers in Europe; females predominate, and most are nonworking housewives.

Belongers. Belongers form 32 percent of the adult population of the United Kingdom. The majority of this group are married, lower-middle-class people, of low to average education. They are generally younger than their other European or U.S. counterparts and can be classified into two types of Belongers. Type 1 is the typical VALS Belonger: passive, oriented toward traditional and family values, and with an overwhelming desire to conform. This group, 19 percent of the population, is concerned about the future and is materialistic and self-sacrificing for the benefit of the family. It is the group most concerned with planning and saving, working for higher pay and more security, although the people would like to have satisfying and interesting work. The males in Type 1 are fifty-five years plus; the surprise is that the females are twenty-five to thirty-four years old. Type 2 Belongers, 13 percent of the population, are active and are the most vociferous and complaining group. Except in their particular areas of concern they are very conventional and conforming—typically Belonger in the nature of their psychological makeup. They have very conservative lifestyles and adhere rigidly to traditional sex roles and family orientation. However, this group is very skeptical about the integrity of large organizations—business, government, and the media. The group is concerned about improving the quality of life, going back to nature, simplifying life, making use of technological developments (while ensuring that the environment will not be spoiled or resources wasted). They also believe that education, examination of one's actions and feelings (a greater emphasis on awareness, emotions, creativity), and interesting and meaningful work will also improve the quality of life. These Belongers are also concerned with physical improvement. Mostly male, the surprising characteristic is their age—from thirty-five upward.

The most likely explanations for the age differences and dual types are twofold. First, the United Kingdom has long been renowned for its tradition and conservatism, characteristics that have continued to place women in roles of wife and mother, working only to supplement the family income. Secondly, another characteristic is the insularity of the British, which makes them unwilling to change or to try new experiences. These characteristics are held by a wide range of the population, differing in age, educational levels, and social class; thus there are younger Belongers and societally conscious Belongers.

Emulators.   Emulators form 16 percent of the population. As with Emulators in other countries they are very status-conscious, materialistic, ostentatious, concerned about physical appearance. Unlike the other Emulators, however, they tend to be older and are predominantly female. In terms of work these differences are manifested in different behavior patterns, because most Emulators are very career oriented. In the United Kingdom career motivation is more for upward social mobility and does not involve job position—except for the male Emulators, who are mostly offspring of Need-Driven and Belonger families. They are willing to be uncomfortable to look better, to sacrifice comfort and practicality in the home for fashion and beauty. They claim no economies, spending their money freely to maintain their position and their lifestyle. Yet they assert that what is most lacking in their lives is money. They are not concerned with social issues unless personally affected and would prefer to see higher unemployment rather than price increases.

Achievers.   In the United Kingdom the Achiever group is too small to be statistically significant. There are several reasons for this. Social status is more a matter of lineage than of success or wealth; although upward mobility is possible, people often are not willing to pay the price—having to leave family and friends behind. An example of this is a very successful and wealthy businessman who feels he can no longer return to his old neighborhood or even to go to a pub on the Mile End Road in London to drink with his old "mates" because they will not accept him. Thus this type of person prefers to remain an Emulator or a Belonger.

Other people who by virtue of their social standing could be classified as Achievers have often had to retrench and become Belongers, either because of financial hardship or because of unwillingness to change. Finally, the high burden of taxes on the very successful and wealthy has increased the number who are becoming Inner-Directed; those small numbers of Achievers who remain (but are too few to be identified from survey data) have strong inner-directed tendencies.

I-Am-Mes.   The United Kingdom does not appear to have a group of I-Am-Mes. There is a group that exhibits some of the self-expressive characteristics of U.S. I-Am-Mes, but they have more Societally Conscious tendencies and therefore have been classified under that heading.

Experientials.   Experientials, 12 percent of the population, are concerned with seeking novelty, excitement, adventure, and experience—even if these activities involve personal and physical risks. They welcome change for its own sake and are pro-technology to the extent that it offers new experiences. They strive for a greater awareness intellectually and sensually and prefer to behave spontaneously rather than habitually. This group wants to be creative, to express their personality and individuality, and to have meaningful work. Opportunity to demonstrate ability and opportunities for advancement are critical factors in their choice of jobs; at the same time they feel a lack of security and an inability to succeed as quickly as they would like. They subscribe to the new values but still see leadership as requiring undue macho masculinity. Predominantly male, this is the youngest and best-educated group in the U.K. typology.

Societally Conscious.   Societally Conscious people, 14 percent of the population, are largely concerned with personal growth and fulfillment through self-expression. They have a strong need for personal freedom, physically and mentally, and a concern with intangible values. They seek to express themselves as individuals, not caring what others may think and rejecting any structure of their lives in favor of spontaneity—which are I-Am-Me characteristics. They are not concerned with appearance or with expressing themselves through material acquisitions; they value personal creativity and meaningful, satisfying work, being in touch with their emotions, and recognition of their motivations. The individual comes before the family, and traditional values are rejected in their belief in equal opportunities, questioning of authority, the value of technological developments, and concern about all social issues. They would rather see price increases than high unemployment and would accept wage restraints to combat inflation. Opportunity to demonstrate ability in a job is a most important requirement, and they are quite willing to see a complete reversal of sex roles in wage-earning and homemaking. This group has a higher proportion of women than men, is generally under thirty-five years old, middle-class, is above average in education, and has a higher proportion of singles.

Integrateds. Estimates for the number of Integrated people in the U.K. are 3 percent of the population—the highest fraction of any nation we have studied. Qualitatively, English Integrateds are the same as those in other countries.

WEST GERMANY

From a basis of almost total destruction, living on minimal resources, the whole nation experienced a *Wirtschaftswunder* (economic miracle) and reached a peak of affluence in less than thirty years following the end of World War II. Many of the social trends in West Germany can be understood only against this background. From practically no functioning industries at the end of World War II, a major industrialized power developed in a relatively short period of time. Unlike Italy, where apparently similar growth took place during the same time, the changes were not traumatic, because West Germany had been industrialized before the war—many of the prewar capitalist families resumed these roles after the war—and therefore did not have to develop from an agrarian society.

Jobs were created, and people could support themselves. Differences in social classes, partly eliminated by the war, were never clearly established again, unlike in the United Kingdom. Overall affluence created a large middle class. People proudly identified themselves with the growing West German industry, and even student protests about big business and multinational corporations in the 1960s and 1970s could not overcome the perceived need for increasing affluence and full employment. Recently, increasing confidence in West Germany's economy is a result of its pride in its industry, in the strength of the mark, and in the popularity of West German goods abroad.

Stability based on affluence, however, does not always imply psychological stability. Attitude surveys have shown that the strong confidence West Germans have in their affluent society is accompanied by a constant feeling of uneasiness, including latent fears, social envy, and apathy in about 60 percent of the population. There are several reasons for this: fear that their affluence will not continue; fear that minor rises in inflation presage the inflationary disaster experienced twice before in this century; fear that the apparently workable democracy developed after World War II will not continue to work; fear among the young that the developments in the late 1920s and early 1930s (in particular, the economic chaos with high inflation and unemployment), leading to the rise of Nazi power and World War II, could occur again. In addition there is the ever-present fear of the U.S.S.R. and the fear that U.S. international policies may become naive, ineffective, and unreliable. Moreover, in society in general there is concern about the falling birth rate, an aging society, and the effect of this on the viability of the social security system. There is concern also about the West German-born offspring of the *Gastarbeiter* ("guest workers" imported particularly from Turkey) being unwilling to support an aging West German population. These fears are played upon, possibly even exacerbated, by political parties, especially in election years.

People find it more comfortable to externalize their fears into some identifiable threat; for many West Germans the Russians, or East Germans as tools of the U.S.S.R., are such a threat. Among younger people, who have only recently been exposed to the history of World War II, a morbid interest in the Nazi period has developed, perhaps because their parents and elders will not talk about it. Afraid of becoming too right-wing and being accused of Nazi sympathies by their peers, they are also afraid of becoming too left-wing and hounded by the right-wing Establishment, of which industry is a part. This has led to a sense of apathy and resignation among the young—a potentially violent state that could be sparked by something to which they respond emotionally. Nevertheless, despite these fears it must be remembered that West Germany is perhaps the most middle-class society in Europe today.

Survivors and Sustainers.   The high standard of living and general level of affluence in West Germany preclude the existence of Survivors in an economic sense (as in the United States). However, data suggest that as many as 11 percent of the population are Survivors constrained by psychological circumstances. They are fearful about their place in society, envious, and afraid that society is no longer stable and that their position may change. Because of this they tend to exaggerate their social positions; they behave as extroverts and are very concerned about physical appearance, going to great lengths to enhance it. The majority of those in this group are women, generally nonworking, who are antibusiness and antiadvertising.

West Germany does not have any Sustainers in the economic, U.S. sense, but it has a surprisingly large proportion of people who exhibit the psychological characteristics of Sustainers. The group has increased rapidly during recent years to its present level of 40 percent of the population. The latent fears of the population, mentioned in the historical-background section, are the cause of the increase, and this trend is likely to continue. The people in this group are predominantly female (60 percent of the group). Sustainers come from all walks of life and span all educational levels. They are concerned about personal appearance and health, suffering from a high level of hypochondria. They have negative feelings toward all aspects of life and are resigned and apathetic, believing that they can have no influence on the future.

Belongers. Only 11 percent of the West German population are Belongers. They have the typical VALS characteristics: middle-aged to old, predominantly female, very much conformist. They adhere to the more traditional values and beliefs and are loyal to their families and friends. While drifting through life, not needing to work too hard or to be self-sacrificing because they are economically better off than their other European and U.S. counterparts, they are more concerned about prestige and standing. It seems likely that this is the group that has lost the most members to the Sustainers during the last few years, as they have aged and grown more fearful.

Emulators. West Germany has the smallest percentage (7 percent of the population) of Emulators in Europe. Predominantly male, fairly young and well-educated, they are very conscious of status. Like other Emulators they are concerned with their physical appearance; but unlike those in other countries they are concerned about their personal safety, particularly if their appearance could be harmed. Thus they are not so likely to drive fast cars or to take other forms of risk.

Achievers. Among the West German population 17 percent have characteristics that are almost identical to those of the U.S. Achiever. West Germany is one of the few European countries where social standing is dependent upon success and wealth, because class differences almost disappeared after World War II. The major differences are that West German Achievers are generally politically active, unlike those in other countries, and they have a stronger social conscience, particularly about the physical environment. They are sufficiently flexible to be good problem-solvers and troubleshooters, but they tend to resist change unless they feel that the change will become accepted as a new norm.

I-Am-Mes.   The only Inner-Directed group in West Germany is I-Am-Mes, although they also exhibit some Experiental and Societally Conscious tendencies. Older than their U.S. counterparts by about a decade, they are equally divided between the sexes and tend to be divorcees or single people. Their occupations are meaningful and self-fulfilling, and their major desire is to make an impact upon society. Unlike the I-Am-Mes elsewhere they have a high level of anxiety, feel emotionally empty, and need leadership. They are ready for change and embrace it willingly, only to find that they are still dissatisfied. They continue to create their own lifestyles without reference to outside or traditional norms. Presently 13 percent of the population is in this group.

Experientials.   There is no Experiential group in West Germany, although some of the I-Am-Mes exhibit Experiential tendencies.

Societally Conscious.   There is no Societally Conscious group in West Germany, although, as in the case of the Experientials, some I-Am-Mes share Societally Conscious concerns.

Integrateds.   We think that perhaps 1 percent of West Germans are Integrateds. As in other countries, these people are marked by exceptional psychological maturity, tolerance, and self-actualization.

PART
IV

SOCIETAL PATTERNS AND THE FUTURE

11

Patterns of Societal Change

Those of us who are optimists see human change as an irregular and faltering upward spiral through the lifestyle stages. It is progress beset by many wrong turns. Sometimes cultural setbacks last for centuries, as in the extinction of the glory that was Greece. Sometimes the sudden decline in levels of maturity is mercifully brief.

In the background of psychological progress usually lies economic and social prosperity. Most but not all surveys[1] suggest that economic well-being tends to accompany overall levels of happiness and that happiness tends to accompany psychological maturity. This is not to say that the people in so-called poor countries are inevitably less happy than citizens of wealthy nations. This definitely is not the case in nations lacking a money economy and free of psychological dependence upon money in its modern forms. But it does tend to be true of economically developing and advanced nations whose members often apply wealth as a yardstick of success.

Our guess is that the human race moves slowly up the values and lifestyle typology as a consequence of its inherent instinct toward development coupled with the staggering increase in the opportunities available for growth that civilization has brought. Consider that only 100 years ago in most of the United States people were born, lived, and died in a circle of fifty miles or less in diameter. In many nations a trip of fifty miles took one to regions where the language was incomprehensible and customs were foreign. Communications other than face to face hardly existed. Consider the opportunities for education, for world knowledge, for meeting people under such circumstances. With luck an individual might meet, say, fifty people suitable to marry. Important friends, chances are, would be pretty much all shaped by similar forces. And so on. The upshot was that individualism inevitably was unable to blossom, unusual talents went unused for a lifetime, and opportunities to grow beyond practical and often preordained roles usually shrank to negligible proportions.

This particular kind of limitation has been vastly ameliorated in the past century by economic and social progress. And with that, we suggest, the human possibility has sprouted like a supernatural potato. The liberating power of economic advance was no where more evident than in the 1960s, when the offspring of successful and prosperous parents introduced Inner-Direction on a massive scale to the American scene and to highly developed nations throughout the world. We look for different kinds of leaps forward to occur in the years ahead.

If the long-term trend in lifestyles continues upward—that is, barring catastrophic reversals in cultural and economic affairs—what will be the patterns of societal change? In what follows we have tried to characterize at the broadest level how and why values change in societies.

THE RHYTHMS OF SOCIETIES

Modern analysts of social change, such as Davies[2] or Johnson,[3] emphasize the role of frustrated expectations—that is, unfulfilled values. Classic macrohistorians sometimes see in history a rhythmic pattern even more akin to what we mean by changing lifestyles. Toynbee,[4] Sorokin,[5] Spengler,[6] and Quigley,[7] for example, have denoted phases of history—even civilizations—with such words as autumn or spring, sensate or ideational, childhood or maturity, gestation or universal empire. The writings of these historians—like analyses of the progress of an individual—portray societies as evolving from stage to stage, sometimes moving in one direction, sometimes in another. There are those who feel this is an outdated way of looking at human affairs, but to us it provides a useful holistic perspective, although no one could argue that all societies are fully or even best explained by such inner rhythms.

One way of putting these rhythms together is schematically shown in Figure 4. The flow as sketched has the shape of the seasons.

Spring. At this stage the society has emerged from the long "winter of discontent" under the influence of a new set of values and perspectives that seem to solve the issues and problems that plagued the society in winter and held it immobile in autumn. There has been a breakthrough, a shift in paradigms, the emergence of a new creative minority, and a

Open   Optimism

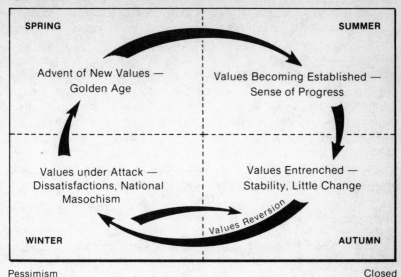

FIGURE 4:
Values Rhythms of a Society

new consensus concerning what is most important. This can be triggered by great events such as victory at war, or it can rise more slowly from the feelings of millions reaching out for a new vision of success and happiness, as happened in the United States of the 1890s and early 1900s. This is a time of high excitement, openness to new ideas, optimism—in short, what might be called a golden age.

Summer. With the passage of the years the glorious freshness of the golden age begins to stale. Ideas that once seemed transcendently different start to become the routines of society and to adjust to the demands of the times. Some speak of the glories of yesterday, but those with longer memories, recalling the stages of winter and autumn, feel a continuing sense of progress. Openness and optimism are still there but are no longer so dominant. The rate of change in people and institutions slows. Politicians and businesspeople pay increasing attention to defensive measures. Parental permissiveness diminishes. Peripheral pleasures—hedonism, sports, romance, status, pride, wealth—loom larger. The days of summer are drawing to a close.

Autumn. When the values so new and exciting in the spring stage have lost their power to move minds and hearts, autumn has set in.

Often this is a prolonged stage marked by rigidity, stability, and rejection of the new. At the same time autumn frequently is a stage of continued success for the society, whether based upon Belonging, Achieving, or some other style. Societal cohesion is likely to be high. Change has slowed to the point where predictions of the future can reliably be based upon the present. It is a comforting, safe, unsurprising time in which to live. So it is, for example, in many a tradition-bound, primitive nation; this style is characteristic of many successful monarchies and dictatorships, of deeply religious societies, of the great Chinese dynasties, and of many much briefer periods of local cultural flowerings. These are times not for the iconoclast but for those of high talent who fit in; they are times that focus on perfection rather than invention, refinement rather than daring, and quietude rather than turbulence.

Winter. Inevitably the calm of autumn is ruffled as new ideas, new values, and new priorities challenge the way things are. At first the dissonant voices are drowned in the societal static. But sooner or later one or another voice will be heard and rebroadcast by people or media closer to the cultural center. It could be a scientist—like Darwin—challenging the beliefs of centuries, or an artist—like Braque or Monet—showing a whole new way of seeing things, or a business leader—like Henry Ford—putting into action an organizational leap forward, or a social leader—like Martin Luther King—insisting on reform. Often the voices of the youthful, the inventive, the restless, and the bored come from many quarters. As the cacophony rises, one of two things usually occurs. The discomfited establishment may move to suppress what is new with whatever means it deems effective. Such efforts can range from the slaughter of millions to wholesale imprisonment to arrest of leaders to mere cosmetic change. Not infrequently, especially in nondemocracies, these reactions create a return to the limited values of the autumn phase. But often, too, such efforts stimulate rather than suppress the mounting dissidence. Dissatisfactions rise, are verbalized in many forms, and ultimately start to penetrate the culture's great institutions—its religions, schools, businesses, and families. Sometimes, as was so evident in the United States in the 1960s, a state of national masochism ensues in which the most cherished traditions of the culture are attacked. From out of this pain and chaos sometimes emerge new viewpoints that develop into new values and new cultural paradigms. This happened in the Golden Age of Greece, in the Italian Renaissance, in the Protestant Awakening, in the Industrial Revolution, in the American Revolution, in postwar Japan—and it is happening today in many a developing country. When the old begins to yield to the new, great changes occur: what was closed and authoritarian transforms to open and permissive, and what was pessimistic transforms to optimistic. In most basic terms what happens is that the cold of winter gives way to springtime, and the cycle begins again.

POWER LINES

A concept important to understanding the apparent swings in lifestyles with the temper of the times is what we like to call "power lines." We have all noticed how national sentiments can shift almost overnight in reaction to local or worldwide events. This phenomenon accounts for swings in political preferences and, on a lesser scale, for trends in fashion or consumption. What seems to occur is that a rather specific idea or perspective gradually or suddenly becomes popular—takes on a fresh element of status—so that it comes into unexpected dominance for some or even for many people. The power line of the idea, so to speak, is dramatically enhanced.

Thus fluctuating power lines are superimposed upon the more fundamental lifestyles of people. For example, pulses of social and fiscal conservatism (or of liberalism) sometimes move through a nation, temporarily changing the emotional timbre of the public as the pulse progresses. A case in point is the wave of conservatism, centered in the Outer-Directeds, that powered Ronald Reagan's election in 1980. Quite often a conservative pulsation is followed by a compensating liberal pulse, such as Kennedy's election following the laissez-faire 1950s. This in turn was eventually followed by Nixon's regime, which in a sense was a return to the initial starting point of the Eisenhower period. This is part of what people mean when they say the more things change the more they remain the same.

It is important to recognize that the ups and downs of the power of a viewpoint are essentially superficial, unlike the change of a society from one set of values to another. It represents, rather, the fleeting ascendancy of one of the many competing perspectives always embedded within some lifestyles. Reverting to our layers-of-an-onion image, a conservative swing could represent the Belonger layer inside an Emulator or a liberal swing could represent the Emulator within an Achiever. To put it another way, the surfacing of the power line of an idea is analogous to a disease bursting forth as the result of the runaway multiplication of germs always present in the body.

In thinking about societal change in the past or in the future, it is essential to distinguish between what reflects undulations in a power line and what flows from the more steadfast and profound evolution of lifestyles.

LEADERSHIP

The role of leadership in changing people and altering values and life-styles is undoubtedly substantial, but it seems also to be exceptionally subtle and elusive. Surely every child is unalterably influenced by the example of parents, brothers and sisters, relatives, and close childhood friends. Among adults such individual influences slacken but do not disappear. For some, great religious, economic, political, athletic, or cultural figures may become personal models for growth. Yet the role of the hero seems definitely to be on the decline owing in part, we feel sure, to the propensity of the media to smash images. The idolized teacher or doctor or boss or even spouse no longer shapes the lives of many. And yet, we think, the role of leadership remains powerful for far more people than recognize it.

Our sense of what has been happening is this: the simplistic, single-entity hero may be vanishing as a guiding light, but taking its place is a fractionated image of perfection. Instead of modeling oneself after, say Dwight Eisenhower or Muhammad Ali or John Lennon or Mom, one models oneself after portions of each of these. As Shakespeare put it: "Featured like him, like him with friends possessed, desiring this man's art and that man's scope." We think this splitting of images is an inevitable consequence of growing psychological sophistication and access to events and personalities from every sector of the globe. An important aspect of this shift is a subtilization of what is admired. Less often is it a clear external characteristic, such as great wealth or great physical prowess, and more often is it an intangible of mind or personality. Admiration for Ali illustrates the point. Although he was a great boxer, he is most admired for his beliefs and his willingness to sacrifice for them. This is in strong contrast to the admiration for Joe Louis a generation earlier. The driving mechanism seems to be that as one becomes aware or fancies that someone else has certain not-altogether-understood admirable qualities, one tries to internalize these virtues in a modern version of "eating the heart of a strong man to become strong."

People who choose intellectual or artistic models seem to operate in the same fashion, although less blatantly. By imitating their model as best they can, they serve to spread and diffuse the influence of the model, after the fashion of ripples spreading from a disturbance in a pond. They themselves often become leaders. This is the disciple mode of leadership, one of the oldest and most effective methods because, with success, the influence of the original model spreads in all directions at a geometric rate.

12

Looking Forward: Toward an Integrated Lifestyle

An important part of the mission of our work at SRI International is to look ahead and to surmise as best we can the "values shape" of the American future. Clearly this is a hazardous undertaking, but, happily, the VALS program was long part of SRI International's Strategic Environment Center, the institution's "futures group." This means we have had intimate access to an extensive body of worldwide research that examines many aspects of the future.[1] However, no matter how encyclopedic the background or what the gifts of individual futurists, we are very sure that no one can foretell what is to come. Hence the intelligent approach is to study plausible alternative scenarios and assess the implications of each. That is what we have done here.

In this work we have tried to be holistic rather than linear, encompassing rather than detailed. In the interest of brevity and clarity we have not thought it wise to document every statement or to explore implications beyond our central concern with values. And, certainly, on more than one occasion we have reached highly speculative conclusions, which we identify as such. We offer no apologies for this because we feel our greatest contribution can be made only if our right brain is much engaged; otherwise, we could not make the leap from what is logical to what we regard as likely. Our thoughts, then, are offered as, we hope, stimulating and useful but certainly not as gospel.

Our approach to looking at shifts in the values of adult Americans is through four scenarios sketching alternative paths through the 1980s. The four scenarios we have elected to examine are:

○ A "Renaissance" future that reflects an extension of many existing trends, but with some crucial discontinuities.

○ A "Bouncy Prosperity" future marked by booming good times and a rapidly growing consumer economy.

○ A "Hard Times" future consisting of creeping, persistent shortages, inflation, unemployment, and lack of economic growth.

○ A "Transformation" future involving a massive shift in the values of Americans toward Inner-Direction and notably a simpler lifestyle.

As a set these four scenarios are designed to give some sense of the range of futures for the United States in the 1980s that we regard as plausible and worth planning for.

A note on plausibility: Some scenarios may be plausible but really cannot be sensibly planned for. Examples include international atomic war, worldwide revolution and the accompanying halt of trade and catastrophic economic depression, massive class-based terrorism in the United States, or wild cards such as the landing on this planet of a spaceship in possession of year-3000 technology.

For each of our scenarios we have provided the basic assumptions that underlie them, the anticipated shifts in the VALS typology, and some of the key social implications.

We have analyzed the Renaissance future in much more detail than the others because its economic underpinnings come closest to representing the status quo extended and hence it warrants particular attention from the standpoint of strategic planning. This does not mean, however, that our Renaissance future is a forecast, since we regard it as altogether unlikely that any single scenario will turn out to be correct over the coming decade. Rather than a forecast, then, we offer four plausible futures with the thought that users of this book will begin by devising planning stratagems to reflect our (or their own) Renaissance economic conditions. The other three futures are designed to indicate maximum plausible shifts away from the status quo trajectory. They provide our judgment of key upper and lower limits to take into account in developing plans reflecting values and lifestyles. In no sense do they exhaust the almost limitless possibilities. Further, aspects of our scenarios may unfold in ways we have not explored. For example, Renaissance and Hard Times might combine into a scenario marked by fits and starts of each and the gradual emergence of an economy that could be called "restructured growth." Our alternative futures, however, should provide planners with a sense of what indicators will best gauge the course taken by the unraveling of events and where contingency plans seem to be needed. Finally—as is not at all improbable—the unfolding future may produce broadly significant trends or events that fall outside the domains we have indicated as plausible. In this event the planner will know that still another scenario must be devised to capture the essence of events to come.

In the pages that follow we first sketch our Renaissance future. We outline the basic economic conditions of this future and proceed to describe demographic and social trends as we think they might develop. This is followed by rather a lengthy discussion of the national "moods" that might accompany such a scenario in the 1980s. Shifts in the numbers of the various VALS groups are then discussed, along with what this means for qualitative trends in values.

The bracketing Prosperity, Hard Times, and Transformation futures are treated in turn, but at less length.

RENAISSANCE FUTURE

The Renaissance scenario assumes for the 1980s a more-or-less straight-line extension of the broad economic, demographic, and social trends of the 1960s and '70s. Our observations concerning national moods and their implications for the coming two decades are much more speculative. Many members of SRI's Strategic Environment Center contributed to the ideas presented here, but the ultimate selection of events is the author's. Although we have suggested the reasoning behind most of our thinking, this book is not the place to go into detail concerning the supporting data.

Economics

This future features real growth in the U.S. GNP (after adjustment for inflation) at a shade under 3 percent annually—not rapid growth, but then again not as low as many seem to anticipate. In 1980 dollars we expect real GNP to rise from $2,630 billion in 1980 to $3,034 billion in 1985 and to $3,500 in 1990. Inflation is likely to average around 7 percent annually over the decade, with higher rates in the first half and lower rates later. The effect will be to cut the value of the 1980 dollar in half by 1990. Personal-consumption expenditures, in 1980 dollars, will expand from about $1,633 billion in 1980 to $1,918 billion in 1985 and $2,210 billion in 1990, for an annual growth rate just under 3.1 percent.

It looks as if the underground economy will continue to expand at rates three or four times higher than that of the measured economy. With high taxes and inflation, incentives to evade taxes through barter or to conduct business in unrecorded cash payments become great. Trafficking in illegal drugs, liquor, prostitution, and gambling are big and growing businesses. Most economists conservatively place the volume of the underground economy at around $300 billion per year— roughly 10 percent of the recorded GNP. (If this seems staggeringly large, consider that the level in Italy is 30 to 40 percent of the measured GNP, and that some observers feel the U.S. level may really be nearly as high!) It is our sense, however, that some trends toward conservatism (discussed later) may blunt the growth of the underground economy.

Energy costs will continue to escalate, but we anticipate no substantial shortages in the decade. Unless technology eliminates large numbers of jobs, unemployment should abate as the number of new entrants into the labor force declines. Women, however, will continue to make up a larger fraction of the work force, though the rate of increase will slow. Worker productivity pretty surely will improve over the recent dismal record. On the international scene we expect a reasonably healthy balance-of-trade figure for the U.S. Even so, the country will become increasingly interdependent with the rest of the world. Indeed, the ratio of U.S. imports and exports to GNP has doubled over the past decade, and this trend is expected to continue throughout the 1980s.

The overall picture here is more favorable than the doomsday futurists portray, yet less bouncy than some hope and prognosticate. In general we think there will be fewer discontinuities and radical shifts in economics than in the spheres of demographics and social trends.

Demographics

Major, if much-heralded demographic changes are looming in the decade ahead. Perhaps least dramatic is population growth itself. The United States population will rise from 226 million in 1980 to 236 million in 1985 and to 247 million in 1990. In terms of age groups the highest growth rates will be in the 35–44 group, followed by the over-65s, and then by the 25–34 cohort. Shrinking groups include, notably, those aged 14–24 and 45–54. An "echo baby boom" will result from the cresting in the prime marriage years of the postwar baby boom combined with a slightly higher birth rate. The fraction of zero- and one-child families will be notably high, with interesting market implications. By one definition the number of households will rise from about 82 million in 1980 to 89 million in 1985 and to 97 million in 1990. Average household size will continue to drop sharply, from 2.75 in 1980 to 2.59 in 1985 and to 2.50 in 1990.

The combination of rapidly rising numbers of households of smaller average size points to major transformations in family structure. By 1990 only 3 or 4 million of the 20 million new households formed over the previous fifteen years will be married couples; the rest will consist of people who are divorced, widowed, or have never been married (i.e., single or living together). In 1990 only slightly over half of all households will be headed by married couples, in contrast to almost 80 percent in 1950. Only 14 percent of all households will consist of married couples with a single breadwinner, in contrast to 43 percent in 1960. This is a picture of remarkably rapid change in the direction of much greater family diversity. And this, of course, will affect both the social scene and the marketplace.

The figures on two-earner families are particularly interesting. In 1977 the average single-earner family had an annual income of about $16,000. Two-earner families with the wife employed full-time in a professional occupation had average incomes of $26,400; those with the wife employed full-time in nonprofessional occupations had incomes averaging $20,000. Net-worth figures and consumption patterns are correspondingly different for these types of households. The market implications of fast-rising household incomes—especially those in the $50,000 and up brackets—are clear and dramatic.

A final demographic trend of major significance is the flow among census regions. Population is expected to rise rapidly in the South and West, while in the Northeast and North Central regions it will hold steady. Growth is likely to be concentrated in key Southern and Western states. In Virginia, the Carolinas, Georgia, and Florida growth could be as high as 20 percent during the decade. In Texas it could be as high as 30 percent. In the West the largest increases will likely be in California, Colorado, and Arizona.

Social Trends

In our view the most important trends of the 1980s will emerge in the social sphere rather than in economics or even demographics– although, of course, all three are intimately intermixed.

Dominating 1980 and 1981 and, we think, at least the first half of the 1980s, is a deep national sense that no one's really in control—a feeling that the economy and, indeed, the society has a life of its own not much related to the past and torn loose from the classic laws that are supposed to govern what happens. This sense of powerlessness flows from almost a decade of inflation combined with unemployment, alternating good and bad times, astronomical interest rates, gyrations in the stock market, and so on—all adding to an incomprehensible and hence dismaying social and economic picture.

Involved is an intense concern by most Americans with the nation's self-image. At one level the focus is on the nation's economic well-being and the tradeoffs required in emphasizing what has been called "reindustrialization" or "economic revitalization" as distinct from the softer issues of "quality of life." At deeper levels underlying this massive concern are such trends as disillusionment with the leadership of essentially every type of institution, loss of faith in the wisdom and expertise of authorities, a dawning realization of the incredible complexity of modern systems and the intricacy of their interconnectedness, and the widespread feeling that things are changing too fast, that people aren't to be trusted, that there are too many regulations and too few principles, that the road ahead is not only rough but blanketed in fog. The sudden advent of a vociferous "moral majority" as a counterforce to widespread hedonism is another sign. The apparent turn toward conservatism among the most youthful of the Inner-Directeds is another. At still deeper levels is what psychiatrist Heinz Kohut calls a "narcissistic character disorder" reflecting family backgrounds that lead to feelings of isolation and disconnectedness.

Many leaders feel that the answer to the American neurosis may be what is variously called "revitalization" of the economic system, or "reindustrialization." The argument is that the U.S. industrial infrastructure is deteriorating and that there are only two long-term options for remedying this state of affairs: Invest in rebuilding it or settle for a lower standard of living. The argument is that the transportation, power, and communication systems need renovation; that major investments are required to find substitutes for foreign oil; that many more resources must go into private capital formation and R&D, because other nations are steadily pulling ahead of us in this regard. According to sociologist Amitai Etzioni[2] a decade of such redevelopment would cost about $650 billion per year, or about 20 percent of GNP. If a "quality-of-life" priority (emphasizing pollution, safety, welfare, culture, and recreation) were to replace the drive toward reindustrialization, the cost might be much less. (Etzioni estimates it at 4.4–6.4 percent of GNP—a figure some observers think is much too low.) Despite this huge difference in costs the weight of contemporary leadership favors reindustrialization, even though many see it as an admission that the postindustrial society is still a long way off. In contrast, writers like economist Robert Hamrin in *Managing Growth in the 1980s*[3] call not for reindustrialization in a past mode (or even if directed toward the so-called information society) but for a wholly new approach to economics, emphasizing qualitative growth rather than quantitative.

Whichever way the reindustrialization-vs.-quality-of-life decision goes, impassioned differences of opinion, perhaps sometimes amounting to national rifts, are likely to result. The reason is profound. The late Angus Campbell, long-time director of the University of Michigan's Institute of Social Research, found in an extensive series of studies called *The Sense of Well-Being in America*[4] that people's sense of well-being stems from a complex array of forces. In sum, well-being depends on the gratification of three basic needs: having (material needs such as food and shelter), relating (love, companionship, solidarity), and being (self-actualization, satisfaction with self). Campbell observed that the U.S. has been entranced with economic indicators identifying only material affluence with "the good life." Material well-being, he says, is losing its capacity to determine psychological well-being for increasing numbers of people. (We would say more people are becoming Inner-Directed.) The point may well be that the nation cannot achieve an economic revitalization without a parallel and comparable "resocialization." Campbell does not feel that the need for material plenty will decline, in view of looming shortages and scarcities, but he also believes the needs for relating and being are likely to become even more important during the balance of the twentieth century. If Campbell is right, and if the nation chooses an "economic revitalization" stance, we are headed for disputatious if not tumultuous times. As a consequence we expect that various national "moods" and "submoods" will come and go, coexist and do battle, in the America of the 1980s. In the next subsection we try to characterize the more important of these.

Moods and Submoods

Our sense of the flow of the American society points to an overarching national mood for the 1980s that will find very different kinds of expressions among the various lifestyle groups. In summary, we see a broad and basic national surge toward what we call "the real thing."

Achievers and Emulators, we think will react to this mood by a response, expressed through the system, involving neoconservatism. Experientials and the Societally Conscious, we surmise, will react more individualistically through artistic pursuits and single-issue politics. I-Am-Mes, in contrast, are likely to have more extreme reactions along the lines of punk rock and a philosophy of nihilism. The response of many Belongers and Need-Drivens, we anticipate, will be to turn more activist in the direction of the Moral Majority.

Such trends, we surmise, will surge and recede for most of the 1980s. This national churning will, however, slowly come to a focus in the 1990s and beyond as a new class of leadership is born among Achievers and, especially, among the Integrateds. This new class will be a kind of person the United States has not yet known: People raised in inner-directed families who switch to Outer-Directedness as youths (just as the children of Achievers today become Inner-Directeds) and some few of whom acquire insights of the Integrateds while still relatively young. These individuals, we hope and believe, will find a way to meld the disparate lifestyle factions into a new coherence. This trend we call, for lack of a better term, "renaissance."

Why do we impute these moods to the 1980s? At heart is the notion that each of the VALS groups will, in its own way, move to take things into its own hands. This is a real phenomenon, not a fantasy. A recent example is the *voluntary* reduction in gasoline usage by American drivers by 8 or 9 percent in a single year. We see voluntary action as the most basic reaction people will have, and are having, to their inability to comprehend the conflicting and confusing social trends sketched earlier. It is a proud and a healthy reaction, drawing strength from national tradition. It suggests—as the polls indicate—that people have more confidence in themselves than in others or in the system. It represents a return to substance over form. It says that the package should not cost more than its contents. Admittedly speculative and difficult to document because no one is yet asking the right questions, we nonetheless find this "mood scenario" plausible and in keeping with the relatively few available empirical clues.

Decade of the Real Thing

What do we mean by a "decade of the real thing?" We mean a shift in mood and values and power lines to seek the down-to-earth, the authentic, the direct, the honest, the unfrilly, the real. It is a rebellion against alienation, mistrust, too much change, too much phoniness, too much that is put on for show, ideologies that are based on intellectual-isms and remote virtues. It seeks to counteract a society marked by fibrillation, fractionalization, and too little sense of its own identity.

We see the "real thing" mood as very broad and with many man-ifestations. Among the Need-Driven it could find expression in a new militancy, which may emerge chiefly in the kind of reactionism we describe later. Belongers will seize it to reinforce tradition and the fundamental virtues as they perceive them. Achievers will exploit it for leadership appeals in business and politics. And the Inner-Directeds will see in this mood confirmation of their experiential and person-centered drives. It will support their impulses toward frugality, the natural, the simple, and the creative. Those patrons of Lady Luck, the Sustainers and Emulators, will probably strive for the real thing more voraciously and dangerously than any other groups, for they, more than others, sense the gap between what is and what they want.

What does a decade of the real thing imply for lifestyles? It implies living by what might be called a "goose-pimple index"—an index that tells you your reaction is genuine. It implies being up front about things and being willing to take the consequences of one's actions. It implies a further decline in the power of mass media and a rise in the power of stiletto media. It implies a drive for significant work and significant personal relationships as a means of overcoming the secondhand and vicarious. More direct living means that most people will be in better touch with themselves—and less afraid of themselves—with all that that implies for personnel, management, marketing, advertising, pack-aging, design, and a dozen other areas of business. It means less intellec-tualism and more emotion. It means women will come into their own more swiftly, emerging more fully as themselves as they drop tradi-tional (mostly male) models of success. It means, most likely, that Americans as citizens, each in his or her own way, will be more willing to do what is required to cope with problems of inflation, scarcities, and ambiguities. But it probably also means more violence and possibly systematic thievery and vandalism by some segments of the population, and this in turn may mean citizen vigilantism and self-arming. In some ways a return to frontier individualism, a decade of the real thing would on balance probably be healthy for most Americans and for the society as a whole, despite the obvious tensions and dangers and conflicts it would produce.

Out of this pervasive mood will come, we think, several distinct movements, each representing the reactions of a different VALS group to the national concern with living by essentials. These are discussed below.

The New Conservatism. Many, many signs point to a gathering wave of new conservatism in America. We have mentioned many such clues earlier in this book, and the daily press is full of further evidence. What we see happening here is the principal reaction of Achievers and Emulators to the "real thing" mood. What are some of the characteristics of this trend toward conservatism as we see it developing during the 1980s?

First, we think one important aspect of the new conservatism results in large part from what might best be called social fatigue* brought about by weariness with battling forces that cannot be pinned down. In addition, however, it gives expression to what Achievers see as plain economic reality—the need for economic revitalization of the existing system. Conservatism will probably slow the rate of change by concentrating on refurbishment of existing methods and technologies rather than invention of the new. More importantly, perhaps, it is likely to change the image of progress to something much less flamboyant and go-go than the nation became accustomed to in the 1960s and 1970s. The trend will probably lead to more insularity, a narrowing of perspective, and a retraction of commitments. Definitions of what is desirable or what can be tolerated are likely to change profoundly, from what is intrinsically good to what interferes least. This points to a more passive, less activist, and less volatile society. There will probably be less interchange among the lifestyle groups and among institutions, less top-down change, less regulation.

Reactionism. A much more negative aspect of conservatism may also come forth during the 1980s. In reactionism the have-nots take the lead. Terrorism, crime, racism, bigotry, and anger substitute for tradition and social fatigue. The key question may turn out to be the levels of violence that occur as part of reactionism. Blockage of progress of the blue collars—not an unlikely prospect in an emerging information-based society—could cause organized and individual responses that may well be severely negative.

We think that three VALS groups are likely to play crucial roles in aspects of this reactionism. Under the economic and social conditions postulated in this scenario, Belongers are likely to have a hard time in the 1980s as their numbers decline, as automation threatens many Belonger jobs, as they drop farther and farther behind technologically, and as many of their values are seen as passé. To overstate it: The '80s will see the decline-but-not-quite-fall of the Belongers. The decade will

---

*We are indebted to James Ogilvy for the invention of this phrase.

be their last hurrah. This last hurrah, we surmise, will take the form of a hardening and narrowing of Belonger values into the most conservative pockets. Something akin to Joe McCarthy Belongerism could emerge. Put another way, the "silent majority" is likely to become more vocal. If this occurs, the trend is likely to be strongly antitechnology, strongly antiprogress, and intensely reactionary.

The time-honored and productive allegiance between Achievers and Belongers is likely to break down, as Achievers tend to move in neoconservative directions and Belongers, instead of being docile followers, move activistically in more reactionary directions. The cleavage will form where the economic values of Achievers come into conflict with the moral values of Belongers. This divisive trend could do a good deal to eliminate the cohesiveness of the middle class as we have known it.

Even more devastating to the health of the society is the role Sustainers could play. It will be recalled that many Sustainers are angry, street-wise, ambitious, and frustrated. They are frustrated because many find no easy admittance to the cultural mainstream represented by Belongers and are forced, if they wish to get ahead, to burrow under the Belongers, so to speak, to the Emulator level. This leaves them psychologically in a fragile state, lacking taproots into the American culture, rejected by the largest and in many ways the most important segment of the population, and forced to play roles for which they are not yet equipped either intellectually or emotionally. We think it not unlikely that Sustainers frustrated in this fashion and with few constructive models at their disposal could become a major force for systematic thievery and even terrorism. Interestingly, some members of Sustainer subgroups, especially those with strong family orientations, will take guidance from their family and ethnic traditions and will not generally respond with violence. These will not seek acceptance by mainstream Belongers but, rather, will maintain their own traditions and hence will not suffer the pangs of national rejection.

Punk, Art, and Single-Issue Politics.   And how will the Inner-Directeds respond to a mood of the real thing? We expect their reactions will be very different from those of Achievers, Belongers, or Sustainers. In fact, the core reaction of each of the three Inner-Directed groups is likely to be unique.

We see the leading edge of the I-Am-Mes as having the most dramatic reaction. Current signs, as identified by Steve Barnett, director of Cultural Analysis at Planmetrics, Inc., point to a "new wave" of attitudes embracing music, fashion, consumption, politics, and personal beliefs. This new wave is most clearly seen in the "punk rock" movement in California and New York. These teenagers and young adults see themselves as an isolated, even beleaguered group. They are anti-natural and reject health foods. They believe both authority and economic growth are irrelevant but feel the system has left them economically disadvantaged irrespective of their personal backgrounds. But they are not politically active. They support technology, especially as it relates to recreation such as music. More than anything, they have almost a sadomasochistic and nihilistic attitude. Many seem to feel that life is a war and the end is near—witness the Talking Heads' song "Life During Wartime" (i.e., now).

The person-centered Experiential group, being more mature than the I-Am-Mes, is likely to respond in less self-destructive ways. As we have said before, we look for Experiential people in the 1980s and 1990s to spearhead a major flowering in essentially all areas of the serious arts. We think artistic expression is a natural development for maturing, sensitive people geared not only to outer excitement but to inner subtlety and the nuance of the situation. For such people, the highest reality is often the deep and private event best expressed through the arts. Significantly, there are and will be enough Experiential people to sustain an artistic flowering, once it has begun, for the Experientials will probably be not only the creators but a major part of the market, too. As Walt Whitman has written: "To have great poets, there must be great audiences, too."

For the Societally Conscious the real thing frequently means intense involvement in economic, political, and social issues. There should be issues aplenty for Societally Conscious people to challenge if neoconservatism and economic revitalization become major trends in the 1980s. Certainly many Societally Conscious people will view revitalization as "backward progress," and they will feel their successes of the past are being threatened. As a result the techniques of single-issue politics are likely to be further refined and perhaps systematized to the point of becoming a permanent national network with continuing issue "headquarters." The 1980s promise to be contentious and tumultuous years for those doing battle with the forces of national economic revitalization.

A possible development of the first importance could be the rapid emergence of entrepreneurship among the Societally Conscious, especially those absorbing some Achiever views prior to acquiring the full Integrated perspective. These people will seek out tasks and businesses they feel are truly worth doing. Money per se will be less important than personal challenge and testing.

Renaissance

From out of the confusions of the 1980s we very speculatively hope that there will come a new order in the 1990s and beyond. The mechanism we foresee involves a new type of leadership that could emerge as the energies of the real thing mood expend themselves. As pointed out in the "Flows" section of Part I, we look for a new type of Achiever to emerge in the 1980s—people with a leadership potential very different from that of conventional Achievers or even of Achievers who are beginning to adopt many of the values of the Societally Conscious. This new type of Achiever will come from inner-directed (especially Societally Conscious and Experiential) families, just as many I-Am-Mes come from Achiever families. Thoroughly aware of inner-directed values, yet no longer convinced that those values lead to the most desirable quality of life, these "new convert" Achievers seem likely to bring an exceptional range of insights and a fresh power of conviction to the fatigued and even jaded ranks of classic Achievers. And we look for this new kind of Achiever, perhaps in the 1990s and surely by the year 2000, to help lead the country beyond neoconservatism and reactionism and punk and art and single-issue politics of the 1980s to what we call "renaissance."

Undoubtedly the forces already are in motion. For the most part, however, the signs are lost in societal static or rendered invisible by forces many times more prominent. So one needs to peer into the crannies of the society to see the signs of a renaissance that we think may cross the nation like the spring—transforming all. We think this transformation may begin in the very late 1980s and continue throughout the 1990s, but it can hardly reach its full flowering until the century to come.

The turning point, we think and hope (and of course we are not alone in either the thought or the hope), will be the emergence of an ideology—a view of what is real and important—that has credibility wide and deep enough to engage the core values of most Americans. Perhaps it is best called a new paradigm that in the deepest sense fills the fissures and holes and discontinuities so many Americans now feel in their personal and work lives. Whether called "renaissance" or some other term, it will give the country a direction and a purpose and a unity so notably lacking today.

Where will this resurgence come from, and what will be its characteristics? In terms of the lifestyle typology we think "new" Achievers and the Inner-Directeds will drive the early stages and that a swelling and different group of Integrateds will take the lead in the 1990s. In that decade we anticipate that enough "new convert" Achievers will have reached the Integrated stage that they can set forth and exemplify the new paradigm to lead the country around the bend from the conflicting moods of the 1980s.

Why do we anticipate this? First, because we think leadership will have to come largely from individuals plus selected firms and communities, not from the central government or large bureaucratic organizations. The remarkable person will be the agent of change. "Thinker-doers" rather than intellectuals or pure pragmatists will be the true leaders. And we see the new generation of Achievers and the new Integrateds as people with these qualities of leadership. Second, by the 1990s and early 2000s we expect the nation to have had enough success that it will, economically and emotionally speaking, be able to afford to refocus attention on nonmaterial aims. In the terms of some historians, this will be a new springtime, a new cycle of "ideation." Third, our computations—given in the next subsection—suggest the fraction of the population holding inner-directed values will reach 33 percent sometime in the 1990s, making them more numerous than either Achievers or Belongers (but still much smaller than the Outer-Directeds as a group). The Inner-Directeds will provide the new Integrated leadership with a potent popular power base.

Finally, what are some of the qualities we think will bring the nation together again? What trends do we surmise will be powerful enough to overcome the divisive moods and reactions of the 1980s as we have sketched them? A few are listed below:

○ Sense of national pride, especially as expressed through individual action

○ Willingness to accept tradeoffs, such as deferring progress in one area that may hinder progress in other areas

○ Decentralization of decision-making

○ Personal involvement with work and national issues

○ Recognition of the contributions and expectations of all stakeholder groups in every enterprise or organization, together with a willingness to share both inputs and outputs

○ Appreciation of other people, other ways, other ideas—of the strengths and weaknesses of both Inner-Direction and Outer-Direction

- Acceptance of many cultures and viewpoints rather than exclusive emphasis on the home culture and viewpoint

- Attention to the spiritual and artistic sides of people

- Awareness of the consequences of acts—as employers, as employees, as consumers, as citizens, as parents, as inhabitants of Earth

- Honoring of the personal, the unique, the mystic

- The ability to be open, direct, moved—to live by the right brain as well as by the left

We are, of course, trying to characterize a society led by Integrated people. Maslow once said he thought a society with 8 percent self-actualizing people would soon be a self-actualizing society. It seems a reasonable figure—every twelfth or thirteenth person. Unhappily, we do not expect the number of Integrateds to reach this level until the year 2000 or beyond. But we see the 1980s with its emphasis on each life-style group doing its own thing, each hypnotized by its own viewpoint almost to the point of blindness, as a final prelude to what could be a sudden rush to the Integrated perspective in the years that follow.

Quantitative Projections

Our estimates of the population in each of the VALS types for 1980 and 1990 under Renaissance conditions are shown in Table 22.

From the quantitative standpoint several points about these projections are central.

- Almost all the growth is concentrated among the Inner-Directeds.

- A decline from 35 to 30 percent of the adult population is anticipated for Belongers—the only substantial negative change.

- Population growth will sustain the absolute numbers of Need-Drivens and Outer-Directeds at about present levels despite shrinkages in percentages.

- Even in 1990 the Outer-Directeds will outnumber the Inner-Directeds by 2.3 to 1. This means that mass markets will continue to flourish, although as a smaller fraction of the whole.

TABLE 22
Renaissance Future: Estimates of Lifestyle Shifts Between
1980 and 1990

	1980		1990	
	PERCENT	NUMBER* (Millions)	PERCENT	NUMBER* (Millions)
Need-Driven	11	17	10	18
Survivors	4	6	4	7
Sustainers	7	11	6	11
Outer-Directed	67	108	60	108
Belongers	35	57	30	54
Emulators	10	16	10	18
Achievers	22	35	20	36
Inner-Directed	20	32	26	47
I-Am-Me	5	8	4	7
Experiential	7	11	9	16
Societally Conscious	8	13	13	24
Integrated	2	3	4	7

*Number aged 18 and over

○ Especially critical for the social scene is the ratio of Achievers to Societally Conscious. The 1980 ratio was 2.7 to 1. By 1990 the ratio is expected to shrink to 1.5 to 1; clearly the Achievers will remain dominant, but less so than now.

○ From a percentage standpoint the fastest growth attends the Integrateds. Frankly, we expect this growth will be largely invisible during the 1980s, but it will leap into prominence during the 1990s. A major surge in numbers is possible, as impressive models of Integrated individuals surface, spurring the conscious switch-over of many people on the brink of that critical psychological advance.

Qualitative Projections

We see the 1980s generally as a period of exaggeration of current value patterns during a difficult period, with spots of intense value change to the point of the emergence of new lifestyles.

Survivors and Sustainers. Improvement in the employment situation—despite more job automation—should be particularly beneficial to Sustainers and to Survivors of working age, but we think it doubtful that the profound anger and even vindictiveness of many members of these groups will abate much because the feelings are based more on relative than absolute conditions.

Belongers. We have already mentioned the maturing—perhaps "overmaturing" is a better term—of Belonger values. We expect that some Belongers will defend their values vociferously (as the Moral Majority shows) and indeed will wax more vehemently traditional. The role of Belongers as the great stabilizers of the American way of life will tend to diminish as they increasingly fall behind the mainstream culture. One of the major questions of the decade is what group, if any, will become the new centerpoint of American values. Just possibly this role will pass to a combination of the more successful Emulators and the less advanced Achievers.

Emulators. Emulators, our guess is, will thrive during the 1980s as the drive toward revitalizing the economy takes hold. In a real way they will grow closer to the Achievers as Achievers and Belongers tend to polarize into quasi-opposed economically conservative and morally conservative groups. The Emulators' nouveau riche aspect and their low social self-assessment should soften in the eighties as their average age rises from twenty-seven to perhaps thirty-two and they find neo-conservatism to their liking. This shift will be truly important if it brings about a new values center (i.e., a new definition of "middle-class") by forming real alliances with Achievers who hold Belonger-type values. If our surmise is correct that Americans on the average are moving up the VALS hierarchy and that Belongers tend to be reverting to a more extreme form of conservatism, it is sensible to expect that the central balancing point of the society will move up from the Belongers to some sort of Emulator/Achiever combine.

It is worth noting that Emulators of the coming decade are likely to be more in the Horatio Alger tradition than any other VALS type. (From one perspective this says that the "values center" of Americans in the 1980s is likely to resemble the Achiever ideal of the turn of the century.) In the past Achievers have outperformed their parents more dramatically than any other group. In the 1980s this attribute is likely to apply more to Emulators, who appear especially well equipped to cope with the negative moods of the decade. However, it is inconceivable that Emulators will displace Achievers as the dominant Outer-Directed Group.

Achievers.   Trends among Achievers have been mentioned earlier. Neoconservative leadership will almost certainly concentrate here. We expect this leadership will embrace a comprehensive agenda not only in economic but in cultural and spiritual matters as well. It will be a vigorous leadership reaching out to touch our daily activities, our modes of doing business, and our most fundamental institutions. We have also mentioned the advent in the late 1980s of a new type of "convert" Achiever, the children of Experiential and Societally Conscious parents. This phenomenon, we think, will produce a new lifestyle not before seen in appreciable numbers in this or any other country.

About 50 percent of Achievers today are more like Belongers than any other VALS type, and 30 percent are more like the Societally Conscious. We surmise that by 1990 this ratio will change to something like 40–40, as successful Achievers tend to draw away from Belongers and toward the Societally Conscious (and some actually become more Societally Conscious than Achiever). As suggested above, the "lower" 40 percent could join values forces with Emulators to create, in a sense, a new values standard for Americans.

The other side of this phenomenon is very different. The values melding of some Achievers and some Societally Conscious people could produce a new "pre-Integrated" VALS type, since such people will be less single-mindedly Outer-Directed or Inner-Directed than in earlier stages, and yet will not yet quite have achieved the depth of blending of viewpoints that marks the truly Integrated person.

Inner-Directeds.   The development of the Inner-Directed group is likely to be especially interesting. The point is not that the Inner-Directeds will grow to be more like the Outer-Directeds, but that a general maturing with the years will enable them to pursue their interests and convictions less flamboyantly and probably more effectively. It means, for example, that fewer will feel the personal need to signal Inner-Directedness by such outward signs as beards, spectacular clothes, and the like. (Yet this will by no means disappear, as the habits of advocates of punk rock show.) It means that growing numbers of closet Inner-Directeds in corporate circles will be free to express their ideas more openly. It means that the political style of the Inner-Directeds will be less confrontive and more subtle as they perfect the techniques of single-issue politics. It means the spectacular attitudinal differences between Achievers and their I-Am-Me children will tend to diminish as it becomes less a requirement to show the split. (This phenomenon is already showing up in the sense that I-Am-Mes tend to be less extreme on some issues—such as legalization of marijuana—than yesterday's I-Am-Mes, today's Experientials. Yet there will be exceptions, as noted above.) It means that men will find it increasingly easy to take up Inner-Directedness despite outer-directed surroundings—again a phenomenon we have noted in the differing male/female ratios of I-Am-Mes and Experientials. More important, the maturing of Inner-Direction as a way of life means that it will gain wider and deeper acceptance by others. Most important of all, perhaps, it means that the experience of Inner-Direction, although less visible, will probably grow deeper, more inwardly rewarding, and more authentic than it ever has been.

We do not take these trends to mean that Inner-Direction will truly be understood by outer-directed people. We expect that denial of its reality and influence will continue, but in more muted terms, if only because the various lifestyle groups will probably live in more emotional isolation from each other during the "real thing" phase.

Integrateds.   A more mature, less volatile inner-directed sector will be conducive to the influence of Integrated people. By 1990, we believe, the Integrateds will be sufficiently numerous, and the "pre-Integrateds" well enough recognized, that leadership based on synthesis of outer and inner perspectives will begin to be seen as the way society in the United States will have to go. And this is a prelude to what we hope will be a flowering of a "renaissance" in the decades to follow.

BOUNCY PROSPERITY FUTURE

If our Renaissance future turns out to be economically too pessimistic, if reality turns to Bouncy Prosperity, projections of the VALS typology would be much affected. By "Bouncy Prosperity" we mean real growth of GNP averaging 4.5 to 5 percent a year, yielding (in 1980 dollars) a maximum GNP of $2,630 billion in 1980, $3,356 billion in 1985, and $4,283 billion in 1990. (Many observers think that this rate of growth is beyond the range of plausibility.) We further assume in this scenario that inflation is brought under control, that international trade picks up resulting in strongly favorable balances, that the energy situation gets no worse, and that problems such as air and water and soil pollution prove to be controllable by technological means. Further, the implication is that social demands (such as those for entitlements) are brought under control, government spending is curbed, and—somehow—

business picks up a major share of the social responsibilities to the disadvantaged. In essence, in this future the fears and worries of the "doomsday" observers prove groundless. The "new economics" work.

Trends and Moods

The surge toward the revitalization of the U.S. economy would proceed with alacrity, with powerful leadership from business and government and with widespread public support. National pride reminiscent of World War II would arise, no doubt bringing with it some isolationist sentiment. "Real thingism" could become almost a cult, penetrating to production processes, merchandising techniques, and management styles. Neoconservatism would be very much in control. The trend toward Integrated leadership, possibly resulting in a new kind of renaissance in the 1990s and beyond, would not materialize.

Bouncy Prosperity would bring busy times of hard work and hard play, less regulation, more competitive business conditions, and good times based on a booming consumer economy reaching down to the least favored segments of the population. The atmosphere would resemble that of the 1950s and the contented years of Eisenhower.

Shifts in the VALS Types

Table 23 shows our sense of how the lifestyle types would shift by 1990 under conditions of Bouncy Prosperity.

TABLE 23
Bouncy Prosperity Future: Estimates of Lifestyle Shifts,
1980 and 1990

	PERCENT IN 1980		PERCENT IN 1990	
Need-Driven	11		7	
Survivors		4		3
Sustainers		7		4
Outer-Directed	67		77	
Belongers		35		35
Emulators		10		12
Achievers		22		30
Inner-Directed	20		14	
I-Am-Me		5		1
Experiential		7		9
Societally Conscious		8		4
Integrated	2		2	

The main trend would be a reversal of the flow from Outer-Direction to Inner-Direction. Bouncy Prosperity is emphatically an Achiever world, so we think the number of Achievers might rise from 22 percent of the adult population today to 30 percent in 1990. Emulators would also increase in numbers. Belongers, instead of losing numbers as in the Renaissance scenario, would hold steady. Their ranks would be replenished by a large influx from the Need-Driven groups, whose proportion of the population would drop by about a third.

The scenario would have complex impacts on the Inner-Directeds. The I-Am-Mes would come close to disappearing because of powerful popular sentiment against "nonreal" and "flibbertigibbet" lifestyles. The Experientials, however, would probably expand in number as prosperity enabled more to do their own things. Their style, however, however, would probably have to change to be less visible and less intrusive. The Experientials would continue to seek much parttime work, but work they would in order to earn money enough to pursue their interests.

We show a fraction of Societally Conscious declining from 8 percent of the population to 4 percent. The reasons very simply are, first, that our Bouncy Prosperity future assumes that many societal issues are being competently handled and, second, that public sentiment is such that the techniques of single-issue politics no longer work. Robbed of many specific issues on one hand and massive public support on the other, we think that the Societally Conscious segment would shrink. However, the shrinkage in numbers would not be overwhelming because the Bouncy Prosperity society would almost surely invade many "quality-of-life" areas about which the Societally Conscious people feel passionately. So many would maintain their convictions even though their political power declined in the face of less popular support.

Table 23 shows no change for the Integrateds. This reflects our belief that Bouncy Prosperity has little to do with the transition to this lifestyle, except that the national mood would be more supportive of Achievers than of Integrated people.

HARD-TIMES FUTURE

The VALS report *Hard Times*[5] provides a fascinating and detailed portrait and analysis of what might happen to U.S. society under a specific hard-times scenario extending throughout the first half of the 1980s.

For our purposes here we have shifted the dates but retained the substance of the argument and conclusions. Our thanks go to the authors of the *Hard Times* study, Marie Spengler and Peter Teige.

The hard-times scenario calls for repeated recessions interspersed with partial upturns, high rates of inflation, and a very small decline in real GNP. The economy would become increasingly erratic and unpredictable, with national unemployment running at 15 percent and as high as 35 percent in certain regions. Average household size would increase as extended families and unrelated individuals band together for economic survival. Crime of all sorts would rise sharply. The underground economy would leap to a third of the GNP. Things would be clearly out of control, growing increasingly unstable.

Trends and Moods

Governmental efforts to avert economic crises would lead to many stopgap measures. Troubled and failing companies and industries would be bailed out through loan guarantees, subsidies, and other government assistance, but at the price of more government control, some of which would amount to quasi-nationalization. There would be a strong demand for more centralization of governmental functions and for big "action" programs designed to solve social problems. The federal bureaucracy would expand once again. It would become pathetically clear that efforts to revitalize the economy have failed. Traditional past-oriented conservatism, not energetic neoconservatism, would be in full swing. The notion of a major move toward Integrated leadership and a national renaissance would seem ridiculous. Indeed, trends would be in the opposite direction, as the nation became less of a "melting pot" and more disdainful of diverse views.

This is a portrait of a nation shriveled into a defensive posture. Along with a compression of values would come pockets of militancy and a sort of Sustainer/Belonger "wash" over the whole of society. Almost everyone would give increased attention to job security, cost of living, and risk avoidance. There would be an increase in basic fear, insecurity, anxiety, dependence, rigidity, compulsiveness, and desire for forceful leadership and for law and order. The Belonging orientation would be evoked by an increased need and desire to group together for mutual support, aid, and comfort in the face of economic adversity. This would be accompanied by increased traditionalism, conventionalism, sense of duty, sentimentalism, conformity, and making a virtue of sameness and fitting in. Closed-mindedness would increase. Isolationism and protectionism would grow. There would be greater suspicion of outsiders and a greater need for recognition and a sense of membership. Links with primary associations—family, relatives, co-workers, company, and neighbors—would be strengthened.

Shifts in the VALS Types

Table 24 shows our estimates of shifts in the lifestyle typology under hard-times conditions. The three dramatic changes are the huge increase in the number of Need-Drivens, the huge decrease in the number of Inner-Directeds, and the elimination of Emulators and I-Am-Mes as groups.

Our thinking, type by type, is as follows:

Integrateds.   These people are mature, balanced, and well-equipped to cope with changing circumstances. Their increase in hard times would be a response to challenge and crisis-induced maturity. The Integrateds would wind up relatively well off.

Societally Conscious.   Most likely of the inner-directed groups to thrive, marked as they are by little unemployment, professional-technical training, multiple careers, diverse skills, and good connections. In general an adaptable, creative, innovative group. The Societally Conscious are likely to be influential in developing responses, organizing, and leading. Many would take government jobs and be active in programs aimed at solving societal ills. Relatively well off. Small increase in percentage.

TABLE 24
Hard-Times Future: Estimates of Lifestyle Shifts,
1980 and 1990

	PERCENT IN 1980		PERCENT IN 1990	
Need-Driven	11		25	
Survivors		4		13
Sustainers		7		12
Outer-Directed	67		60	
Belongers		35		39
Emulators		10		1
Achievers		22		20
Inner-Directed	20		12	
I-Am-Me		5		0
Experiential		7		2
Societally Conscious		8		10
Integrated	2		3	

Experientials.   Being less stable and more dependent on financial security, many Experientials would be likely to revert to family values of achieving or belonging, or to make commitment to Societally Conscious lifestyles. Big drop in percentage.

I-Am-Mes.   Extreme attention to self would become an unaffordable luxury. I-Am-Mes would revert to family values of achieving or belonging, thus in effect disappearing from the scene.

Achievers.   Well positioned occupationally and financially; likely to have the skills to deal with crises; many with latent entrepreneurial capacities gravitate to growth areas. Many would feel threatened and defeated, and would experience lowered self-esteem with lost status. Hardening of attitudes, cynicism, arrogance. In-movement from inner-directed groups; out-movement mostly to belonging. Small drop in percentage.

Emulators.   Importance of appearance greatly diminished in hard times. Emulators would be forced to abandon hope of affluence, refocus on belonging and sustaining needs. Many would become embittered, alienated, hostile. Essentially disappear.

Belongers.   Many Belongers are well prepared for hard times being financially conservative, with high equity in their homes, and having secure occupations sustained by strong support groups. A portion is much more vulnerable, especially younger people and the elderly who depend on pensions and savings. Many of the latter would be forced into sustaining and surviving modes. Big in-migration especially from Achievers and Emulators, resulting in sharp growth in percentage.

Sustainers.   Many are well adjusted to living close to poverty, but newcomers to this group face more difficulty. Some would be forced below the poverty line to the Survivor level. Major increase in underground economic activity, especially unreported cash odd jobs, a "flea market" network to dispose of stolen goods, and bartering to get by. A likely source of criminal activity of various kinds. Hard times would create a large growth in percentage.

Survivors.   Perhaps the least changed, since they are living in hard times already; greater numbers could lead to competition or to collective action. Many Sustainers and Belongers and some Emulators would take on survival characteristics. The biggest increase in percentage of any group.

TRANSFORMATION FUTURE

This scenario postulates a major trend toward managerial decentralization of governmental and other organizational activities accompanied by a massive shift in values toward Inner-Direction and, particularly, voluntary simplicity. The driving forces include sharply deteriorating conditions brought about by pollution, growing scarcities of key raw materials and energy, critical international tensions between have-not and have nations, and an abject admission by traditional leaders in business and government that they don't know how to cope with the awesome array of problems facing them. What happens is that individuals, one by one, decide to take things into their own hands—to live more frugally, to tread more lightly on the Earth, to find rewards in inner rather than external domains.

The Transformation future would incorporate many new elements, most of them now centered in inner-directed lifestyles. For example, it would include the twin ethics that futurist Theodore Roszak sees as the basis of change in his book *Person/Planet: The Creative Disintegration of Industrial Society*[6]: (1) an ecological ethic emphasizing the "rights" of the Earth, and (2) the "right to personhood"—that is, the right to have the institutions of society support each person's search for self-realization. This kind of a decentralized society would pay more attention to the importance and potentials of third-sector institutions, such as informal (not underground) economics, voluntary associations, and intentional communities. The role of work would become much less impersonal than at present, with many more options for part-time occupations, job shifts, and a melding of work and play. It is very likely that many new forms of private enterprise would proliferate, including Freda Libaw's[7] concept of a "creative corporation" that specifically incorporates consumers in its policy decisions; "Briarpatch industries," which collaborate to provide services or manufactured products, often on a cooperative basis with books open to all; or a variety of other types of "new cottage industries," often based on the principles set forth by Schumacher in *Small Is Beautiful*.[8] Finally it should be noted that the emergence of a Transformation society would show large regional differences, probably being best developed in the West and in New England, finding least acceptance among the more traditional states of the South and the Midwest.

GNP in the Transformation future would decline, probably by hundreds of billions of dollars. At the same time public spending for the Need-Drivens might increase, driven by compassion on the part of inner-directed leaders, but the main approach would be to create millions of part-time jobs (which Inner-Directeds tend to prefer) so that unemployment would fall and the Need-Driven predicament might actually improve.

Trends and Moods

Obviously this kind of scenario would be profoundly disturbing to outer-directed people, and violent ideological wars would occur between the outer- and inner-directed factions. Dreams of revitalizing the economic system would have to be abandoned. Meanwhile, the Inner-Directeds would be proclaiming that the nation at last is moving into a postindustrial era. And, under the leadership of a growing Integrated group, a real start would be made toward what we have called "renaissance."

Any period so fractionalized by transition would be difficult. Passions would probably run high, and politics might well be chaotic. But it probably also would be a time of great inventiveness, soaring hopes, and (for the Inner-Directeds especially) extremes of idealism and patriotism. Perhaps the critical questions are whether the U.S. economy and society could survive so radical a transition and remain a substantial and reliable member of the world community, and whether democratic traditions could weather the transition without veering off either into some form of benign socialism or even to rule by a self-appointed "aristocracy" in the Orwell style.

Shifts in the VALS Types

Table 25 presents our estimates for 1980 and 1990 for the Transformation scenario.

By 1990 the Inner-Directeds would jump to a third of the population and outnumber Achievers by 2:1. Narcissistic I-Am-Me types would not thrive in the ideological and high-purpose setting of this future, but the number of Experientials would probably grow moderately. In contrast the Societally Conscious group would more than double. The Transformation future, in fact, would be dominated by Societally Conscious philosophies. Their leadership would be subtly but importantly supported and augmented by the growing Integrated group.

We see the number of Belongers holding fairly steady in this scenario—theirs being a deep-rooted, hard-to-change lifestyle responsive to people albeit not to all people. Emulators and Achievers, however,

TABLE 25
**Transformation Future: Estimates of Lifestyle Shifts,
1980 and 1990**

	PERCENT IN 1980		PERCENT IN 1990	
Need-Driven	11		10	
Survivors		4		4
Sustainers		7		6
Outer-Directed	67		52	
Belongers		35		32
Emulators		10		4
Achievers		22		16
Inner-Directed	20		33	
I-Am-Me		5		3
Experiential		7		11
Societally Conscious		8		19
Integrated	2		5	

would suffer large losses as it became clear that the system based on industrial values simply was no longer working. The younger Emulators and Achievers would probably switch to Inner-Direction, leaving a residuum of older, more traditional people in those outer-directed groups. These people would undoubtedly have intense preserve-the-empire sentiments. Because many would be in positions of power, they surely would not be docile concerning the course of events.

We think that the Need-Drivens might rather like the Transformation future for the very practical reason that society would be serious about finding them jobs and providing adequate welfare for cases in which jobs were inappropriate or unavailable. Overall, however, we look for relatively little change in this VALS sector.

ON SHAPING THE FUTURE

It is tempting—a siren call, really—to try to evaluate the probabilities of various scenarios for the future actually coming to pass. But no one is wise enough or learned enough (we wish we could add brash enough) to do so with any real chance of success. So we decline to indulge in this game. However, choosing which future one would *like* to have come to pass is quite another matter. Such a preoccupation is eminently worthwhile and, taken seriously, most instructive because it tells so much about oneself. If you feel so inclined, you may choose a specific future as especially desirable, or you may choose a class of futures. Having made such a choice, what can you do as an individual to help bring about that future?

At SRI International what we do is talk and write about the futures we find good, saying why this or that appeals or charms and why another repels. We try to avoid routine judgments (which bore) and do our best to reflect the full gamut of attractions in what strikes us as favorable. In our judgment it is more effective to accentuate the positive rather than the negative, partly because so few do, partly because the very act of thinking about and talking about a future tends to make it more real and more possible. We try to emphasize what is alive and alert and on the move. The point is that many people are inexperienced in thinking about options for the future. They find it hard to look over the walls of the ruts in which they are imprisoned. If things have gone wrong for them personally, they have trouble believing things could be better. If they were raised in conventional surroundings, a Transformational society is as unbelievable as science fiction. So the problem is to build a context, a setting, a real-life portrait of what could reasonably be and what it would mean, not in sweeping generalities but in the everyday terms of living. The scenario is one of the best ways of doing this. At SRI we have devised scenarios to deal with scores of issues, large and small. A recent book, *Seven Tomorrows*,[9] presents seven societal scenarios for the 1980s based largely on SRI studies.

In addition we think it essential to live in the way you think the world should be. If voluntary simplicity is your vision of the ideal society, you should live the simple life. By being what you believe—a task of supreme difficulty—you become a living advertisement for the kind of future you believe in. In the long run this may be the most effective of all ways of shaping the future.

Some of us have more opportunities than others to sketch and perhaps even to live our notions about what we want of the future. But in my experience the most effective persuaders are those who do not have gilt words in which to frame the essence of reality. I shall not forget the words of a dark-haired woman, raised in Central Europe, who told me her idea of the good society: "It is where I can smile without fear."

APPENDIX

Other Typologies

It is perhaps worth noting that the VALS theory-based approach to identifying types of people is fundamentally different from the usual approaches. In this appendix we sketch three kinds of typologies: market, social, and business. Brief comments are offered on why these approaches did not suit our purposes.

MARKET TYPOLOGIES

Most dependable market typologies are developed through so-called psychometrics. This involves factor analysis of various attitudes, interests, psychological characteristics, opinions, and selected activities into clusters that define different kinds of people. The following list shows some clusters developed statistically, chiefly for purposes of market research.

SOME MARKET TYPOLOGIES

○ Bachelor, newlywed, full nest I, full nest II, empty nest, solitary survivor

○ Active achiever, self-indulgent pleasure-seeker, traditional homebody, blue-collar outdoorsman, business leader, successful traditionalist

○ Worriers, sociables, independents, sensories

○ Push-button woman, identity seeker, weight-watching worrier, body acher, affluent hedonist, aromatic male, soothers

○ (female only) Old-fashioned traditionalist, militant mother, chic suburbanite, contented housewife, elegant socialite

○ (male only) Retiring homebody, successful professional, frustrated factory worker, devoted family man, self-made businessman

○ Swinger, unisex person, easy rider, multistylist

○ (female only) Freshman wife, freshman mother, senior mother, mother emeritus, consultant grandmother

○ Outgoing optimists, conscientious vigilants, apathetic indifferents, self-indulgents, contented cows, worriers

○ Traditionalists, complainers, authoritarians, self-actualizers, losers, loners

○ Early adopters, appearance-conscious shoppers, carefrees, traditional department store shoppers, apathetic shoppers

○ Experimental, transitional, traditional

○ Traditionalists, new conformists, forerunners, autonomous, retreaters

○ Moralists, new conformists, forerunners, materialists, retreaters

Although groupings developed through cluster analysis are often vivid and exceedingly useful for understanding aspects of consumer behavior, they have three weaknesses from our standpoint. First, most tell us rather little about behavior outside the marketplace. Second, such systems tend to be weak in explaining the inner whys of behavior even when they superbly describe the behavior itself. These two weaknesses probably could be overcome, but the third weakness is fatal for an approach such as ours, which seeks to enfold the individual, the marketplace, and the society into an interlocked system that reveals both how a change in one area is likely to affect all others areas, and how the typology can be used for systematic forecasting of changes in the sizes and properties of the groups. Primarily because cluster analysis fails to show how groups interrelate (and hence is not suitable for cross-impact analysis or forecasting), it was not an appropriate starting point for our research. There is no reason, however, why clusters identified through standard psychographics cannot be dovetailed with the life-style approach, once the characteristics of the conceptually conceived lifestyle groups have been empirically confirmed via field research.

SOCIAL TYPOLOGIES

Social typologies, such as those listed below, turned out to be less useful to us than we initially anticipated and for much the same reason that cluster analyses are flawed: Interconnections among groups are unclear or unsystematic, although many do imply a continuum.

SOME SOCIAL TYPOLOGIES

○ Poor, middle-income, rich

○ Lower-class, middle-class, upper-class

○ Conservative, moderate, liberal

○ Low-brow, middle-brow, high-brow

○ Mainstream, counterculture

○ Consciousness I, consciousness II, consciousness III

○ Formalistic, sociocentric, personalistic

○ Traditionalists, anarchists, liberated, reformers, counter-culturalists

○ High social consciousness, low social consciousness

○ Innovators, early adopters, early majority, late majority, laggards

○ Movers, makers, preservers, takers, changers, escapers, seekers

○ Embracers, rejectors, indifferents, inadequates

○ Conformity, innovation, ritualism, retreatism, rebellion

- ○ (business scene only) Organization man, jungle fighter, craftsman, gamesman

- ○ Dionysian, promethean, buddhistic

THE MACCOBY TYPES

Michael Maccoby in *The Gamesman*[1] proposes an interesting typology of businesspeople. He identifies four basic types: the Organization Man,[2] the Jungle Fighter, the Craftsman, and the Gamesman. Although we did not explicitly employ them in our work, these types fit quite neatly into our framework, as the following notes indicate.

Organization Man. This is the conformist, the unexperimental person who follows the rules more or less unquestioningly. The type is little changed from the 1950s, when Whyte first described the phenomenon. Dress, whether the gray flannel suit of yesterday or the three piecer of today, is flawlessly inoffensive, but not necessarily cheap. Orders are taken without retort and, indeed, with gratitude. Adherence to rules is absolute, support of company policy relentless. Innovations are made to be rejected. In our terms this, of course, is the Belonger.

Jungle Fighter. Jungle Fighters, as Maccoby says, come in two varieties: the lion and the fox. The lion's style involves intimidation, bombast, soapboxing, credit-taking, boasting, and often crudities and lying. The fox's crafty manipulative schemes are marked by artful artifice, skilled silences, purposeful misinterpretations, flattery, groveling, hypocrisy. What Geoffrey Chaucer described as "the smiler with the knife under his cloak" is the fox Jungle Fighter. Jungle Fighters in the trades are most likely to be Sustainers. Those among the ranks of executives are most often Emulators.

Craftsman. This is the person whose greatest pleasure is to construct a perfectly modeled plan or concept. The craftsmanship of the work is almost more important than its workability. Such people tend to be idealistic, careful, sensitive, committed, intelligent, impractical. Often they are loners. Frequently they are much admired by their coworkers, who tend to be protective of them. Such people seldom rise to the very top of the modern corporate hierarchy because they tend to be poor managers and disinterested salesmen. The Craftsman is clearly inner-directed and could be either Experiential or Societally Conscious, depending on the nature of his or her interests.

Gamesman.   The Gamesman, as Maccoby describes him, is the truly modern business leader. He or she is relatively young, intellectually gifted, works for a high-technology company, and is intensely absorbed in work. Far from being a loner like the Craftsman, the Gamesman builds and leads a team. The Gamesman's highest pleasure is to put together elaborate plans that often involve high risks. The business venture is at heart a game full of art, luck, and more than anything skill. The Gamesman is highly trained, thoroughly knowledgeable, energetic, hard-working, and happy in work. Strikingly, the Gamesman has almost no interest in societal issues. So here is a portrait of one kind of contemporary, successful Achiever.

The VALS 1980 Field Survey

METHODOLOGY

The VALS 1980 Survey was based on a national probability sample of households with telephones (excluding military and other institutions). Random digit-dialing techniques were used to locate households. Within each contacted household the appropriate respondent was selected through the Trodahl-Carter random-selection procedure.[3] All English-speaking adults aged eighteen years or older were eligible. Once the selected respondent was reached, his or her participation in the mail survey was solicited, and he or she was asked several demographic and attitudinal questions. Results of this telephone screening were used as a guide in making follow-up phone calls and in sample control.

Sample control was maintained by several procedures. The total sample of telephone numbers (5,728, including nonworking, business, and government numbers) was segmented into thirds, and at least 80 percent of all contact attempts were required to be resolved (as refusals, completed interviews, etc.) in the first sample segment before the second sample segment was released for initial contact. Similarly, at least 80 percent of all contact attempts in the first two segments were required to be resolved before the third segment was released. In addition, *all* numbers in the total sample eventually had to be resolved (as completed interview, refusal, ineligible respondent or household, or unable to contact), which means that all potential households had an equal probability of selection. Time periods for contact attempts were segmented. No second contact attempt could be made in the same time segment as the first, and no more than one-third of all contact attempts could be made during weekday calling hours. Up to seven contact attempts in all were made to each phone number. All initial refusals were recontacted in an attempt to deal with the potential bias of refusals. Nearly one-third of initial refusals eventually were enrolled in the survey.

To increase returns from persons who were sent mail questionnaires, a five-dollar bill was attached to each questionnaire, and three follow-up calls, spaced ten to fourteen days apart, were made to nonrespondents. (A pretest of the mail questionnaire with 200 respondents found that individuals who were sent ten dollars were not more likely to respond than were those sent five dollars.) A fourth follow-up call was made to specific types of households underrepresented in early returns. This last procedure was possible because an analysis of household data from the screening questionnaire was performed on every 500 questionnaires returned to enable us to spot problem areas and to compensate for them during follow-up procedures.

The completion/response rates for the survey were as follows:

- 79 percent of all respondents who were contacted by phone and who agreed to receive the mail questionnaire returned completed questionnaires.

- 67 percent of all respondents who were contacted by phone (including those who did not agree to receive the mail questionnaire) returned completed questionnaires.

- 48 percent of all households contacted by phone (including those in which the designated respondent could not be contacted, refused to be interviewed, or was ill) returned completed questionnaires.

SURVEY QUESTIONS

The following questions were asked in the VALS 1980 Survey. Most of the market-oriented items were posed by clients of the VALS program at SRI International. Wording of questions, pretesting, and conduct of the survey were under the direction of Drs. Stephen Crocker and Susan Russell of SRI. Results have been compiled in terms of the specific responses of eight of the nine lifestyle types, Integrateds being omitted for reasons explained elsewhere. Over 1 million data points were developed in the survey. Please note that the questions below do not include the options to be checked. The questionnaire had no write-in items.

ATTITUDES

1. Following is a series of statements. Please indicate how much you agree or disagree with each one by checking the box which comes closest to how you feel. (Choices were: Disagree Strongly, Disagree Mostly, Disagree Somewhat, Agree Somewhat, Agree Mostly, Agree Strongly.)

   a. Financial security is very important to me.
   b. I want to live every moment to its fullest.
   c. I'd say I'm rebelling against the way I was brought up.
   d. I believe that "industrial growth" should be limited.
   e. Generally speaking, most people are trustworthy and honest.
   f. Everything is changing too fast today.
   g. In general, it's more important to understand my inner self than to be famous, powerful, or wealthy.
   h. My greatest achievements are ahead of me.
   i. I believe a woman can work outside the home even if she has small children and still be a good mother.
   j. I certainly am more conventional than experimental.
   k. Saving time is important to me.
   l. I like to try new and different things.
   m. It's very important to me to feel I am a part of a group.
   n. I'm usually on the go all day long.
   o. Overall, I'd say I'm very happy.
   p. I want to get ahead financially.
   q. TV is my main form of entertainment.
   r. I'm a "spender" rather than a "saver."
   s. I would rather spend a quiet evening at home than go out to a party.
   t. My family is the single most important thing to me.
   u. I think I have more self-confidence than most people.
   v. I like to think I'm a bit of a swinger.
   w. A woman's life is fulfilled only if she can provide a happy home for her family.
   x. I like myself pretty much the way I am.
   y. I feel that I have more good qualities than most people.
   z. Whenever I shop for major items, I tend to buy the best product or nothing at all.
   aa. My social status is an important part of my life.
   bb. I act on my hunches.
   cc. Air pollution is a major worldwide danger.
   dd. I often feel left out of things going on around me.
   ee. I think we are spending too much money on improving and protecting the environment.
   ff. It is wrong for an unmarried man or an unmarried woman to have sexual relations.
   gg. Women should take care of running their homes and leave running the country up to men.

hh. It would be best for the future of this country if the United States continues to take an active part in world affairs.

ii. I'd say I'm rebelling against the way things are in general.

jj. The purchase and use of marijuana should be legalized.

kk. A sense of accomplishment is perhaps the most important reward in a job.

ll. Conservation of natural resources is extremely important to me.

mm. I am as effective as most people in getting done what is important to me.

nn. I think we are spending too much money on military armaments.

2. During the last three years would you say your financial situation has been getting worse, has it stayed the same, or has it been getting better?

3. How satisfied are you with your present financial situation?

4. How much satisfaction do you get from each of the following in your life?
   a. Your job (whether you work, keep house, or go to school)
   b. Nonwork activities such as hobbies.
   c. Your friends.

5. About how much confidence would you say you have in the following groups in our country?
   a. Elected officials
   b. Leaders of major companies
   c. Leaders of the military

6. Please indicate whether you think the following aspects of today's products are worse, about the same, or better than they were ten years ago.
   a. Quality of today's products
   b. Safety of today's products
   c. Labeling and information about products
   d. Quality of service received
   e. Companies satisfying consumer complaints

7. On balance, do you think that the demands by the consumer movement have resulted in lower prices, made no difference, or have they resulted in higher prices?

8. In the past year have you complained to a store or manufacturer about a product or service?

9. Suppose an organized consumer group were to be set up in your local area to put pressure on all retailers who sold the products of a certain manufacturer that the group felt were inferior or harmful. Which *one* of the statements below would best describe your feelings (assuming you agreed the products were indeed inferior or harmful)?
   a. I wouldn't care one way or the other.
   b. I would certainly not join and would oppose its activities.

    c. I would probably not join but would support its goals.

    d. I would probably join the group and take an active part in it.

    e. I would certainly join the group and take an active part in it.

    f. Not sure what I would do.

10. How important to you is energy usage in home appliances?

11. How important do you think it is that people in your area insulate their homes?

12. How much have the gasoline shortage and higher gasoline prices affected your pleasure travel by motor vehicle?

13. To what extent do you agree or disagree that there is an energy crisis—that is, a major shortage of natural gas and oil available to the United States?

14. In general, how accurate do you believe the following are as sources of information about the energy situation?
    a. Federal government
    b. Public utilities
    c. Oil companies

15. To what extent, if any, do you feel that public utility companies (gas, electric, and telephone) *operate with the interest of the consumer in mind?*

16. To what extent, if any, do you believe that public utility companies *encourage energy conservation* among gas and electric consumers?

BACKGROUND INFORMATION

1. What is your marital status?

2. What is your current age?

3. What is the highest level of formal education you have completed?

4. What is the highest level of formal education *your father* completed?

5. What ethnic group do you consider yourself to be a member of?

6. Your sex:

7. How many children in each of the following age categories do you have *living at home* with you?
    a. Under 6 years old
    b. 6–11 years
    c. 12–17 years
    d. 18 years or older

8. How many children in your family (if any) are living away from home?

9. Generally speaking, do you usually think of yourself as a Republican, a Democrat, or an Independent?
   a. IF YOU ARE A REPUBLICAN OR DEMOCRAT, would you call yourself a strong or not very strong Republican or Democrat?
   b. IF YOU ARE AN INDEPENDENT, do you think of yourself as closer to the Republican or Democratic party?

10. In terms of your political outlook, do you usually think of yourself as: very conservative, somewhat conservative, middle of the road, somewhat liberal, very liberal

11. How long have you lived at your current residence?

12. (IF YOU HAVE LIVED AT CURRENT RESIDENCE THREE YEARS OR LESS): Where did you live just prior to moving to your current residence?

13. In what type of dwelling do you live?

14. Do you own or rent your home?

IF YOUR HOME IS A SINGLE FAMILY DWELLING (A HOUSE) OR A MOBILE HOME, PLEASE ANSWER QUESTIONS 15–18. IF YOUR HOME IS A TOWNHOUSE OR CONDOMINIUM, PLEASE SKIP TO QUESTION 19.

15. About how old is the dwelling you live in?

16. Has the dwelling ever (to your knowledge) been *totally* remodeled or renovated within the last 5 to 10 years?

17. Have any of the following kinds of activities been completed on your dwelling *within the last 12 months?*
   a. Total remodeling or renovation (both inside and outside)
   b. Addition of one or more rooms
   c. Remodeling of one or more rooms
   d. Normal maintenance (painting, wallpapering, minor repairs to structure, etc.)
   e. System replacement (e.g., replacement of roof, siding, plumbing, heating system, electrical wiring, air conditioning, etc.)
   f. Lot improvement (fences, patio, landscape, garage, etc.)
   g. Other (please specify)

18. During the last 2 years, have you contacted a public utility or equipment manufacturer about the cost of solar heating for your home (excluding swimming pool)?

19. Which *one* of the following categories best describes your occupation? [sixteen categories follow]

20. What was your *major* activity during the last week? [eight categories]

21. (IF YOU ARE CURRENTLY EMPLOYED), are you *primarily* self-employed or are you employed by a company or other organization?

22. If you were asked to use one of the following terms to describe your social class, which would you choose? [five categories]

23. What is the total income that *you personally* received in 1979 from all sources before taxes?

24. What is your total *household* income in 1979 from all sources before taxes?

MEDIA HABITS

Movie Viewing

1. During the last 12 months, how many times did you go to a theatre *to see a movie*?

2. In general, how much influence does each of the following sources of information have in helping you to decide which movie to attend?
   a. Movie *ads* in magazines and newspapers
   b. Movie *reviews* in magazines or newspapers
   c. Movie *ads* on TV
   d. Movie *reviews* on TV
   e. Radio advertising
   f. Recommendations by friends or relatives

3. If you had the choice, how often would you prefer to watch a full-length current movie at home on your TV set, without commercials or interruptions, rather than going to a movie theatre to see the same movie? Please assume the costs are the same.

Television Viewing

1. In an average week, about how much time do you spend each *weekday* (Monday-Friday) watching *commercial or educational* television during each of the time periods listed below?

	Eastern or Pacific Time Zone	Central or Mountain Time Zone
a.	7–10 AM	6–9 AM
b.	10 AM–1 PM	9 AM–Noon
c.	1–4:30 PM	Noon–3:30 PM
d.	4:30–8 PM	3:30–7 PM
e.	8–11 PM	7–10 PM
f.	11 PM–2 AM	10 PM–1 AM

2. About how much time do you spend per day each *weekend* (Saturday and Sunday) watching *commercial or educational* television during each of the time periods listed below?

	Eastern or Pacific Time Zone	Central or Mountain Time Zone
a.	7–10 AM	6–9 AM
b.	10 AM–1 PM	9 AM–Noon
c.	1–4:30 PM	Noon–3:30 PM
d.	4:30–8 PM	3:30–7 PM
e.	8–11 PM	7–10 PM
f.	11 PM–2 AM	10 PM–1 AM

3. How much time in an average week do you spend watching educational television?

4. How often do you usually watch each of the following types of programs on *commercial or educational* TV?
   a. Morning news ("Today Show," or "Good Morning America," etc.)
   b. Afternoon news (3–5 p.m.)
   c. Early evening news (5–7 p.m.)
   d. Late evening news (10 p.m. or later)
   e. Mystery or crime dramas
   f. Comedies
   g. Variety shows
   h. Game shows
   i. Soap operas
   j. Movies
   k. Talk shows
   l. Sports programs
   m. Children's shows
   n. Nature or wildlife shows

5. To what extent do you think each of the following describes *commercial* television (not educational television)?
   a. Interesting
   b. Educational
   c. In bad taste
   d. Exciting
   e. Unimaginative

6. In general, would you say *commercial* television is getting worse, staying about the same, or getting better than it was 10 years ago?

Radio Listening

10. On an average *weekday* (Monday through Friday) about how much time do you spend listening to the radio during each of the time periods listed below?
    a. Early morning to noon
    b. From noon to 5 p.m.

c. 5–8 p.m.
d. 8–11 p.m.
e. After 11 p.m.

Reading Newspapers and Magazines

1. About how often do you read a daily and a Sunday newspaper?
    a. Daily newspaper
    b. Sunday newspaper

2. When you read a newspaper, how often do you read parts or all of the following sections?
    a. Business/finance
    b. Classified advertising
    c. Comics
    d. Entertainment
    e. Feature writers' columns
    f. Food/cooking
    g. Main news section
    h. Sports
    i. Travel

3. How often do you read parts or all of the following types of magazines?
    a. Business (*Business Week, Fortune*, etc.)
    b. Major news (*Time, Newsweek*, etc.)
    c. Television (*T.V. Guide*, etc.)
    d. General sports (*Sports Illustrated, Sports*, etc.)
    e. Human interest (*People, Us*, etc.)
    f. Tabloids (*National Enquirer, The Star*, etc.)
    g. Automotive (*Car and Driver, Motor Trend*, etc.)
    h. Specific sports (*Skiing, Tennis*, etc.)
    i. Domestic (*Woman's Day, Family Circle*, etc.)
    j. Men's magazines (*Playboy, Penthouse*, etc.)
    k. Fashion (*Mademoiselle, Vogue*, etc.)
    l. Educational (*National Geographic, Smithsonian*, etc.)
    m. Home or Garden (*Sunset, House & Garden*, etc.)
    n. Commentary (*New Republic, Co-Evolution Quarterly*, etc.)
    o. Literary (*Saturday Review, New Yorker*, etc.)

Reading Books

1. About how many books have you read in the past 12 months?

2. Have most of these been fiction or nonfiction books?

3. Are most of the books you have read hardcover or softcover books?

4. Are any of the books you have read in the past 12 months condensed or shortened versions of complete books?

5. Does anyone in your household belong to a book club?

ACTIVITIES

(Respondents, in most cases, were asked to select among seven or eight frequencies ranging from "not at all" to "once a week or more often" or "five times a week or more often.")

1. How often do *you* engage in each of the following activities?

Sports and Outdoor Recreation

a. Backpacking
b. Baseball, basketball, softball, or football
c. Bicycling
d. Camping overnight
e. Flying/gliding as a sport or hobby
f. Fresh or salt water fishing
g. Golf
h. Hunting
i. Jogging
j. Motorboating
k. Outdoor gardening as a hobby (flowers or shrubs)
l. Vegetable gardening
m. Sailing
n. Scuba or skin diving
o. Snow skiing
p. Squash, handball, or racquetball
q. Swimming
r. Tennis
s. Water skiing

2. How often do you engage in each of the following activities? For seasonal activities, please indicate the frequency during the season.

Attendance at Sporting and Other Events

a. Attend professional sporting events (football, boxing, golf, etc.)
b. Attend college or high school sporting events
c. Go to horse races
d. Attend pop or rock concerts
e. Attend night clubs or discos
f. Attend theatre (plays, musicals) or concerts
g. Attend an X-rated movie

h. Attend opera, ballet, or other dance performance
i. Visit art galleries or museums in your local area
j. Attend a theme or amusement park
k. Attend encounter, transcendental meditation, or similar groups
l. Play video games in arcades or commercial establishments

3. How often do *you* engage in each of the following activities?

Indoor Recreation and Hobbies

a. Play a musical instrument
b. Listen to records and/or tapes
c. Paint, draw, or sculpt (art)
d. Write poetry/fiction/nonfiction for pleasure
e. Engage in crafts (ceramics, leather working, pottery, etc.)
f. Do woodworking or carpentry
g. Knit/crochet/do needlework
h. Design your own or others' clothes
i. Sew to make something
j. Sew to repair or mend something
k. Do repair or fix-up projects around the house
l. Go bowling
m. Exercise in a gym
n. Play pool or billiards
o. Play cards—bridge
p. Play cards—poker
q. Play chess
r. Play backgammon
s. Yoga or meditation at home

4. How often do *you* engage in each of the following activities?

Shopping and Related Activities

a. Purchase items through the mail
b. Purchase items by phone
c. Use trading stamps to purchase items
d. Use coupons in magazines or newspapers to purchase items
e. Return an unsatisfactory product
f. Shop in large discount stores (K-Mart, etc.)
g. Shop in major department stores
h. Purchase a newspaper or a magazine at a newsstand
i. Shop in convenience food markets ("7–11," etc.)
j. Purchase drugs in discount drug stores
k. Shop at second-hand stores

l. Shop in specialty stores (i.e., those specializing in specific kinds of products—jewelry, furniture, liquor, toys, books, clothing, and so on)

5. How often do *you* engage in each of the following activities?

Eating, Drinking, and Food Preparation

a. Bake bread at home
b. Bake pastries at home
c. Cook outdoors (backyard, patio)
d. Preserve foods at home
e. Eat out at or bring food home from fast food restaurants
f. Give dinner parties

6. How often do *you* engage in each of the following activities?

Business Travel

a. Travel by air for business purposes
b. Travel abroad for business purposes
c. Stay at hotels/motels during business travel
d. Use rental cars for business travel
e. Use a travel agency for business travel

Vacation or Pleasure Travel

a. Travel by air for pleasure (vacation) purposes
b. Travel abroad for pleasure
c. Stay at hotels/motels while vacationing
d. Use rental cars for pleasure travel
e. Use a travel agency for pleasure trips
f. Take trips in a recreational vehicle (RV) such as a motor home, travel trailer, or camper

7. How often do *you* engage in each of the following activities?
a. Write letters to friends and relatives
b. Send or give greeting cards
c. Telephone friends or relatives locally
d. Telephone friends or relatives long distance
e. Telephone friends or relatives internationally
f. Borrow books/magazines from local library
g. Use audio-visual materials at local library
h. Work at a second job, including free-lancing
i. Visit phone company offices
j. Type personal letters at home
k. Type at home to earn extra money
l. Work on own car or other motor vehicle

Eating and Food Preparation Patterns

1. In general, what kind of food brands do *you* personally think are most trustworthy with respect to quality?
   a. Store brands
   b. National brands
   c. Imported brands
   d. No difference

2. What one meal do you *most often* eat away from home (excluding business and travel)?
   a. Breakfast
   b. Lunch
   c. Dinner

3. What kind of restaurant do you eat in *most often?*
   a. Fast food
   b. Coffee shop
   c. Small informal restaurant
   d. Formal restaurant

4. What time of the week do you most often go to restaurants?
   a. Weekends
   b. Weekdays
   c. Both about equally

5. Which of the following do you engage in on a *regular* basis?
   a. Collect cooking gadgets
   b. Collect recipes
   c. Eat desserts
   d. Eat vegetarian meals
   e. Eat dinner while watching TV
   f. Eat between-meal snacks

Cigarette Smoking

1. Have you personally *ever* smoked cigarettes?

2. Have you smoked cigarettes at any time during the past month?
   a. (IF HAVE SMOKED IN PAST MONTH) How long have you been smoking?
   b. (IF HAVEN'T SMOKED IN PAST MONTH) How long ago did you *stop* smoking?

3. On the average, about how many cigarettes do you smoke per day?

4. What type of cigarette do you usually smoke?

Vitamins and Nutrition

1. How often do you take vitamins or nutritional supplements?

2. Which of the following best describes your reducing diet habits?

3. How much attention do you pay to keeping yourself healthy?

4. In general, how important is nutritional label information on a food item package in your decision whether or not to buy that food item?

5. How much attention do you pay to each of the following?
   a. The amount of sugar in foods you eat
   b. The amount of salt in foods you eat
   c. The amount of vitamins in foods you eat
   d. The amount of caffeine you consume
   e. The possible effects of additives in foods you eat
   f. The amount of saccharin you consume
   g. The nutritional quality of food you eat

Alcoholic Beverages

1. During the last 12 months, did you drink any alcoholic beverages?

2. About how often do you drink each of the following domestic and imported wines in your home or at a restaurant?
   a. California wines
   b. Other domestic wines
   c. French
   d. German
   e. Italian
   f. Portuguese/Spanish
   g. Domestic champagnes or sparkling wines
   h. Imported champagnes or sparkling wines

3. About how often do you drink each of the following kinds of liquors in your home or at a restaurant?
   a. Bourbon
   b. Canadian
   c. Gin
   d. Scotch
   e. Tequila
   f. Vodka
   g. Rum

4. About how often do you drink domestic and imported beers?
   a. Domestic beers
   b. Imported beers

5. About how often do you have a cocktail or alcoholic drink (not wine or beer) before dinner when dining in a restaurant?

Medical

1. Have you had a complete medical check-up in the past 12 months?

2. How many times have you visited a doctor about *your* own health (not children or spouse's) in the past 12 months?

3. Have you heard the term "holistic health"?

Teaching and Learning

1. Do you have any children who are currently attending school in grades one through twelve?

2. Do any of these children use a calculator in their schoolwork?

3. Are these calculators provided by the school, or did you buy them?
   a. Provided by the school
   b. Bought one or more

4. Do you expect to buy a calculator (or another calculator if you have already bought one) for any of your children while they are in school?

5. To what extent do you agree or disagree with this statement: "Elementary schools should use calculators to help children learn mathematics."

6. Have you spent $50 or more to provide instruction (not books or materials) in basic skills such as reading, writing or arithmetic, for any of your children (other than sending them regularly to private schools)?

7. Have you (or your spouse) spent $50 or more for *you* to take an educational or training course in any subject since you completed your formal education?

8. Have you engaged in any of the following types of educational activities since you completed your formal education?
   a. Foreign language courses
   b. Enrolled in correspondence courses
   c. Attended night school, college, or other courses

FINANCIAL ISSUES

1. Please indicate the extent to which you agree or disagree with each of the following statements. Please note that there is no right or wrong answer to any question.
   a. With the rate at which inflation is going, it pays to be in debt, since you will always pay the debt back in cheaper dollars
   b. It is unwise to buy anything on time other than a house or a car
   c. When it comes to financial matters, I consider myself an expert
   d. I'd rather spend my money on things such as art, gold, and gems than invest in stocks, bonds, etc.

    e. It seems as though I use my credit cards more and more all the time

    f. With the current high rate of inflation, I doubt that I will be able to keep up my current standard of living five years from now

    g. I find that I use credit cards less these days than I did a few years ago

    h. I feel I am an important customer to some of the financial institutions I deal with

2. How many VISA/Bankamericard *accounts* are held by members of your household?

3. How many MasterCard *accounts* are held by members of your household?

4. Which of the following kinds of credit cards (if any) are held by members of your household? (Diner's Club, Carte Blanche, American Express, Gasoline/oil company, Auto rental, Department or specialty store, None of the above)

5. For which of the following types of purchases would you say you *usually* use credit cards?
    a. Gasoline
    b. Mail order or phone purchases
    c. Department or specialty store purchases
    d. Business travel
    e. Other business expenses
    f. Pleasure travel
    g. Personal entertainment
    h. Other (please specify)
    i. None of the above

6. Whom do you consider to be the *chief* decision maker in your household for each of the financial areas listed below?

    a. Banking accounts
    b. Insurance
    c. Investments
    d. Loans

7. The following kinds of services are offered at several kinds of financial institutions. Please check the appropriate boxes to indicate which kinds of institutions your household uses (if any) for each service listed.
    a. Savings accounts
    b. Home mortgages
    c. Auto loan(s)
    d. Other personal loans

8. Does anyone in your household have a checking account?
    a. Is the *total* balance on *all the checking accounts in your household* usually less than $1,000 or more than $1,000?

9. Does anyone in your household have any mutual funds or money market funds?
   a. What is the total current market value on all these funds held by members of your household?

10. Does anyone in your household have a savings account, savings bond or certificate, credit union account, T-bill account, etc.?
    a. What is the total balance on all these accounts held by members of your household?

11. Does anyone in your household have any stocks or bonds?
    a. What is the total current market value of *all your* household's stocks and bonds?

12. Do you own your home (rather than rent or lease)?
    a. If you were to sell your home and pay off the mortgage, about how much money would you have left from the sale?

13. Does anyone in your household own any investment real estate, such as a vacation home, apartment or rental property, commercial building, farm, ranch, or undeveloped land?
    a. If you were to sell *all* this investment real estate and pay off whatever loans you may have on it, about how much money would you have left from the sale?

14. Do members of your household have any loans (*other than your home mortgage*), checking overdrafts, or margin accounts on which the *total owed is more than $1,000?*
    a. What is the *total* amount owed on *all these loans*, etc.?

15. Do members of your household have credit card balances totaling more than $100 *on which you/they are paying a finance charge?*
    a. What is the total amount of *all balances on which members of your household are paying finance charges?*

16. Does anyone in your household have a stockbroker?
    a. What was the approximate value of *all transactions* (both purchases and sales) made by your household through a stockbroker in 1979?

17. At the present time, what do you believe to be the *total value of all assets* belonging to you and other members of your household?

18. At the present time, what do you believe to be the *total value of all liabilities and debts* owed by you and other members of your household?

19. Does your household have homeowner's or renter's insurance?

20. Does anyone in your household have an Individual Retirement Account (IRA)?

21. Does anyone in your household have a Keogh account?

22. Which members of your household (if any) have the following kinds of insurance?
    a. Individual life insurance (purchased individually through an agent)
    b. Group life insurance (purchased through or paid for by employer, union, professional or fraternal organization, etc.)
    c. Health or major medical insurance
    d. Disability insurance

23. What kind(s) of *individual* life insurance is carried by members of your household?

24. From whom was this *individual* life insurance purchased?

25. How important a part of your household's financial security do you feel individual life insurance is?

26. If you were buying life insurance, how interested do you think you would be in life insurance that allowed you to increase or decrease the amount of your coverage (and the premiums you would pay) as major events occurred in your life (e.g., getting married, having a child, children grown up, and so on)?

27. Please indicate whether *you believe* a woman should have life insurance under each of the following circumstances.
    a. She is the sole support of the family
    b. She contributes about half of the family income
    c. She is a full-time housewife, with children under 12 living at home
    d. She is a full-time housewife with no children
    e. She is single (divorced or never married) with no children
    f. She is a full-time housewife, with children 13–18 living at home

HOUSEHOLD INVENTORY AND PRODUCT USE
Household Appliances

Which of the following appliances does anyone in your household *own?* Please do not include appliances that are used but not actually owned.
    a. Refrigerator/freezer combination
    b. Refrigerator (separate from freezer)
    c. Freezer (separate from refrigerator)
    d. Gas cooking range
    e. Electric cooking range
    f. Microwave oven
    g. Food processor
    h. Dishwasher
    i. Garbage disposal
    j. Trash compactor
    k. Color television set

l. Black-and-white television set
m. Clothes washer/dryer combination
n. Clothes washer (separate)
o. Clothes dryer (separate)

Household Equipment and Tools

Which of the following does anyone in your household *own?*
a. Burglar alarm
b. Smoke or fire alarm
c. A total home security system
d. Water filtration equipment
e. Room air conditioning unit
f. Central air conditioning unit
g. Water bed
h. Home encyclopedia set
i. Decorator telephone
j. Telephone answering machine
k. Telephone extension for the home
l. Lawn/patio furniture
m. Chain saw
n. Motorized lawnmower
o. String grass trimmer

Home Electronic Equipment

Does anyone in your household *own* any of the items listed below? If yes, how often are they used?
a. Pocket calculator
b. Electric typewriter
c. Manual typewriter
d. Citizen's band mobile radio
e. Hi-fi stereo component set
f. Blank recording tapes or cassettes
g. Prerecorded tapes or cassettes
h. Video games
i. Video tape or disk recording equipment
j. Personal computer (not calculator)
k. Home movie equipment
l. Exercise equipment at home

Recreation and Sports Equipment

Does anyone in your household own any of the equipment listed below? If yes, how often are they used?
a. Camping and backpacking equipment

    b. Racing bicycle
    c. Sailboat
    d. Powerboat (powered by outboard motor)
    e. Motorcycle
    f. Handgun
    g. Rifle
    h. Permanently installed home swimming pool

Motor Vehicles

1. How many licensed motor vehicles (cars, vans, or trucks) does your household own? Please do *not* include motorcycles or other two-wheel vehicles.

2. Please record the make (Ford, Olds, Toyota, etc.), model (Pinto, Cutlass, Celica, etc.) and year of each licensed motor vehicle in your household in the spaces below.

3. What is the body style of each vehicle?
Newest
2nd Newest
3rd Newest

4. Was/Is this vehicle—
Newest
2nd Newest
3rd Newest

5. About how many miles in an average year do you or others drive each vehicle?
Newest
2nd Newest
3rd Newest

6. What are the *three* main uses of each vehicle?
Newest
2nd Newest
3rd Newest

7. Who is the primary driver of each vehicle?
Newest
2nd Newest
3rd Newest

8. If you were to buy a car this year, how important would each of the following items be in your purchase decision? Please assume that this would be the car that you personally would drive most often.
    a. Convenient dealer location for servicing car
    b. Passenger seating capacity
    c. Exterior or interior styling

   d. Price or deal offered
   e. Ease of handling, driving
   f. Riding comfort
   g. Gas mileage
   h. Durability and reliability
   i. Future trade-in or resale value
   j. Prestige
   k. Power and pickup
   l. Cost of service and repairs
   m. Safety features
   n. Diesel engine
   o. Overall quality
   p. Value for the money

9. All things considered, given a choice between an American-made and foreign-made car with the same price and accessories, which would you buy?

Auto Insurance

1. When was the *most recent* time *you* changed auto insurance companies?

2. How important were each of the following in your decision to change auto insurance companies?
   a. Dissatisfied with settlement of a claim
   b. Better coverage, plan, or policy through another company
   c. Better rates, price
   d. Moved from area served by company
   e. Other important reasons
   f. Don't know or remember why I/we changed insurance companies

Photography

1. During the past year, how often have you *personally* taken any photographs?

2. Which of the following cameras do members of your household *own*, and how often do *you personally* use each of them?
   a. Instamatic
   b. Instant
   c. 35 mm
   d. 35 mm reflex
   e. Movie camera
   f. Large and medium format camera
   g. View camera

3. Do you usually buy a national or store brand of film?

4. Do you usually ask for a brand of film by name?

5. Do you have your own darkroom?

6. How important are each of the following as reasons why you engage in photography?
   a. An outlet for creative or artistic abilities
   b. To earn money
   c. To have a record of memories
   d. Showing photos to friends or relatives
   e. Giving photos to friends or relatives
   f. Meeting other photographers

Pets

1. Does your household have any pets? By "pets," we mean a tame animal kept for pleasure rather than for food or other purposes.

2. Which of the following pets does your household have?
   a. Dogs or puppies
   b. Cats or kittens
   c. Hamsters, gerbils, or mice
   d. Birds
   e. Horses, donkeys, etc.
   f. Fresh water or salt water fish

3. During the last year, about how often did you take one or more of your pets to a veterinarian?

4. Which type of dog food do you *usually* feed your dog?

5. Which type of cat food do you *usually* feed your cat?

Buying Patterns

1. Who in your household *usually* does the shopping for each of the following?
   a. Non-prescription medicines
   b. Men's personal grooming and health aids
   c. Women's personal grooming and health aids
   d. Groceries, non-alcoholic beverages and cleaning products
   e. Alcoholic beverages
   f. Home security equipment (e.g., burglar alarms, smoke detection, etc.)
   g. Home appliances
   h. Furniture and major home furnishings (e.g., couch, dining room table, etc.)
   i. Audio-visual equipment for television (e.g., video tape decks or games, etc.)

　　j. Television sets
　　k. Hi-Fi/Stereo equipment
　　l. Calculators
　　m. Motor vehicles
　　n. Boats

Brand Purchases

1. How frequently do you buy "generic" *prescription drug products*—that is, prescriptions that are sold under their scientific name rather than their commercial brand name?

2. How often do you buy the store's own brand in grocery products rather than national brands?

3. Considering the grocery products you buy, would you say you usually stick to one brand or do you switch brands?

4. What is the *major reason* you switch from one brand to another?

5. Listed below are some statements people make about the reasons they buy personal grooming aids for themselves. To what extent do each of these describe you?
　　a. I buy personal grooming aids to maintain my personal appearance
　　b. I buy personal grooming aids to maintain my youth or look younger
　　c. I buy personal grooming aids to improve my feelings about myself

Special Household Services and Appliances

Below is a brief list of special household services and appliances. Please indicate your degree of interest in them. Consider only your interest in the *product itself*, and do not decide whether or not you are interested based on what you think it would cost.
　　a. A service which pays bills by telephone rather than by check
　　b. A complete home controller device which could turn lights on and off throughout the house, adjust the heat, open and close the drapes, activate burglar alarms, etc.
　　c. A home computer which would keep track of what household items you need, tell you your checking account balance, tell you what sales are going on in local stores, and provide information about new products
　　d. An automatic telephone dialing service
　　e. An intercom system in your home

Clothing Use

How often do *you* buy each of the following types of clothing?

Men's Clothing
　　a. Dress shirts (that is, those with which you might wear a tie)

    b. Sports/casual shirts
    c. Sport coats
    d. Suits
    e. Slacks
    f. Jeans
    g. Bath or lounging robes

Women's Clothing
    a. Dresses
    b. Skirts
    c. Slacks
    d. Jeans
    e. Fur coat, jacket, or stole
    f. Bath or lounging robes
    g. Bras

Product Use

About how often do *you* (*not* other members of your household) use each of the following?

Nonprescription Medicines
    a. Pain relievers or headache remedies
    b. Cold remedies
    c. Nasal spray or drops
    d. Antacid products
    e. Laxative products
    f. Hemorrhoid products
    g. Sleep aids
    h. Keep alert/stay alert aids

Personal Grooming, Beauty, and Health Aids
    a. Dental floss
    b. Device for massaging the body
    c. Shampoo
    d. Feminine hygiene spray
    e. Mouthwash
    f. Hand lotion
    g. Aerosol underarm deodorant
    h. Stick underarm deodorant
    i. Pump spray underarm deodorant
    j. Baby oil or body lotion
    k. Talcum powder
    l. Aftershave lotions
    m. Cologne or perfume
    n. Hair coloring
    o. Aerosol hair spray

p. Pump hair spray
q. Facial moisturizers
r. Facial cleansing creams
s. Eye make-up (liner, mascara, etc.)
t. Contact lenses

Cleaning Products
a. Detergent boosters or non-chlorine bleaches
b. Chlorine bleaches
c. Laundry pretreatment products
d. Dry cleaning soil or stain removers
e. Carpet or rug cleaning products
f. Furniture polishes
g. Glass/window cleaners
h. All-purpose household cleaners ("409," "Fantastik," etc.)
i. Aerosol bathroom cleaners
j. Toilet bowl cleaners
k. Drain-pipe cleaners (chemical or mechanical)
l. Air fresheners

Food
a. "Organically" grown fruits or vegetables
b. Fresh, frozen, or canned seafood
c. Canned meat
d. Canned pasta
e. Frozen TV dinners
f. Prepared canned or frozen Chinese foods
g. Prepared canned or frozen Italian foods
h. Prepared canned or frozen Mexican foods
i. Steak sauce
j. Brown or spicy mustard
k. Potato or corn chips
l. Pretzels
m. Almonds
n. Regular peanuts
o. Dry roasted peanuts
p. Cashews
q. Canned soups
r. Instant soups
s. Canned vegetables
t. Frozen vegetables
u. Cake mixes
v. Pudding mixes
w. Gelatin dessert (Jell-O, etc.)
x. Candy
y. Regular gum

z. Sugarless gum
aa. Pancake mix
bb. Pancake syrup
cc. Cold breakfast cereals
dd. Hot breakfast cereals
ee. "Natural" grain cereals
ff. Breakfast/meal replacement bars or milk additions (e.g., Instant Breakfast)

Nonalcoholic Beverages
a. Fruit juices
b. Fruit juices (e.g., Hi-C or noncarbonated soft drinks)
c. Sugar-free carbonated soft drinks (sodas)
d. Regular carbonated soft drinks (sodas)
e. Carbonated or sparkling mineral water
f. Tea (including instant tea)
g. Regular coffee (ground or instant)
h. Decaffeinated coffee (ground or instant)
i. Flavored instant teas or coffees

Specific Foods and Products

1. About how much margarine does your household use in an average week?

2. Which of the following brands of margarine does your household use most often? (Blue Bonnet, Chiffon, Fleischmann's, Imperial, Land O'Lakes, Mazola, Mrs. Filbert's, Nucoa, Parkay, Promise, Saffola, store label brand, no specific brand, have no idea.)

3. When members of your household buy margarine, how important is each of the following reasons?
a. Health considerations
b. Price
c. Taste

4. About how much butter does your household use in a week?

5. Which of the following brands of peanuts, cashews, and almonds do you buy *most often*?

6. During the last 6 months or so, which of the following have you bought for yourself or as gifts?
a. Dinnerware (plates, cups, bowls, etc.) for myself
b. Dinnerware as a gift
c. Oven/bakeware (casserole or baking dishes, etc.) for myself
d. Oven/bakeware as a gift
e. Rangetop cookware (sauce pans, frying pans, etc.) for myself
f. Rangetop cookware as a gift

7. During the last 6 months or so, which of the following kinds of watches have you bought for yourself or as a gift?
    a. Mechanical (windup) watch for myself
    b. Mechanical (windup) watch as a gift
    c. Battery operated watch (*no* digital face) for myself
    d. Battery operated watch (*no* digital face) as a gift
    e. Digital watch for myself
    f. Digital watch as a gift

8. Do you have any indoor plants?

9. About how many indoor plants are there around your home?

The 1980 VALS Algorithm

The questions that follow constitute the 1980 short-form VALS algorithm or lifestyle classification system. For the reasons set forth elsewhere we are not at liberty to reveal the weightings of each item by lifestyle types. Without these weightings it is not possible to convert the items into lifestyle rankings. This form of the algorithm was worked out under the direction of Dr. Stephen Crocker starting from the sixty items used to derive the results reported in this book. We wanted a short form less for our research than for the convenience of clients of the VALS program seeking to apply the values and lifestyles approach to their specific problems. The objective of this analysis was to produce a condensed version of the algorithm with the following characteristics:

○ Individual items included in the algorithm were the best discriminators among VALS types.

○ The condensed version classified persons into the same types as the full algorithm (internal reliability).

○ The condensed version classified persons into the same types as the VALS staff (external reliability).

○ The condensed and full algorithms produced consistent results when analyzing dependent variables such as activities or consumption patterns.

DISCRIMINANT ANALYSIS PROCEDURES

The objective of the discriminant analysis was to produce a minimum number of items with the most evident discriminating power—those items that classified persons into the same types as the full algorithm. Over sixty demographic and attitude items were used as a "full" or "complete" algorithm for classifying 1980 survey respondents. These items were entered into the analysis as either continuous or dummy variables, depending upon whether they approached the interval level of measurement. For example, age was entered as a continuous variable, whereas party identification (e.g., strong Republican, not very strong Republican, etc.) was entered as several separate dummy variables.

The discriminant analysis functions were derived from one-half the sample (1,356) and tested for predictability on the other half of the sample.* This procedure is important because it enables one to test the results produced by the discriminant analysis on a sample that is independent of its derivation, and thus makes it possible to see how well the algorithm would work when used in another sample. The procedure is also important for another reason. By comparing the results in both samples, one can avoid the pitfall of fitting the data well to the sample on which the algorithm is based without improving predictability in another sample, i.e., "curve-fitting."

The discriminant analysis was accomplished using two basic methods. The program was set up to select from among the total item pool the most discriminating items in a stepwise fashion (e.g., adding items one at a time) until maximum prediction was obtained and further discriminating power could not be improved with any additional items (the F-level of significance was set at .05). In addition, a discriminant analysis was performed beginning with the total item pool and asking the program to *delete* stepwise those items that did not adequately discriminate among groups. The results of both the analyses produced a basic set of items that was exactly the same except for a single item.

The results of the analysis were then reviewed in an attempt to pare down the number of items even further. The ten individual items with the highest classification function coefficient (Fisher's Linear Discriminant Function) for *each* VALS type (Survivor, Sustainer, etc.) were selected as the preliminary set of items for the algorithm.† The discriminant analysis was performed again on this smaller number of items to see if a reduction in agreement in classification occurred between the full algorithm and the condensed version. The results showed only about 1-percent loss in agreement with this reduced item pool.

---

* In the 1980 survey respondents and their spouses were administered all potential VALS classification items. Hence, the total sample used for classifying individuals was 2,713.

† The data were standardized for this operation.

To further improve agreement in classification between the condensed and full versions of the algorithm, another analysis procedure was undertaken. Additional discriminant analyses were run *adding* various conceptually derived combinations of variables. For example, to the basic set of items was added another group of five items that were the most powerful from the remaining number in discriminating Emulators from the rest of the types. The purpose was to see if adding these five items might improve the percentage agreement in classification between the full and condensed versions of the algorithm for Emulators. Similar attempts were made by adding item packages reflecting the Experiential and Societally Conscious types. These analyses produced an addition of three items to the basic set mentioned earlier. This set of items constituted the final, condensed version of the 1980 algorithm.

CONSISTENCY OF CLASSIFICATION BETWEEN THE COMPLETE AND REDUCED VERSIONS

The condensed algorithm was tested for agreement with the full algorithm in three ways. The first was percentage agreement between cases classified by both the full and condensed versions. The overall level of agreement is 86 percent. The level of agreement by VALS type is:

SURVIVORS	SUSTAINERS	BELONGERS	EMULATORS	ACHIEVERS	I-AM-ME	EXPERIENTIAL	SOCIETALLY CONSCIOUS
82%	81%	94%	85%	88%	84%	78%	70%

The lower rate of agreement for the Inner-Directed types overall is not surprising, given that this survey was the first attempt to classify them. Among the Inner-Directeds, the I-Am-Me group has the advantage of easier classification because they are most often single persons living alone. Both the Experiential and Societally Conscious types have no singular demographic constellation that facilitates classification. Their distinction is mainly based on attitudinal differences, and the set of items used in our first survey attempt is not likely to be the optimal set.* Nevertheless, the overall level of agreement is quite high and indicates that both full and condensed algorithms classify the large majority of persons into the same VALS type.

* Work is proceeding to find more discriminating items.

RELIABILITY WITH EXTERNAL SCORING OF VALS TYPES

Prior to the development of weight scores for the algorithm, members of the VALS staff were asked to identify 100 prototypical cases representing eight VALS types in the first 210 questionnaire returns. These cases were identified on a "gestalt" basis, scanning the responses to a number of questionnaire items and developing an overall impression. This analysis took place before the statistical work on the algorithm began so that this classification would not be affected by that work. The classifications developed by the algorithm were compared to the "gestalt" classifications. There was a 72-percent agreement between the two methods of classification.

CONSISTENCY OF ANALYSIS RESULTS PRODUCED BY BOTH FORMS OF THE ALGORITHM

One of the questions that users of the reduced form might ask is, "Will I get the same analysis results if I use the reduced form?" To test this question, data on twenty activities and twenty household products were compared for consistency of results between the complete and reduced algorithms. Bivariate tables were run comparing extent of activity and product use by VALS types. In only one case out of the forty comparisons was there any statistically significant percentage difference. We feel, therefore, that for market purposes the results provided by the reduced form are essentially the same as the complete form.

ALGORITHM ITEMS

Below appear the specific items used in the condensed 1980 VALS algorithm. The numbers and letters are as they appear in the questionnaire itself.

ATTITUDES

In this part of the survey, we are interested in your attitudes about a number of social and economic issues.

1. Following is a series of statements. Please indicate how much you agree or disagree with each one by checking the box which comes closest to how you feel.

	DISAGREE STRONGLY	DISAGREE MOSTLY	DISAGREE SOMEWHAT	AGREE SOMEWHAT	AGREE MOSTLY	AGREE STRONGLY
(Please Check One Box for Each Item)	(1)	(2)	(3)	(4)	(5)	(6)
c. I'd say I'm rebelling against the way I was brought up.........	☐	☐	☐	☐	☐	☐
g. In general, it's more important to understand my inner self than to be famous, powerful, or wealthy	☐	☐	☐	☐	☐	☐
h. My greatest achievements are ahead of me	☐	☐	☐	☐	☐	☐
i. I believe a woman can work outside the home even if she has small children and still be a good mother.................	☐	☐	☐	☐	☐	☐
m. It's very important to me to feel I am part of a group..........	☐	☐	☐	☐	☐	☐
o. Overall, I'd say I'm very happy..	☐	☐	☐	☐	☐	☐
s. I would rather spend a quiet evening at home than go out to a party....................	☐	☐	☐	☐	☐	☐
w. A woman's life is fulfilled only if she can provide a happy home for her family	☐	☐	☐	☐	☐	☐
cc. Air pollution is a major worldwide danger	☐	☐	☐	☐	☐	☐
dd. I often feel left out of things going on around me..........	☐	☐	☐	☐	☐	☐
ff. It is wrong for an unmarried man or an unmarried woman to have sexual relations..........	☐	☐	☐	☐	☐	☐
gg. Women should take care of running their homes and leave running the country up to men..	☐	☐	☐	☐	☐	☐
hh. It would be best for the future of this country if the United States continues to take an active part in world affairs	☐	☐	☐	☐	☐	☐

jj. The purchase and use of
     marijuana should be legalized... ☐   ☐   ☐   ☐   ☐   ☐

nn. I think we are spending too
     much money on military
     armaments .... ☐   ☐   ☐   ☐   ☐   ☐

2. During the last three years would you say your financial situation has been getting
   worse, has it stayed the same, or has it been getting better?
   (Please Check.Underline{One} Box)

   ☐ 1. Getting worse

   ☐ 2. About the same

   ☐ 3. Getting better

3. How satisfied are you with your present financial situation?
   (Please Check One Box)

   ☐ 1. Very dissatisfied

   ☐ 2. Mostly dissatisfied

   ☐ 3. Mostly satisfied

   ☐ 4. Very satisfied

4. How much satisfaction do you get from each of the following in your life?
   (Please Check One Box for Each Item)

	LEVEL OF SATISFACTION				
	NOT MUCH	SOME	A GREAT DEAL	AN EXTREME AMOUNT	DOESN'T APPLY TO ME
	(1)	(2)	(3)	(4)	(8)
a. Your job (whether you work, keep house, or go to school).	☐	☐	☐	☐	☐
b. Nonwork activities such as hobbies	☐	☐	☐	☐	☐
c. Your friends................	☐	☐	☐	☐	☐

5. About how much confidence would you say you have in the following groups in our
   country?
   (Please Check One Box for Each Group)

	LEVEL OF CONFIDENCE				
	NO CONFIDENCE	A SMALL AMOUNT	SOME	A FAIR AMOUNT	A GREAT DEAL
	(1)	(2)	(3)	(4)	(5)
b. Leaders of major companies ...	☐	☐	☐	☐	☐
c. Leaders of the military	☐	☐	☐	☐	☐

BACKGROUND INFORMATION

The following background information questions are included only to help us interpret your responses on other questions. Your responses here and throughout the questionnaire will be held <u>strictly</u> confidential.

1. What is your marital status?
   (Please Check <u>One</u> Box)

   ☐ 1. First marriage   ☐ 5. Widowed

   ☐ 2. Second or later marriage   ☐ 6. Separated

   ☐ 3. Living together, not married   ☐ 7. Single, never married

   ☐ 4. Divorced

2. What is your current age?
   (Please Check <u>One</u> Box)

   ☐ 1. 18–24   ☐ 5. 45–54

   ☐ 2. 25–29   ☐ 6. 55–64

   ☐ 3. 30–34   ☐ 7. 65 and over

   ☐ 4. 35–44

3. What is the highest level of formal education you have completed?
   (Please Check <u>One</u> Box)

   ☐ 01. Grades 1–8   ☐ 07. First year of college

   ☐ 02. Grade 9   ☐ 08. Second year of college

   ☐ 03. Grade 10   ☐ 09. Third year of college

   ☐ 04. Grade 11   ☐ 10. Graduated college (4 years)

   ☐ 05. Graduated high school   ☐ 11. Attended or completed graduate school

   ☐ 06. Technical School

4. What is the highest level of formal education <u>your father</u> completed?
   (Please Check <u>One</u> Box)

   ☐ 01. Grades 1–8   ☐ 07. Second year of college

   ☐ 02. Grade 9   ☐ 08. Third year of college

   ☐ 03. Grade 10   ☐ 09. Graduated college (4 years)

   ☐ 04. Grade 11   ☐ 10. Attended or completed graduate school

   ☐ 05. Graduated high school   ☐ 11. Don't know

   ☐ 06. First year of college

5. What ethnic group do you consider yourself to be a member of?
   (Please Check <u>One</u> Box)

   ☐ 1. Caucasian or white

   ☐ 2. Black

   ☐ 3. Hispanic or Spanish Origin

   ☐ 4. Other (please specify): _____

9. Generally speaking, do you usually think of yourself as a Republican, a Democrat, or an Independent?
(Please Check One Box)

☐ 1. Republican (Please Answer Question 9a)

☐ 2. Democrat (Please Answer Question 9a)

☐ 3. Independent (Please Answer Question 9b)

9a. IF YOU ARE A REPUBLICAN OR DEMOCRAT, would you call yourself a strong or not very strong Republican or Democrat?
(Please Check One Box)

☐ 1. Strong Republican

☐ 2. Not very strong Republican

☐ 3. Not very strong Democrat

☐ 4. Strong Democrat

9b. IF YOU ARE INDEPENDENT, do you think of yourself as closer to the Republican or Democratic party?
(Please Check One Box)

☐ 1. Closer to the Republican Party

☐ 2. Not close to either party

☐ 3. Closer to the Democratic Party

10. In terms of your political outlook, do you usually think of yourself as:
(Please Check One Box)

☐ 1. Very conservative

☐ 2. Somewhat conservative

☐ 3. Middle of the road

☐ 4. Somewhat liberal

☐ 5. Very liberal

20. What was your major activity during the last week?
(Please Check One Box)

☐ 01. Working full time (30 hours or more)

☐ 02. Working part time (less than 30 hours)   (Please Answer Question 21)

☐ 03. Have a job but not at work due to illness, vacation, strike, etc.

☐ 04. Looking for work, unemployed, laid off

☐ 05. Attending school

☐ 06. Retired   (Please Skip to Question 22)

☐ 07. Keeping house

☐ 08. Other (please specify): _____

_____

21. Which one of the following categories best describes your occupation?
(Please Check One Category)

☐ 01. Professional or technical (e.g., accountant, artist, computer specialist, dentist, engineer, lawyer, librarian, nurse, physician, scientist, teacher, technician, writer, etc.)

☐ 02. Manager or administrator (except on a farm)

☐ 03. Sales worker (e.g., insurance salesman, realtor, salesclerk, stockbroker, etc.)

☐ 04. Clerical worker (e.g., bank teller, bookkeeper, cashier, office clerk, postman, secretary, teacher's aide, telephone operator, etc.)

☐ 05. Crafts worker (e.g., baker, carpenter, electrician, foreman, jeweler, mechanic, painter, plumber, tailor, etc.)

☐ 06. Machine operator (e.g., bus driver, conductor, factory worker, truck driver, operator of other kinds of machines)

☐ 07. Laborer (except on a farm) (e.g., carpenter's helper, fisherman, garbage collector, stock handler, teamster, warehouseman, etc.)

☐ 08. Farmer or farm manager

☐ 09. Farm foreman or farm laborer

☐ 10. Service worker (except in a private household) (e.g., barber, bartender, cook, dental assistant, dishwasher, firefighter, janitor, nursing aide, police officer, usher, waiter, etc.)

☐ 11. Private household worker

☐ 12. Government or military worker

☐ 13. Other (please specify your job title and describe briefly what you do): _____

_____

_____

_____

22. If you were asked to use one of the following terms to describe your social class, which would you choose?
(Please Check <u>One</u> Box)

☐ 1. Lower class   ☐ 4. Upper-middle class

☐ 2. Lower-middle class   ☐ 5. Upper class

☐ 3. Middle class

23. What is your total <u>household</u> income in 1979 from all sources before taxes?
(Please include here <u>all</u> income received by <u>anyone</u> in your household.)
(Please Check <u>One</u> Box)

☐ 01. Less than $5,000   ☐ 07. $25,000 to $29,999

☐ 02. $ 5,000 to $ 7,499   ☐ 08. $30,000 to $39,999

☐ 03. $ 7,500 to $ 9,999   ☐ 09. $40,000 to $49,999

☐ 04. $10,000 to $14,999   ☐ 10. $50,000 to $74,999

☐ 05. $15,000 to $19,999   ☐ 11. $75,000 to $99,999

☐ 06. $20,000 to $24,999   ☐ 12. $100,000 and over

Size of residence area (Coded from ZIP Codes)*

1. Large central city (250,000 or more)

2. Medium central city (50–250,000)

3. Suburb of large central city

4. Suburb of medium-sized central city

5. Not within an SMSA (Standard Metropolitan Statistical Area) and open country within large civil divisions, e.g., township division, small city, town, or village.

*The responses to this question must be inferred by a research analyst using U.S. census maps and population statistics.

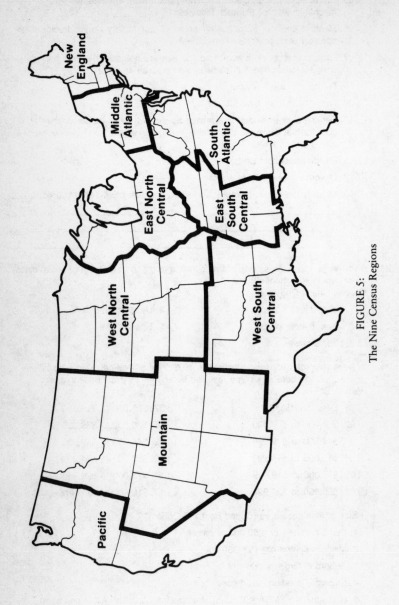

FIGURE 5:
The Nine Census Regions

TABLE A-1
Demographics of the Lifestyle Groups
(All in percent except as noted)

	SURVIVORS	SUSTAINERS	BELONGERS	EMULATORS	ACHIEVERS	I-AM-MES	EXPERIENTIALS	SOCIETALLY CONSCIOUS	SAMPLE AVERAGE
Median age (years)	66*	33	52	27	43	21*	27	39	40
Sex—female	77*	55	68	47	40	36*	55	52	54
Marital status									
Married	24	49	77	57	83*	1*	53	70	67
Widowed	50*	4	13	1	2	0*	1	3	7
Divorced or separated	10	21*	5	15	8	0*	9	16	9
Living together	0*	6	1	5	1	0*	9*	2	2
Single	17	19	4*	23	7	98*	28	8	15
Children at home									
Under age 6	7*	27	14	28*	14	**	22	26	18
Age 6 thru 11	2*	28	18	21	21	**	19	32*	20
Age 12 thru 17	11*	31*	17	15	27	**	18	25	20
Ethnic group									
Caucasian	72	64*	95*	79	95*	91	91	86	90
Black	26*	21	3	13	2*	3	2*	7	5
Hispanic	2	13*	2	6	1*	4	1*	1*	3
Other	0*	2	1	2	2	2	6*	5	2
Education									
8th grade or less	37*	12	10	1	2	0*	0*	1	6
9–12th grade	42	69*	64	62	30	38	25	14*	46
Technical school	2*	4	4	9*	8	5	9*	4	6
1–3 years college	9*	12	15	23	27	50*	29	24	22
College graduate	2*	3	3	3	18	3	26*	19	10
Graduate school	7	0*	4	3	15	5	12	39*	11
Social class									
Lower	35	46*	21	40	4*	19	15	9	19
Middle	50	42*	65*	55	55	59	62	58	59
Upper	15	12	14	5*	41*	22	23	33	22

TABLE A-1 (continued)

Demographics of the Lifestyle Groups

(All in percent except as noted)

	SURVIVORS	SUSTAINERS	BELONGERS	EMULATORS	ACHIEVERS	I-AM-MES	EXPERIENTIALS	SOCIETALLY CONSCIOUS	SAMPLE AVERAGE
Party									
Republican	15	9*	23	13	58*	20	15	14	27
Democratic	60*	50	49	48	19*	33	30	30	38
Independent	25	41	28	39	24*	48	55	57*	35
Politics									
Conservative	53	29	46	25	66*	30	21*	28	43
Middle-of-road	28	48*	44	46	27	18*	33	20	35
Liberal	19	23	10	29	8*	52	46	53*	23
Occupation									
Work full time	11*	39	34	85*	70	38	53	73	54
Work part time	11	11	7	4*	8	9	13*	8	8
Self-employed	0*	6	13	8	21*	3	13	10	13
Looking for work	3	15*	2	3	1*	1*	2	2	3
Professional or technical	3	2*	3	9	29	3	27	59*	18
Manager or admin.	0*	2	2	6	17*	1	7	5	6
Sales worker	0*	2	2	8*	6	6	2	2	4
Clerical worker	5	3*	9	22*	6	13	12	4	10
Crafts worker	3	6	7	15*	7	11	5	2*	8
Machine operator	0*	23*	8	15	4	4	5	1	7
Laborer	0*	3	2	5*	1	4	4	0*	2
Farmer	0*	2*	2*	1	2*	0*	1	1*	2*
Service worker	11	13*	5	3	2	5	3	1*	4
Homemaker	21	23	28*	4	13	0*	12	5	16
Student	3	3	1*	4	1*	44*	7	2	4
Retired	47*	3	20	0*	3	0*	1	3	9
Household Income (1979):									
under $5,000	78*	20	8	3	2*	27	7	2*	8
$5,000— 7,499	22*	22*	9	5	1*	17	8	3	7

	SURVIVORS	SUSTAINERS	BELONGERS	EMULATORS	ACHIEVERS	I-AM-MES	EXPERIENTIALS	SOCIETALLY CONSCIOUS	SAMPLE AVERAGE
$7,500—9,999	0*	18*	10	7	2	8	4	2*	6
$10,000—14,999	0*	18	20*	16	4	16	10	10	14
$15,000—19,999	0*	7	16	32*	8	5	13	12	14
$20,000—24,999	0*	3	16	19*	9	9	16	18	14
$25,000—29,999	0*	5	12	12	20*	5	20*	14	14
$30,000—39,999	0*	3	6	4	24	**	11	25*	12
$40,000—49,999	0*	2	2	1	16*	**	6	7	6
$50,000—74,999	0*	2	1	1	10*	**	1	4	3
$75,000—99,999	0*	0*	0*	0*	2*	**	1	1	1
over $100,000	0*	0*	0*	0*	3	**	1	0*	1
average for 1979 (000$)	5	11	17.3	18.3	31.4	8.8	23.8	27.2	18
Place of residence									
Large or medium city	48	47	25*	50*	30	47	46	42	35
Suburbs	33	20*	24	37	49*	33	33	27	33
Small town or open country	19	33	51*	13*	21	21	22	32	32
Census region									
New England	5	10	5	6	8	9	4*	13*	7
Mid-Atlantic	18	15	12*	16	14	21*	19	15	15
East North Central	14*	16	20	21*	19	21*	19	20	19
West North Central	11*	9	11*	8	7	7	4*	5	8
South Atlantic	18	15	16	20*	12	20*	9*	9*	15
East South Central	9	6	12*	3*	7	3*	4	5	7
West South Central	16*	12	9	10	10	6*	10	10	10
Mountain	7*	6	6	3*	5	5	6	5	5
Pacific	3*	10	8	15	19	9	24*	19	14

*Highest or lowest (or tied) of lifestyle groups.
**Instances in which some I-Am-Mes have apparently answered in terms of their parents, not themselves, thus invalidating the data.

281

TABLE A-2
Attitudes of the Lifestyle Groups
(percent)

	SURVIVORS	SUSTAINERS	BELONGERS	EMULATORS	ACHIEVERS	I-AM-MES	EXPERIENTIALS	SOCIETALLY CONSCIOUS	SAMPLE AVERAGE
Feel most people are honest	54*	58	82	62	83*	68	79	73	76
Am rebelling against things	68*	58	47	48	33*	38	38	44	44
Believe inner self is more important	81*	85	96*	88	86	88	96*	92	91
Think greatest achievements are ahead	61	82	59*	89	68	99*	94	83	73
Would rather stay home than go to party	84*	62	81	61	71	42*	58	74	71
Often feel left out of things	57	63*	36	51	20*	43	22	28	34
Feel things are changing too fast	91*	87	82	69	59	51*	53	61	69
Family is most important thing to me	93	86	97*	91	95	78*	86	86	92
Believe unmarried sex is wrong	57	26	58*	18	44	20	10*	15	39
Believe woman's place is in the home	56*	42	48	18	26	19	4	3*	30
Agree working women can be good mothers	43*	58	46	77*	43*	52	77*	72	55
Am conventional, not experimental	75	65	84*	72	77	41*	48	51	71
TV is my main entertainment	65*	61	57	52	42	31	28*	33	47
Feel it is important to be part of a group	75*	73	71	64	58	74	53	47*	64
Overall am very happy	80*	81	96*	83	94	90	96*	87	91
Feel have more self-confidence than others	66*	75	70	68	84*	74	74	80	75

	SURVIVORS	SUSTAINERS	BELONGERS	EMULATORS	ACHIEVERS	I-AM-MES	EXPERIENTIALS	SOCIETALLY CONSCIOUS	SAMPLE AVERAGE
Am a bit of a swinger	14	55	12*	41	22	69*	36	27	26
Agree social status is important	51	77	45	49	47	78*	40	31*	47
I often act on hunches	68	74	62*	68	66	80*	78	70	67
Believe marijuana should be legalized	12*	45	13	52	17	47	61*	39	28
U.S. should be active in world affairs	73	72	78	74	89*	60*	82	83	80
Believe air pollution is a major danger	84	86	81	83	68*	90	87	91*	81
Agree too much is spent protecting environment	59*	50	39	29	44	20	11*	13	34
Believe industrial growth should be limited	58*	50	51	52	28*	53	58*	58*	48
Agree too much is spent on military	43	29	26	30	11*	32	49*	38	27
Get great deal of satisfaction from job	33*	33*	75	38	77*	58	67	72	67
Get great deal of satisfaction from nonwork activities	26*	59	66	60	68	80	94*	65	67
Get great deal of satisfaction from friends	61	61	79	55*	71	90	96*	62	74
Have good deal of confidence in elected officials	29	11*	41*	19	31	28	26	19	30
Have good deal of confidence in company leaders	31	12*	32	22	48*	23	22	16	31
Have good deal of confidence in military leaders	40	34	61*	40	57	50	33	23*	49

TABLE A-2 (continued)
Attitudes of the Lifestyle Groups
(percent)

	SURVIVORS	SUSTAINERS	BELONGERS	EMULATORS	ACHIEVERS	I-AM-MES	EXPERIENTIALS	SOCIETALLY CONSCIOUS	SAMPLE AVERAGE
Believe quality of products is improving	20	17*	21	24	30*	25	21	22	24
Believe products are getting safer	40	39*	51	67	68*	58	67	64	59
Believe labelling is getting better	68	61*	81	87	85	88*	88*	87	83
Believe quality of service is improving	15	17	11	12	12	21*	7*	8	12
Have returned unsatisfactory product in past year	59*	71	76	86	89	86	88	95*	83
Have complained to store in past year	48	43*	45	66	69*	59	68	68	58
Believe consumer movement has increased prices	80*	75	63	57	66	63	53*	57	62
Agree energy crisis is real	64	39*	51	45	57	54	64	66*	54
Believe fed. gov't accurate source of energy info	45*	23	24	16*	22	31	23	21	23
Believe public utilities accurate source of energy info	26	27	26	14*	23	30*	23	16	23
Believe oil companies accurate source of energy info	24*	16	13	10	20	12	12	7*	14

*Highest or lowest (or tied) of lifestyle groups.

284

TABLE A-3

Financial Status of the Lifestyle Groups (percent)

	SURVIVORS	SUSTAINERS	BELONGERS	EMULATORS	ACHIEVERS	I-AM-MES	EXPERIENTIALS	SOCIETALLY CONSCIOUS	SAMPLE AVERAGE
Strongly agree financial security is important	68	76*	54	55	55	49	47	38*	53
Strongly agree want to get ahead financially	47	74*	40	60	41	49	47	28*	44
Mostly very satisfied with present finances	26	15*	70	32	72*	44	63	61	60
Finances improving in past 3 yrs.	7*	15	29	31	56*	41	52	44	38
Expect to maintain std. of living over next 5 yrs.	12*	34	30	37	48	51	58*	48	40
Am a spender, not a saver	36*	66	38	60	47	72*	61	54	49
Am a financial expert	28	42*	31	26	39	12*	23	28	30
It pays to be in debt, due to inflation	21	22	20*	26	39*	24	33	38	28
Better to spend on art/gold/gems	17*	28	27	39	31	41*	35	37	32
It is unwise to buy on time	57*	42	53	48	54	41*	42	45	50
Have credit card(s) in household	45*	54	66	74	87*	**	83	83	74
Credit card balance under $100	81*	73	69	45	57	**	41*	48	60
Of those over $100:									
$100– 500	75*	53	58	42	47	**	48	38*	49
$501–1,500	25*	29	31	45*	40	**	34	44	37
over $1,500	0*	18*	12	13	13	**	18*	18*	14
Have checking account(s) in household	56*	66	89	90	97*	**	91	93	90
Checking account(s) balance over $1,000	5*	8	19	10	30*	**	19	22	21
Have mutual/money mkt funds in household	13	6*	17	8	31*	**	17	20	19
Value mutual/money mkt funds:									
under $5,000	***	***	28	47	25*	**	56*	41	33
$5,001–20,000	***	***	33	27*	42	**	27*	47*	37
$20,001–50,000	***	***	29*	27	21	**	18	6*	22
over $50,000	***	***	10	0*	12*	**	0*	6	8

TABLE A-3 (continued)

Financial Status of the Lifestyle Groups (percent)

	SURVIVORS	SUSTAINERS	BELONGERS	EMULATORS	ACHIEVERS	I-AM-MES	EXPERIENTIALS	SOCIETALLY CONSCIOUS	SAMPLE AVERAGE
Have savings acct/certifs, etc. in household	49*	57	86	85	91	**	90	92*	86
Value savings acct, etc.:									
under $5,000	79	76	61	86*	57*	***	80	69	66
$5,001–$20,000	11*	22	30*	11*	30*	***	18	27	26
$20,001–$50,000	11*	3	8	1*	9	***	1*	4	6
over $50,000	0*	0*	1	2	4*	***	2	1	2
Have stocks or bonds in household	5*	17	28	24	50*	**	29	43	33
Value stocks or bonds:									
under $10,000	***	***	80	90*	60*	***	78	84	74
$10,001–$50,000	***	***	13	9*	24*	***	11	9*	16
$50,001–$100,000	***	***	6	0*	8*	***	3	7	6
over $100,000	***	***	1	2	8*	***	8*	0*	4
Have investment real estate in household	7*	15	22	13	35*	**	23	24	23
Money left from sale of real est. invest:									
under $10,000	***	***	33	36*	24*	***	29	33	29
$10,001–$50,000	***	***	33	48*	39	***	29*	45	36
$50,001–$100,000	***	***	16	4*	14	***	16*	15	15
over $100,000	***	***	17	12	24	***	26*	8*	19
Own own home	45	45	82	58	87*	***	53	76	73
Have home mortgage	50*	54	57	59	76*	***	50*	73	61
Money left from sale of home:									
under $10,000	***	46*	20	41	9*	***	17	17	19
$10,001–$50,000	***	38*	59*	49	46	***	54	56	53
$50,001–$100,000	***	8*	18	9	33*	***	24	22	22
over $100,000	***	2	2	1*	11*	***	4	5	6
Have loans outstanding	10*	28	27	45	44	**	50*	41	37
Amount over $1,000 owed on loans:									
$1,000–$5,000	***	***	67	79*	60	**	55	53*	64

	SURVIVORS	SUSTAINERS	BELONGERS	EMULATORS	ACHIEVERS	I-AM-MES	EXPERIENTIALS	SOCIETALLY CONSCIOUS	SAMPLE AVERAGE
$5,001–$20,000	***	***	26	17*	27	**	38	41*	28
$20,001–$50,000	***	***	4	4	5	**	0*	6*	4
over $50,000	***	***	4	1	7*	**	7*	0*	4
Household has a stockbroker	2*	3	6	5	25*	**	11	15	11
Transaction value thru stockbroker, 1979:									
none	***	***	44*	***	33	**	40	30*	35
$1–$10,000	***	***	41	***	40	**	33*	43*	41
$10,001–$50,000	***	***	12*	***	17	**	13	26*	17
over $50,000	***	***	3	***	9	**	13*	0*	7
Value of household assets:									
under $5,000	52*	32	6	18	1*	**	15	8	10
$5,001–$10,000	5	19*	7	14	2*	**	11	5	8
$10,001–$25,000	23*	13	14	13	7*	**	16	7*	11
$25,001–$50,000	11	17	22*	18	10*	**	13	14	16
$50,001–$100,000	8*	17	35	31	32	**	24	36*	31
$100,001–$500,000	0*	2	15	5	41*	**	16	29	20
$500,001–$1,000,000	0*	0*	1	2	4	**	5*	2	2
over $1,000,000	0*	0*	1	0*	3*	**	1	0*	1
Debts or liabilities:									
none	58*	28	34	11	10	**	7*	12	21
$1–$5,000	31	37*	24	31	14*	**	36	19	25
$5,001–$10,000	10	9*	13*	9*	12	**	10*	12	12
$10,001–$25,000	7*	14	14	18	22*	**	13	17	17
$25,001–$50,000	0*	8	11	24	24	**	21	30*	17
$50,001–$100,000	0*	5	3	5	13*	**	8	8	6
$100,001–$500,000	0*	0*	1	2	4*	**	4*	2	2
over $500,000	0*	0*	0*	0*	1*	**	0*	0*	0

*Highest or lowest (or tied) of the lifestyle groups.
**Instances in which some I-Am-Mes have apparently answered in terms of the parents, not themselves, thus invalidating the data.
***Cell size too small for meaningful results.

NOTES AND INDEX

Notes

Foreword

1. Kenneth J. Cooper, Hawkins Stern, and Arnold Mitchell, *Consumer Values and Demand*. Business Intelligence Program, SRI International, 1960.
2. Arnold Mitchell and Mary Lou Anderson, *The Arts and Business*. Business Intelligence Program, SRI International, 1962; Eli Brandes and Arnold Mitchell, *A Cultural and Social Framework*. Business Intelligence Program, SRI International, 1964; Arnold Mitchell and Edith Wyden, *The Negro American*. Business Intelligence Program, SRI International, 1966; Arnold Mitchell, *Alternative Futures: An Exploration of Humanistic Approaches to Social Forecasting*. Educational Policy Research Center, SRI International, 1967; Arnold Mitchell and Mary K. Baird, *American Values*. Business Intelligence Program, SRI International, 1969; Arnold Mitchell, O. W. Markley et al., *Toward Master Social Indicators*. Educational Policy Research Center, SRI International, 1969; Arnold Mitchell, T. J. Logothetti, and R. E. Kantor, *An Approach to Measuring Quality of Life*. Research and Development Program, SRI International, 1971; Arnold Mitchell, *Life Ways and Life Styles*. Business Intelligence Program, SRI International, 1973; Arnold Mitchell et al., *Consumer Values*. Business Intelligence Program, SRI International, 1974; Arnold Mitchell, "Trends in Ways of Life," in *Alternative Futures for Environmental Policy Planning: 1975–2000*. Environmental Protection Agency, Washington, D.C., 1975; Arnold Mitchell et al., *Handbook of Forecasting Techniques* (3 vols.), Fort Belvoir, Va., Institute for Water Resources, U.S. Army Corps of Engineers: 1975; Duane Elgin and Arnold Mitchell, *Voluntary Simplicity*. Business Intelligence Program, SRI International, 1976; Peter Schwartz and Arnold Mitchell, *The Art of Exploratory Planning*. Business Intelligence Program, SRI International, 1976; Arnold Mitchell, *Alternative Future Societal Factors for Long-Range Research Planning: Volume 2, Consumer Typology*. SRI International for the Monsanto Company, 1977.
3. Arnold Mitchell and Mary K. Baird, *American Values*. Business Intelligence Program, SRI International, 1969.
4. A. H. Maslow, "Hierarchy of Human Needs," in *Motivation and Personality*. New York: Harper & Row, 1954.
5. Arnold Mitchell, *Life Ways and Life Styles*. Business Intelligence Program, SRI International, 1973.
6. Duane Elgin and Arnold Mitchell, *Voluntary Simplicity*. Business Intelligence Program, SRI International, 1976.
7. Duane Elgin, *Voluntary Simplicity*. New York: William Morrow, 1981.
8. Arnold Mitchell, *Consumer Values: A Typology*. Values and Lifestyles Program, SRI International, 1978; Arnold Mitchell, *Social Change: Implications of Trends in Values and Lifestyles*. Values and Lifestyles Program, SRI International, 1979; Arnold Mitchell and DCM Associates, *Attitudinal and Other Correlates of Values*. Values and Lifestyles Program, SRI International, 1979; Arnold Mitchell, *Belonging*. Values and Lifestyles Program, SRI In-

ternational, 1979; Arnold Mitchell and DCM Associates, *Trends in Values: 1973–1978*. Values and Lifestyles Program, SRI International, 1979; Donald Michael, Arnold Mitchell, William Royce, Peter Schwartz, and Joop de Vries, *Values and Strategic Planning*. Values and Lifestyles Program, SRI International, 1980; Arnold Mitchell, *Values and Activities*. Values and Lifestyles Program, SRI International, 1981; Arnold Mitchell, *Flows in the VALS Typology*. Values and Lifestyles Program, SRI International, 1981; Arnold Mitchell, *Proximities of the VALS Types*. Values and Lifestyles Program, SRI International, 1981; Arnold Mitchell, *The VALS Typology: Summary 1981*. Values and Lifestyles Program, SRI International, 1981; Arnold Mitchell, *Values Scenarios for the 1980s*. Values and Lifestyles Program, SRI International, 1981.

9. Bill Huckabee, *Values in Merchandising*. Values and Lifestyles Program, SRI International, 1979; Marie Spengler and Lynn Rosener, *Business Uses of Values and Lifestyles*. Values and Lifestyles Program, SRI International, 1979; DCM Associates and VALS Staff, *The Demographics of Values*. Values and Lifestyle Program, SRI International, 1979; Peter Schwartz and James Ogilvy, *The Emergent Paradigm: Changing Patterns of Thought and Belief*. Values and Lifestyles Program, SRI International, 1979; DCM Associates and VALS Staff, *Regional Patterns of Values*. Values and Lifestyles Program, SRI International, 1979; Dustin Macgregor, *The Home*. Values and Lifestyles Program, SRI International, 1979; Bill Huckabee, *Managing in Diversity*. Values and Lifestyles Program, SRI International, 1980; James Barrell and J. W. Waters, *Consumer Motivation*. Values and Lifestyles Program, SRI International, 1980; Richard Ferguson, *Regulation: A Social Values Perspective*. Values and Lifestyles Program, SRI International, 1980; Marie Spengler and Peter Teige, *Hard Times*. Values and Lifestyles Program, SRI International, 1980; Donald N. Michael, *The New Competence: The Organization as a Learning System*. Values and Lifestyles Program, SRI International, 1980; Gloria Esdale and Stephen Crocker, *Values and Consumption Patterns*. Values and Lifestyles Program, SRI International, 1981; Christine MacNulty, *Values and Lifestyles in Western Europe*. Values and Lifestyles Program, SRI International, 1981; James

Ogilvy and Philip Kohlenberg, *Values and Religion*. Values and Lifestyles Program, SRI International, 1981; R. Meimei Pan, *Foods, Beverages, and Values*. Values and Lifestyles Program, SRI International, 1981; Catherine Chavez and Barbara Casey, *Values and Financial Behavior*. Values and Lifestyles Program, SRI International, 1981.

10. R. F. Stewart, O. J. Benepe, and Arnold Mitchell, *Formal Planning: The Staff Planner's Role at Start-Up*. Business Intelligence Program, SRI International, 1965; Arnold Mitchell and Charles Turk, *An Approach to Strategic Planning*. SRI International for the Budd Company, 1977; William S. Royce and Arnold Mitchell, *Stakeholder Values and Corporate Success*. Business Intelligence Program, SRI International, 1980; Arnold Mitchell et al., *Social Trends in Food Retailing*. SRI International for Coca Cola Retailing Research Group, 1980; Arnold Mitchell, "Changing Life Ways and Corporate Planning," in R. J. Allio and M. W. Pennington, eds., *Corporate Planning: Techniques and Applications*. New York: American Management Association, 1979; Arnold Mitchell, "An Approach to Measuring Quality of Life," in *The Quality of Life Concept: A Potential New Tool for Decision Makers*. Washington, D.C., The Environmental Protection Agency, 1973; Arnold Mitchell, "Human Needs and the Changing Goals of Life and Work," ed., in Fred Best, *The Future of Work*. Englewood Cliffs: Prentice-Hall, N.J.: 1973.

Chapter 1

1. David Riesman, Nathan Glazer, and Reuel Denney, *The Lonely Crowd*. New Haven: Yale University Press, 1950.

2. Duane Elgin, *Voluntary Simplicity*. New York: William Morrow, 1981.

Chapter 2

1. Arnold Mitchell and Mary K. Baird, *American Values*. Business Intelligence Program, SRI International, 1969.

2. A. H. Maslow, "Hierarchy of Human Needs," in *Motivation and Personality*. New York: Harper & Row, 1954.

3. Clare W. Graves, "Human Nature Prepares for a Momentous Leap." *The Futurist* (April, 1974).

4. Jane Loevinger, "The Meaning and Measurement of Ego Development." *The American Psychologist* (March, 1966).

5. David C. McClelland, *Studies in Motivation*. New York: Appleton-Century-Crofts, 1955, and *The Achieving Society*. New York: Van Nostrand, 1961.

6. Erik H. Erikson, *Childhood and Society*, 2nd ed. New York: W. W. Norton, 1963.

7. Lyman W. Porter and Edward E. Lawler, *Managerial Attitudes and Performance*. Homewood, Ill.: Richard D. Irwin, 1968.

8. Erich Fromm, *The Sane Society*. New York: Holt, Rinehart and Winston, 1955.

9. O. J. Harvey, David E. Hunt, and Harold M. Schroder, *Conceptual Systems and Personality Organization*. New York: John Wiley, 1961.

10. R. F. Peck and R. J. Havighurst, *The Psychology of Character Development*. New York: John Wiley, 1960.

11. Lawrence Kohlberg, *The Philsophy of Moral Development*. New York: Harper & Row, 1981.

12. Anthony G. Athos, "Is the Corporation Next to Fall?" *Harvard Business Review* (January, 1970).

13. Clyde Kluckhohn, "Have There Been Discernible Shifts in American Values During the Past Generation?" in E. E. Morison, ed., *The American Style: Essays in Value and Performance*. New York: Harper & Row, 1958.

14. Douglas McGregor, *The Human Side of Enterprise*. New York: McGraw-Hill, 1960.

15. A. H. Maslow, "Theory Z," in W. G. Bennis and E. H. Schein, eds., *New Developments with the Human Side of Enterprise*. New York: McGraw-Hill, 1969.

16. R. E. Kantor, *Psychological Theories and Social Groupings*. Educational Policy Research Center, SRI International, 1969.

17. E. L. Shostron, *Personality Orientation Inventory*. San Diego, Calif.: Educational and Industrial Testing Services, 1969.

18. Jerome S. Bruner et al., *A Study of Thinking*. New York: John Wiley, 1956.

19. David Levinson, *The Seasons of a Man's Life*. New York: Ballantine, 1978.

20. William Bridges, *Transitions*. Reading, Mass.: Addison-Wesley, 1980.

21. Michael Maccoby, *The Gamesman*. New York: Simon and Schuster, 1976.

22. Michael Maccoby, op. cit.

Chapter 3

1. William Bridges, *Transitions*. Reading, Mass.: Addison-Wesley, 1980.

2. Clare W. Graves, *On the Theory of Value*, mimeographed paper, 1967.

3. Bridges, op. cit.

4. David Levinson, *The Seasons of a Man's Life*. New York: Ballantine, 1978.

5. Roger L. Gould, *Transformations*. New York: Simon & Schuster, 1978.

6. Carl G. Jung, *Man and His Symbols*. Garden City, N.Y.: Doubleday, 1964.

7. Joseph Campbell, *The Masks of God: Creative Mythology*. New York: Viking Press, 1968.

8. Eric Berne, *Transactional Analysis in Psychotherapy*. New York: Grove Press, 1961.

9. Gould, op. cit.

10. Peter Schwartz and James Ogilvy, *The Emergent Paradigm: Changing Patterns of Thought and Belief*. Values and Lifestyles Program, SRI International, 1979.

11. Willis Harman, "The Coming Transformation." *The Futurist* (February, 1977).

12. Gould, op. cit.

13. Bridges, op. cit.

Chapter 5

1. Based on and quoted from Robert Coles, "Like It Is in the Alley." *Daedalus* (Fall, 1968).

Chapter 7

1. This account utilizes information from Bayard Webster, "A Day with the Whales." *The New York Times* (September 22, 1981).

Chapter 9

1. Virginia H. Hine, "The Basic Paradigm of a Future Socio-Cultural System." *World Issues* (April/May, 1977).

Chapter 10

1. Christine MacNulty, *Values and Lifestyles in Western Europe*. Values and Lifestyles Program, SRI International, 1981.

Chapter 11

1. George Gallup et al., *Human Needs and Satisfactions: A Global Survey*. Dayton, Ohio: Charles F. Kettering Foundation; Princeton, N.J.: Gallup International Research Institutes, 1977.

2. James C. Davies, ed., *When Men Rebel, and Why*. Riverside, N.J.: Free Press, 1971.

3. Chalmers Johnson, *Revolutionary Change*. Boston: Little, Brown 1966.

4. Arnold Toynbee, *A Study of History*. London: Oxford University Press, 1972.

5. Pitirim A. Sorokin, *Social and Cultural Dynamics*. New York: Bedminster Press, 1963.

6. Oswald Spengler, *The Decline of the West* (abridged edition). New York: Knopf, 1962.

7. Carroll Quigley, *The Evolution of Civilizations*. New York: Macmillan, 1961.

Chapter 12

1. See, for example, Paul Hawken, James Ogilvy, and Peter Schwartz, *Seven Tomorrows*. New York: Bantam, 1982.

2. Amitai Etzioni, "Choose America Must—Between 'Reindustrialization' and 'Quality of Life.'" *Across the Board* (October, 1980).

3. Robert D. Hamrin, *Managing Growth in the 1980s: Toward a New Economics*. New York: Praeger, 1980.

4. Angus Campbell, *The Sense of Well-Being in America: Recent Patterns and Trends*. New York: McGraw-Hill, 1979.

5. Marie Spengler and Peter Teige, *Hard Times*. Values and Lifestyles Program, SRI International, 1980.

6. Theodore Roszak, *Person/Planet: The Creative Disintegration of Industrial Society*. Garden City, N.Y.: Doubleday, 1979.

7. F. B. Libaw, "The Creative Corporation." *Innovation* (1970).

8. E. F. Schumacher, *Small is Beautiful*. New York: Harper & Row, 1973.

9. Hawken, Ogilvy, and Schwartz, op. cit.

Appendix

1. Michael Maccoby, *The Gamesman*. New York: Simon & Schuster, 1976.

2. Terms and concept from William H. Whyte, *The Organization Man*. New York: Simon & Schuster, 1956.

3. Barbara E. Bryant, "Respondent Selection in a Time of Changing Household Composition." *Journal of Marketing Research* (May, 1975).

Index

By the year 2000, 2 out of 3 Americans could be illiterate.

It's true.

Today, 75 million adults… about one American in three, can't read adequately. And by the year 2000, U.S. News & World Report envisions an America with a literacy rate of only 30%.

Before that America comes to be, you can stop it… by joining the fight against illiteracy today.

Call the Coalition for Literacy at toll-free **1-800-228-8813** and volunteer.

Volunteer Against Illiteracy. The only degree you need is a degree of caring.

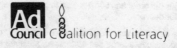

Ad Council   Coalition for Literacy

Warner Books is proud to be an active supporter of the Coalition for Literacy.

GLASSBORO STATE COLLEGE